Spoken Corpora
in Applied Linguistics

Linguistic Insights

Studies in Language and Communication

Edited by Maurizio Gotti,
University of Bergamo

Volume 51

PETER LANG

Bern · Berlin · Bruxelles · Frankfurt am Main · New York · Oxford · Wien

Mari Carmen Campoy & María José Luzón (eds)

Spoken Corpora
in Applied Linguistics

· · · · · · · · · · · · · · · · · · ·

PETER LANG

Bern · Berlin · Bruxelles · Frankfurt am Main · New York · Oxford · Wien

Bibliographic information published by Die Deutsche Bibliothek
Die Deutsche Bibliothek lists this publication in the Deutsche National-
bibliografie; detailed bibliographic data is available on the Internet at
‹http://dnb.ddb.de›.

British Library and Library of Congress Cataloguing-in-Publication Data:
A catalogue record for this book is available from *The British Library,*
Great Britain

Library of Congress Cataloging-in-Publication Data

Spoken corpora in applied linguistics / Mari Carmen Campoy &
María José Luzón (eds).
    p. cm. — (Linguistic insights, ISSN 1424-8689 ; v. 51)
Includes bibliographical references.
ISBN 978-3-03-911275-3 (alk. paper)
1. Oral communication—Research—Methodology. 2. Corpora (Linguistics)
3. Language and languages—Study and teaching—Research—Methodology.
I. Campoy, Mari Carmen, 1967- II. Luzón, María José, 1969-
P95.3.S66 2007
418—dc22
                              2007040281

This book has been funded by a grant from the *Conselleria d'Empressa,
Universitat i Ciència* (Spain) (GV05/172).

GENERALITAT VALENCIANA
CONSELLERIA D'EMPRESA, UNIVERSITAT I CIÈNCIA
D.Gral. d'Investigació i Transferència Tecnològica

ISSN 1424-8689
ISBN 978-3-03911-275-3

© Peter Lang AG, International Academic Publishers, Bern 2007
Hochfeldstrasse 32, Postfach 746, CH-3000 Bern 9, Switzerland
info@peterlang.com, www.peterlang.com, www.peterlang.net

Printed in Germany

Contents

III. Teaching and Learning Languages through Oral Corpora

Preface

The last few decades have witnessed an increased interest in corpus linguistics, fostered by the easy availability of language corpora. Although spoken corpora are more difficult to compile and may require more sophisticated processing tools, there is a growing awareness of the importance of such corpora as resources for the analysis of spoken language. This has led us to devote a volume to this kind of corpora, including papers from leading researchers in the field.

The papers in this volume illustrate research which relies on the analysis of spoken corpora to inform different areas related to spoken language, such as language change and variation, pragmatics and grammar of spoken discourse, the teaching of English as a foreign language or oral academic discourse. The number and variety of spoken corpora used for the pieces of research reported in the book attest to the interest that these corpora have arisen in the last years and to the great efforts devoted to their analysis and compilation.

The first introductory chapter provides an overview of current research on these corpora in an attempt to give an overall perspective of their different applications, some of which are illustrated throughout the papers presented in the book. Although these papers do not exhaustively represent the range of spoken corpora studies, we believe they provide a good example on the developments in this field.

After this introductory chapter, the book includes papers in two areas: (i) the use of spoken corpora for language research, and (ii) the teaching and learning of languages through spoken corpora.

In the second chapter of the volume, Mauranen presents an overview of research carried out in the field of English as Lingua Franca (ELF). The various studies discussed in this chapter may be seen as a breakthrough in the use of English as an international language and point to new ways of understanding the strategies that speakers from different L1 backgrounds may and do develop to enhance communication among them in real (non-classroom) situations. In this context, the *English as Lingua Franca in Academic Settings* corpus (*ELFA*) is introduced as a means to develop research which suggests ways to deal with the demands of present day EAP.

The following three chapters explore oral discourse in academic contexts. In their chapter Cortes and Csomay merge their research methodologies to describe the use of a particular type of recurrent word combinations, *lexical bundles*, in the beginning stages of university classroom talk, as defined in special Vocabulary-Based Discourse Units. The findings of their exploratory study contribute important information to the lexico-grammatical analysis of the language used in the different stages of the university class.

Drescher examines differences in the way that people with different identity characteristics (e.g., male student / female professor) used a set of sex-related linguistic and pragmatic variables (e.g., hedges, hesitations and fillers) in different situations. The analysis in this chapter provides insights into the varied and complex ways in which speaker and addressee identities interact with register and affect linguistic behaviour.

García investigates how speakers occupying various social roles and contexts accomplish their communicative goals through pragmatic language use. Results illustrate differences in the use of pragmatic utterances by situation type (i.e., office hours, service encounters, study groups) and speaker role (i.e., student, professor, service provider). By means of quantitative and qualitative analyses of corpus samples, García shows that native speakers use a great variety of pragmatic functions in different situations, and also use different lexical and grammatical patterns in the realizations of these pragmatic functions.

The chapter by Pérez Guerra illustrates the use of spoken corpora to explore the features of orality. Starting from the hypothesis that text types can be graded in terms of complexity, he compares the linguistic complexity of what he regards as two text types of the same language: spoken and written Present-day English. For this purpose, he focuses on the complexity of constituents functioning as unmarked preverbal subjects in declarative sentences in *The British National Corpus*.

In their contribution Mendes and Bacelar present an analysis of the grammaticalization process undergone by *daí* 'from there' in European Portuguese. Their chapter reveals the different semantic and pragmatic values of the word and shows how it has progressed from a deictic form to a discourse marker, with both functions in use in contemporary Portuguese.

In the first paper of the second part of the volume, Tono reviews spoken learner corpora bringing new insights from one of the biggest learner oral corpora, the *NICT JLE*, a corpus containing more than 1,200 Japanese EFL learners' oral interview transcripts. The corpus allows for research across nine spoken language proficiency levels. Tono tackles one of the hottest issues in the field: how research on spoken learner corpora highlights the need to evaluate oral and written performance by means of different parameters. Research undertaken using the *NICT JLE* corpus clearly points towards ways in which NLP techniques may help in the detection of learner errors and proficiency levels.

Osborne reflects on the validity of retracing, length of runs and pauses and speech rate to determine how effective they may be in evaluating learners' fluency when speaking a foreign language. Results are contrasted across different proficiency levels and against native speaker data. His research suggests that corpus-based analysis of these data may help to assess learners in a more effective and clear way. In the discussion of these three points, this author also provides interesting comments on their complexity and to which extent they may be good predictors of fluency.

Cheng's study on the use of interruption in textbooks reveals how corpus-based techniques may be particularly useful in assessing the adequacy of textbook input. Thus, by contrasting textbooks with native and other speakers of English, she shows empirical evidence on major differences between interruption realisations in real life communication (in this case taken from the HKCSE corpus) and educational materials. This author also argues on the need of teaching materials where contextualisation is given a priority status, thus providing learners with relevant data to obtain higher achievements in their language reception and production.

De Cock compares routinized building blocks in spoken learner and native speaker corpora. This comparison highlights the importance of recurrent word sequences which are seen as representative exponents of both speech types. Thus, de Cock's contrast of these two corpora provides us with insightful comments on which routines are typical of native speakers and should be emphasised in learning and teaching contexts and which routines are typically followed by learners and how they differ from one another. De Cock opens her research not only to a limited number of words in a block, but to different combinations ranging from two to six word sequences.

Farr advocates for a corpus-based research on language use in professional practices, where corpus information may be used to examine interaction in professional contexts. In her chapter, the analysis of a corpus including feedback sessions between student teachers and their tutors (the POTTI corpus) reveals the strengths and weaknesses of such interactions, suggesting ways to develop further research in professional communication.

We hope that the present volume will be a step in the direction of reflecting the diversity of spoken corpora research and knowledge and that it may generate fruitful discussion in the field.

I. Introduction

MARÍA JOSÉ LUZÓN, MARI CARMEN CAMPOY,
MARÍA DEL MAR SÁNCHEZ AND PATRICIA SALAZAR

Spoken Corpora: New Perspectives in Oral Language Use and Teaching[1]

1. Introduction

Research based on spoken corpora is scarcer than that based on written corpora because the former are difficult to compile and work with for a number of reasons, such as the arduous job of data collection, the time consuming and complex transcriptions, and the design of tools which should cater for the idiosyncrasies of the recorded and transcribed material. Despite these obstacles, there is a growing number of researchers engaged in the analysis of spoken corpora, both to reveal specific features of spoken language and to derive pedagogical applications from the results of such analysis.

The volume *Spoken Corpora in Applied Linguistics* is a collection of papers which explore the opportunities for the analysis of authentic data that spoken corpora offer and illustrate the challenges involved in doing research with such corpora. In an attempt to provide a framework for the book, in this introductory chapter we present a survey of spoken corpora and review current research on these corpora. We comment in more detail on three fields in which results deriving from corpus analysis of oral data may contribute to important advances: academic and professional English as used in various contexts, language learning, and interpreting.

1   The research carried out for the writing of this paper has been financed by the Generalitat Valenciana. Conselleria d'Empresa, Universitat i Ciència (Project code: GV05/172).

2. Overview of spoken corpus typology

The first spoken corpus to become available (the *LLC London-Lund Corpus of Spoken English*) was based on the *Survey of English Usage* (*SEU*, 1959, University College London) and on the *Survey of Spoken English* (*SSE*, 1975, Lund University). In spite of the great effort involved in the compilation and transcription of the first spoken corpora, they had some drawbacks that more recent corpora have partly overcome, e.g., unavailability of the original sound recordings, or restrictions on the spoken data they contain. In the 1980s and 1990s there appeared spoken corpora as part of "megacorpora" such as the *COBUILD* corpus (with a spoken sub-corpus of 20 million words) or the *BNC* (with a spoken sub-corpus of 10 million words). Similarly, the *CANCODE* (*Cambridge and Nottingham Corpus of Discourse in English*) is the spoken part of the *Cambridge International Corpus*. These corpora have a larger size and include much more varied data than earlier corpora. The data for the *CANCODE*, for instance, were recorded at hundreds of locations across the British Isles and include a wide variety of situations: casual conversation, people working together, people shopping, people finding out information, discussions, and many more types of interaction.

Spoken corpora can be compiled taking into account one or several different criteria:

1. National variety represented in the corpus. Although many languages other than English have already developed spoken corpora (e.g., the Spanish oral corpus *COREC, Corpus Oral de Referencia del Español Contemporáneo*), corpora related to the English language far outnumber those in any other language. The most frequent ones are British corpora (e.g., the *LLC*, the *Longman British Spoken Corpus*, the *CANCODE*) and American corpora (e.g., the *Switchboard Corpus, the Longman Spoken American Corpus,* the *Santa Barbara Corpus of Spoken American English*). However, there are various projects involving the collection of spoken data in other English-speaking countries around the world, e.g., the *Wellington Corpus of Spoken New Zealand,* the *International Corpus of English* (*ICE*). The primary

aim of the *ICE* is to collect material for comparative studies of English worldwide. Fifteen research teams around the world have been preparing one million word electronic corpora of their own national or regional variety of English (United States, Australia, Hong Kong, Singapore, etc). De Klerk (2006) studies Xhosa English, a variety of English spoken as a second language in South Africa, in a corpus of over half a million transcribed words, collected from 317 speakers, consisting entirely of spoken, unrehearsed language.

2. Dialectal variety/varieties, e.g., the *Freiburg English Dialect Corpus*, with data collected in 43 different countries in 9 major dialect areas, the *IviE Corpus* (*Intonational variation in English,* English Intonation in the British Isles)*,* with recordings from different major or mainstream British dialects, or the *Limerick Corpus of Irish English*.

3. Range of time covered by the texts. *The Diachronic Corpus of Present-Day Spoken English* contains 400,000 words from *ICE-GB* (collected in the early 1990s) and 400,000 words from the *London-Lund Corpus* (late 1960s – early 1980s).

4. The age of the speakers. The data for some corpora is the spoken language of children (*CHILDES – Child Language Data Exchange System, POW – Polytechnic of Wales Corpus*), adults (*MAELC – The Multimedia Adult ESL Learner Corpus*), or teenagers (*COLT – The Bergen Corpus of London Teenage Language*, the *SACODEYL* corpus – *System Aided Compilation and Open Distribution of European Youth Language* – a multilingual and multi-functional corpus, containing European teen talk in the context of language education).

5. The text types and genres represented in the corpus and the domains to which they belong. There are some spoken corpora focusing on academic or professional English, e.g., *MICASE – Michigan Corpus of Academic Spoken English, BASE – British Academic Spoken English Corpus, CPSAE – Corpus of Spoken Professional American English*. There are also domain specific corpora, e.g., the *ATIS* (*Air Travel Information System*) corpus, whose aim is to provide data for research into how to set up dialogue systems for giving flight timetable information, or the *TRAINS* corpus, consisting of problem-solving dialogues dealing with the transport of goods by means of cargo trains.

6. Native or non-native producers of the texts. Although in most corpora the data collected belong to native speakers, some spoken corpora consist of material from learners of a second or a foreign language, e.g., the *LINDSEY Corpus* (*Louvain International Database of Spoken English Interlanguage*), or the Japanese learner corpus *NICT JLE* (Tono, this volume). In other cases the corpus consists of interactions between non-native speakers of English who use it as a lingua franca, e.g., *VOICE – Vienna Oxford International Corpus of English, ELFA – English as a Lingua Franca in Academic Settings*; or interactions between expert speakers (*SUE, Successful Users of English*; see Promodou 2003).

There are many other features that are considered when compiling, transcribing, marking-up and annotating oral corpora, e.g., the corpus format (machine readable texts or transcripts, audio recordings of different kinds, available tools and links between various formats in one or more corpora), the kind of tagging (for example, grammatical, pragmatic, phonetic, semantic, or stylistic features), the software that may be used for analysing the texts and the outcomes the software offers, the purpose of the corpus and its intended users (lexicographers, linguists, teachers, students), the size and availability of the corpus. All these features can help to highlight the differences and similarities between different spoken corpora, leading to a better understanding of research possibilities and classroom (or other) applications.

3. What can spoken corpora tell us about language use?

The potential applications of spoken corpora depend to a great extent on the criteria used for their compilation and codification. A spoken corpus annotated at multiple linguistic levels (i.e., corpora which provide annotation for phonetic, prosodic, syntactic, semantic, pedagogic, and discourse information) can be a highly useful resource to investigate how a specific feature at one level maps to a feature at another level. There are many areas where spoken corpora can be used, e.g., in the field of discourse analysis, to carry out research on the nature of orality and on the features of spoken discourse as compared with written discourse, in the field of speech technology, as a tool to develop phonological and prosodic models for speech technologies or to evaluate speech recognition systems. Due to space constraints, here we will only describe some pieces of research that illustrate how spoken corpora are being used in the areas that are most related to the topics covered in this volume.

One of the most evident applications of spoken corpora is research into phonetics, intonation and prosodic features, and this was the focus of some of the earlier research with these corpora (e.g., Knowles 1992, Wichmann 1991). Within this area, some researchers have focused on corpus-based studies of discourse prosody. For instance, Wichmann (2004), in her research on the intonation of please-requests, showed that the word *please*, which can be a full verb or a request marker, is realised prosodically in different ways that correlate with its semantic or pragmatic function.

A more recent line of research is the investigation of whether there is a special grammar of spoken English, a question that can only be answered thanks to the availability of sufficiently large spoken corpora. Leech (1998) considers that there are three possible answers to this question: "(i) spoken English has no grammar at all: it is grammatically inchoate; (ii) spoken English does not have a *special* grammar: its grammar is just the same as the grammar of written English; (iii) spoken English *does* have a special grammar – it has its own principles, rules and categories, which are different from those of the written language". Based on the results of research leading to a large corpus-based grammar of English (*Longman Grammar of Spoken and Written English*), which studied and compared a corpus of about 20 million words from the *Longman Spoken and Written English Corpus*, Leech (1998, 2000) supports the second answer. He considers that there is just one English grammar, and that conversational grammar is just a rather special implementation of the common grammar of English, which can be contrasted with other registers: both speech and writing make use of the same overall grammatical repertoire, but some features "might be overwhelmingly commoner in one than the other" (Leech 1998). Carter and McCarthy (1995) have used corpus analysis tools to explore features of spoken grammar and seem to support the third answer. They argue that there are many grammatical features inherent to speech which have been largely neglected by standard grammars and ELT materials, since these are mostly based on the analysis of written discourse, e.g., structures such as the "dislocated topic" of *This little shop ... it's lovely* or the "wagging tail" of *Oh I reckon they're lovely. I really do whippets.* These are features which result from the dynamic interactive nature of spoken discourse and therefore are not present in written discourse. Proponents of this view claim that the description of English spoken discourse for teaching purposes should be based on corpus analysis, which reveals regularities and patterns (Carter and McCarthy 1995).

In an attempt to define the features of spoken grammar, a great number of corpus-based studies have focused on how specific grammar items are used in spoken discourse, sometimes comparing structures in spoken and written discourse (Adolphs and Carter 2003, Berglund 2000, Tao and McCarthy 2001). More recently, Sinclair and Mauranen (2006: 9) propose a grammar where "the observed features of spoken text are given genuinely equal status vis-à-vis written text". This grammar has at its core a cyclical style of analysis in contrast to top-down grammars, where a "single pass" analysis and description is carried out, a method which seems to be inadequate, specially for some (less formal) language varieties. This grammar differs significantly from other proposals in that it considers written and spoken language together as data for analysis under the same methodology and terminology.

Spoken corpora are also being used to analyse the features of orality (De Haan 2002, O'Connell *et al.* 2004). O'Connell *et al.* (2004) analysed eight TV news interviews for markers of orality/ literacy (back channeling, hesitations, interruptions, contractions and elisions, first-person singular pronominals, interjections, and tag questions) and found that the most evident markers of orality were hesitations and first-person singular pronominals. Pérez Guerra (this volume) compares written and spoken English by quantifying several linguistic factors which are considered to be determinant of complexity. The purpose is to analyse linguistic complexity in English spoken texts.

The analysis of pragmatics and discoursal strategies is another challenging and promising line of research, despite the difficulties involved in compiling and coding corpora suitable for this kind of research (see Garcia, this volume). Part of this research focuses on individual items, such as discourse markers, back channel devices and fixed expressions. For instance, Beeching (2001) explores the role of the pragmatic particle *enfin* when it is used as a corrective, both to introduce a repair and in its mitigating or hedging role. Andersen (1997b) used the *Bergen Corpus of London Teenage Language* (COLT) to research the use of *like* as a discourse marker in London teenage speech. She concludes that *like* has a wide range of uses, many of which do not fit the labels which categorize this word in Standard English (e.g., verb or preposition/conjunction), and considers it as a multifunctional discourse marker. Buchstaller (2003) studies the co-occurrence of quotative verbs with mimetic enactment (i.e., the direct representation and total imitation of an event) based on two corpora of U.S. American English (the *Switchboard Corpus* and the *Santa Barbara Corpus of Spoken English)*. The paper shows that *be like* and *go* are synchronically used as quotative items for mimetic performances instead of quotative devices such as *say* and *think*.

A relatively small number of studies have concentrated on conversational acts, moves and exchanges (e.g., Koester 2002, Thomas and Wilson 1996). An example of this kind of research is the "Language in the workplace" project, whose aim is to study communication based on a corpus of real interactions in New Zealand workplaces. The goal of the project is "to identify and analyse features of effective interpersonal communication in a variety of workplaces from a sociolinguistic perspective" (Holmes 2000: 2). García (this volume) uses samples from the spoken portion of the *Spoken and Written Academic Language Corpus* to study the types of pragmatic functions that occur in this corpus and how these functions are realized linguistically. The results show great variability in the types of pragmatic functions speakers used in different situations (e.g., office hours, service encounters, study groups) and in the linguistic realization of these pragmatic functions. This study illustrates the suitability of spoken corpora as a resource to study language variation.

Spoken corpora are being used to study how language varies depending on the situation, on the text type or domain, on the region where it is spoken, or on variables such as social class, gender, age, etc. Some pieces of research draw on spoken corpora to explore variational pragmatics, in spite of the difficulties involved in working comparatively with spoken corpora. Studies of variational pragmatics may involve the use of two different spoken corpora to compare specific pragmatic features in two different languages or in two different varieties. The *COLA* corpus (*Corpus Oral de Lenguaje Adolescente* – Oral corpus of teenage language) is being used for this purpose. This is a corpus of informal language spoken by teenagers in Madrid and other Spanish speaking cities (e.g., Santiago de Chile, Buenos Aires, La Habana). The *COLA* corpus follows the same pattern as the *COLT* (*Bergen Corpus of London Teenage Language*) and *UNO* (*Språkkontakt och ungdomsspråk i Norden*) corpora, which makes it possible to carry out comparative analyses between the language spoken by Spanish, English and Nordic teenagers. For example, Stenström (2005, 2006) compares the use of some prominent features of teenage language (e.g., intensifiers, pragmatic markers, taboo words) in *COLT* and *COLAm* (*COLA* Madrid). In general, intensifiers are more frequent in the Madrid girls' conversations (Stenström 2005), but taboo words are more often used by the English middle/upper class girls than by the Spanish ones (Stenström 2006). The most popular ones were *fuck* and *joder*, which have the same meaning.

Other researchers have used other spoken corpora for similar studies. Müller (2004) investigates the use of the discourse marker *well* by German EFL speakers and compares the results with the use of this marker by American native speakers (NS). Of the twelve functions of *well* found in the data, nine were used more by the EFL than by the native speakers. Adolphs and O'Keeffe (2005) use the *Cambridge and Nottingham Corpus of Discourse in English (CANCODE)* and the *Limerick Corpus of Irish English* (*LCIE*) to compare listenership response tokens (i.e., mm, yeah, umhum) in British and Irish English. They examine the data at the level of variational pragmatics to find any possible correlation of forms, functions and/or frequency with variables such as speaker relationship, context and spoken genre.

Some spoken corpora are suitable to carry out studies of intercultural pragmatics. This is the case of the *Hong Kong Corpus of Conversational English*, consisting of recordings of conversations between Hong Kong Chinese and non-Cantonese speakers (mostly native speakers of English). This corpus can be used to study specific pragmatic elements in intercultural conversations. For instance, Cheng and Warren (2002) compare how *actually* is used by native and nonnative speakers of English in Hong Kong in intercultural conversations.

Several spoken corpora have been compiled taking into account sociolinguistic parameters, which makes it possible to use these corpora for sociolinguistic research. For instance, Andersen (1997a) uses two corpora with sociolinguistic annotation, the *COLT (The Bergen Corpus of Teenage Language)* and the spoken component of the *British National Corpus*, to determine whether there are distributional differences between teenage and adult conversation in the use of pragmatic markers, i.e., words such as *cos, like, innit, well, oh*. Stubbe and Holmes (1995) analysed the *Wellington Corpus of Spoken New Zealand English* to examine the frequency and type of pragmatic devices such as *you know* and *eh* used in oral New Zealand English. They found that *you know* and *eh* were more frequently used by working-class speakers than by middle-class speakers. They also found correlations with age and gender. Drescher (this volume) analyzes differences in the way that people in interactions involving different combinations of speaker/addressee sex and roles (e.g., a male student talking to a female professor) used a set of pragmatic and linguistic variables (e.g., hedges, hesitations and fillers) associated in the literature with gender and power relations.

Another frequent use of spoken corpora is the comparison of specific grammar features in different geographical varieties. Nelson (2004) examines the different ways of negating lexical *have* (e.g., *I don't have (any) money / I haven't any money / I haven't got any money / I have no money / I've got no money*) in corpus data from Great Britain, New Zealand, India, Hong Kong, and Singapore. The results show that the Outer Circle varieties (Hong Kong, India, Singapore) form a very distinct group of their own, in terms of the negation of lexical *have*. Tottie and Hoffman (2006) use instances of question tags extracted from the *British National Corpus* and the *Longman Spoken American Corpus* to investigate the differences between British English and American English as regards the use of "canonical" tag questions such as *It's raining, isn't it?, It's not raining, is it?*, or *It's raining, is it?* They found differences in frequency, in polarity types and operators in tags, and in pragmatic functions of tags in both varieties.

Spoken corpora are also being fruitfully used to investigate variation according to genres, registers, and contexts. Most of these studies have focused on academic discourse. Together with learner corpora, research based on English corpora made up of academic and professional discourse conforms most of the present volume. Academic English as used in various contexts is seen in Drescher, García and Cortés and Csomay, where analysis is carried out in different language use situations including university lectures, office hours, service encounters, study groups, and classroom management sessions. Mauranen's paper also focuses on academic English, in this case English as lingua franca in academic settings (*ELFA*). The number of papers devoted to academic and professional discourse in this volume attests to the appropriateness of using spoken corpora to analyse this type of discourse. We consider, therefore, that this application merits special attention.

4. Corpus-based research on academic and professional discourse

The *TOEFL 2000 Spoken and Written Academic Language (T2K-SWAL) Corpus* was constructed to fill the gap in large-scale empirical investigations of spoken academic registers. This corpus is made of spoken and written language at university, including both academic registers (e.g., classroom teaching and textbooks) and non-academic registers (e.g., service encounters). As an example of the kind of research performed with this corpus, we can mention Biber's (2003) Multi-Dimensional (MD) analysis of university spoken and written registers. A statistical factor analysis, using a large number of linguistic features (e.g., number of contractions, number of nominalizations), was performed and four major "dimensions" of variation were identified: (1) oral vs. literate discourse; (2) procedural vs. content-focused discourse; (3) narrative orientation; (4) academic stance.

A productive area of research is the analysis of complex lexical units in academic registers. Biber and Conrad (1999) studied the use of "lexical bundles" (sequences of words that commonly co-occur in a register, e.g., *one of the most, if you look at...*) in conversation and academic prose and found that the two registers differ in the types of lexical bundles. In a later study, Biber, Conrad and Cortés (2004) compare the lexical bundles in classroom teaching and textbooks to those found in their previous research on conversation and academic prose (Biber and Conrad 1999). The results show that classroom teaching uses more stance and discourse organizing bundles than conversation does, and, at the same time, classroom teaching uses more referential bundles than academic prose. Cortés and Csomay (this volume) examine the position of lexical bundles in the first few Vocabulary-based Discourse Units identified in university lectures.

A great deal of studies on oral academic discourse have used the *MICASE* corpus (*Michigan Corpus of Academic Spoken English*) to analyse a variety of issues. Here we will only comment on some examples of the kind of research that is being carried out with this corpus. Some pieces of research analyse the function of specific lexical items that seem to be especially frequent in academic speech. This is the case of studies which examine the expression of evaluation and other metadiscursive items (e.g., Lindemann and Mauranen 2001, Mauranen 2003, Poos and Simpson 2002). Lindemann and Mauranen (2001), for instance, investigate the roles of *just*, an item that is among the most frequent in distinguishing academic speech data from comparable written data. Poos and Simpson (2002) study the use of the hedges *kind of* and *sort of* in academic spoken English and show that the functions of these devices are rather diverse. They are not only used to express inexactitude, but also to soften the force of a stance or opinion, or to mitigate a criticism or request. Swales and Burke (2003) examine the function of evaluative adjectives and intensifiers across academic registers. Biber (2006) makes use of a different corpus (the *T2K-SWAL Corpus*) to compare the marking of stance in four academic spoken and written registers: classroom teaching, class management talk, textbooks and written course management language. Mauranen (2003) analyses the organising and socialising role of some metadiscursive items related to argumentation (e.g., *argue, claim, observe*). The analysis shows that different verbs are used differently: in different types of speech and by different speaker categories. For instance, *argue* is more frequently used by senior faculty members and is also more frequent in monologues.

Some smaller corpora have been designed with the purpose to examine features of a specific genre, and thus, include only instances of such genre. Farr (2003) uses a corpus of spoken English from an Irish university setting to examine three strategies of engaged listenership (minimal response tokens, non-minimal tokens, and simultaneous speech and interruptions) in meetings between tutors and graduate students. The results show that these strategies differ quantitatively and functionally. Webber (2005) uses a spoken corpus consisting of plenaries and paper presentations given at international medical conferences by competent speakers of English of various nationalities to analyse whether characteristics of the conversational mode are used in these genres as a resource for creating a relationship with the audience. Crawford (2004) uses a corpus of lecturers given by visiting academics (both L1 and L2 speakers) at the University of Florence, to compare the use of interactive discourse in these lectures and in a corpus of classroom lectures taken from the MICASE corpus.

Another important area which is currently gaining field is that of the compilation and analysis of *English as Lingua Franca* (ELF) corpora. In *English as Lingua Franca* corpora (ELF), the research interest shifts from data obtained from an ideal or native-like speaker to the use of English as communication tool between speakers with different L1 backgrounds in academic and professional contexts. As Mauranen suggests in this volume in a paper devoted to English as lingua franca in academic settings (ELFA), it is not enough to make use of academic and business language corpora including English native speakers' oral production: it is essential to incorporate ELF corpora to gain a more realistic view on English as used for international purposes among NNS and between NS and NNS. In the study of ELF it is crucial to bear in mind that we are talking about speakers with different language backgrounds, and thus, as Seidlhofer (2005: 340) states:

> ... the features of English which tend to be crucial for international intelligibility and therefore need to be taught for production and reception are being distinguished from the ('non-native') features that tend not to cause misunderstandings and thus do not need to constitute a focus for production teaching for those learners who intend to use English mainly in international settings.

Spoken corpora of professional language are harder to find. The *Cambridge and Nottingham Spoken Business English Corpus* (*CANBEC*) gathers a variety of spoken business samples such as presentations, informal meetings, or telephone conversations that take place in companies. These companies are representative of diverse business situations since they range from small to big multinational companies thus being a good example to examine interactions in different contexts where interaction between professionals may differ from one enterprise to another.

Science, engineering, technology, law, medicine, finance, and other professions are taken into account by *PERC*, the *Professional English Research Consortium*, which develops corpus data including spoken and written discourse used by working professionals and professionals-in-training to engage in workplace speech. Other examples of spoken corpora made up of professional language are the *Corpus of Spoken Professional American-English* (*CSPAE*), which is made up of interactions in professional settings (academic and White House press conferences); or the *Hong Kong Corpus of Spoken English* which contains among other spoken text types, professional speech. The *Spoken Chinese Corpus of Situated Discourse* (SCCSD) is a multimodal corpus (Audio/Video chunks linked to transcripts) with transcribed and annotated recordings of Mandarin Chinese spoken in China, including speech in a variety of activities, among which is workplace discourse in Chinese.

5. Spoken corpora and language learning

A field where spoken corpora are taking on a prominent role is that of second language learning. Although most corpus-based research in the language learning context relies on native speaker (NS) corpora, other kinds of corpora, such as *English as Lingua Franca* corpora or *learner corpora* are gaining a roothold in the SLA realm. Learner corpora are "systematic computerized collections of texts produced by language learners" with specific compilation criteria that differentiates them from native speaker corpora such as including level and L1 of learners (speakers), language acquisition type (instructed/naturalistic) and task setting (Nesselhauf 2004: 125, 130). They are used for the comparison of language use between different groups of learners and between learners and native or expert speakers (de Cock, this volume; Granger 1998). Spoken learner corpora do not have a peripheral role anymore, as attested by projects on learner corpora such as the *Louvain International Database of Spoken English Interlanguage* (*LINDSEI*), which contains data from English language learners with different mother tongue backgrounds. However, there are still few spoken learner corpora when compared with written learner corpora, which may be in part due to the difficulties involved in their compilation.

In the teaching of spoken skills there are still many things that may be observed and learnt by contrasting native speaker and learner corpora. O'Keefe *et al.* (2007:140 ff) analyse listener responses in native speaker corpora to see how different contexts call for different responses and to study the functions that those responses have in spoken events. They suggest that learners should be encouraged not only to exchange information but also to use language in order to keep good relationships with other people so as to achieve successful communication.

The exploitation of corpora to create teaching materials has undergone a significant change during the last decade. Although Carter and McCarthy (1995: 144) have argued that corpora may be a "useful resource for teachers and learners", it seems that until recently they have not had much remarkable impact on pedagogic material, except for learner dictionaries (Nesselhauf, 2004). This may be due to the fact that, as Williams (1988: 45-46) suggests, textbook writers do not consult appropriate corpora when designing materials. However, despite claims pointing to the static nature of materials and the use of intuitive judgements, it seems that things are changing. Corpus-based research comparing textbooks and natural language production is growing (e.g., Frazier 2003, Römer 2005) and textbooks are beginning to integrate the use of corpora. Carter and McCarthy (1997) designed a textbook for spoken English with extracts from a spoken language corpus. Römer (2005) focuses on progressives in a variety of settings (written and spoken), comparing, among other aspects, the functions and contexts where progressives occur in spoken British English and the way they are presented in instructional settings and materials, deriving useful pedagogical implications. Cheng (this volume) analyses interrupting strategies in textbooks in contrast to data obtained from a spoken corpus of intercultural speakers in communicative contexts. Recent textbooks (such as the *Touchstone* series published by Cambridge University Press) clearly show that the use of corpora in the design of teaching materials is no longer a future enterprise but one that is already generating fruitful results.

In the same way that the use of "real language" in textbooks and other pedagogical materials has been a much debated issue within the language teaching community, in compiling learner corpora authenticity and the conditions in which these corpora are gathered generate much debate among researchers. The degree of authenticity of the tasks from which language databases are developed and the relationship among speakers may be questioned from different angles. For instance, (oral) exams – which are the base for some learner corpora – are not always representative of what the student knows, since they are done under some degree of pressure. Interviews with teachers may have a similar pressure effect. Various degrees of spoken language knowledge are also missed: in a written task the student may revise the results, while in an oral task this is not always possible to the same extent (they may use self-correction but not revise the whole production or event after they have finished), even in cases where some preparation would be natural in a real situation. It is interesting to note that some corpora combine data obtained through different degrees of guidance (see Osborne, this volume), from free to semi-guided to guided tasks. Another aspect which affects oral production is the partner with whom one has to carry out a conversation, since the ability of the other person to communicate and the real life relation-ship between the language learners may facilitate or hinder their own production (contrast for instance the pairs student / student and student / teacher or expert/non-expert).

The use of corpus-based information in language teaching has contributed considerably to changes in the way spoken and written corpora are compiled and used. Previous corpus use for language teaching purposes relied to a great extent on concordances and the identification of collocates in order to focus on lexical and gram-matical patterns. But pedagogically oriented corpora are currently experiencing a shift from focus on concordance to focus on text and text selection: the challenge now lies in the enhancement of the connection between the concordance, or bottom-up approach to corpus use, and the top-down, text-oriented approach. In the inter-section, understanding and application of both approaches lies the future of corpora in learning environments, as suggested in figure 1:

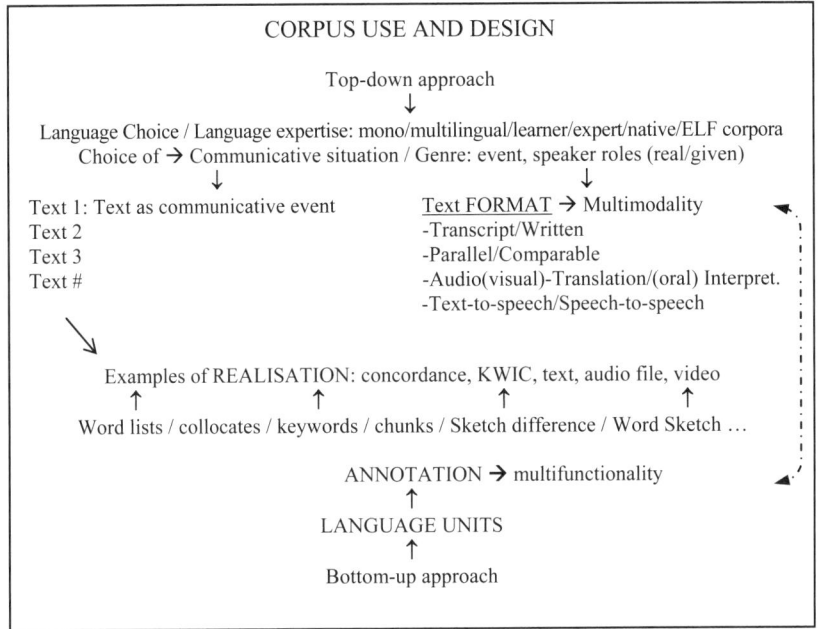

Figure 1. Pedagogic and user oriented corpus exploitation and design.

Thus, instead of dealing with texts outside the communicative event in which they were created, corpora such as the *ELISA* corpus (*English Language Interview Corpus as a Second-language Application*) are designed combining access and information about a communicative event and other similar events in the application. As well as integrating the text approach, new annotation models based on pragmatic information and on methodological issues are provided. The *ELISA* corpus (Braun 2006) annotates, for instance, grammatical keys devised to point out grammatical issues which may be valuable or worth working within a language learning context.

In this context, multimodality (different communication modes combined in one text where interaction between these modes is necessary to fully or better understand the text) plays an essential role, especially in spoken corpora such as the *ELISA* corpus, which includes audiovisual materials, (commented) transcripts, translations, informative and illustrative materials among other informational devices. The *Multimedia Adult ESL Learner Corpus* (*MAELC*) takes a step further to develop not only a multimedia corpus, but a corpus capable of showing learning stages, thus facilitating longitudinal studies (Reder *et al.* 2003). In the *MAELC*, classroom codes and student language may be merged in the same corpus search, allowing researchers to study the correlation between pedagogical activities and student language development.

6. Spoken corpora and interpreting

Corpus linguistics is also becoming very popular among translation scholars, since this new area of research allows a rapid and accurate examination of large amounts of naturally occurring language. The use of corpora is extending towards the area of interpreting. Considered as subsumed under translation, interpreting research is often based on anecdotal data (Shlesinger, 1998). The advent of corpora, mainly of oral corpora, is introducing new models of research that can benefit this area. However, the use of corpus-based methodology in the study of interpreting poses some problems. According to Shlesinger (1998:2), there are two main obstacles that have to be overcome in order to achieve a full-fledged paradigm of corpus-based interpreting studies. The first one is related to transcription:

> While the input [...] may often be available in machine-readable [...] form, the interpreters' output is not. For all the advances of modern technology, transcription is still a labour-intense and arduous process which poses a major methodological hurdle.

As other scholars state, the problem is not transcription alone but the fact that many elements of spoken communication are so subtle that it is impossible to grasp all of them (Cook 1995, O'Connell and Sabine 1993, Shlesinger 1998). A second obstacle, also related to features of spoken communication, is that researchers have to keep in mind paralinguistic dimensions of language such as intonational subtleties.

Despite these difficulties, the use of corpora offers numerous advantages in the area of interpreting research. The application of corpus linguistics to interpretation provides information about grammatical constructions, discourse patterns, lexical density, etc. Moreover, as Shlesinger (1998) adds, interpreting can benefit from the design of comparable and parallel corpora. Regarding comparable corpora, this author proposes the development of three separate collections of texts in the same language: interpreted texts, original oral discourses delivered in similar settings, and written translations of the texts. Shlesinger (1998: 3) points to the following benefits of her proposal:

> This would allow for the identification of patterns specific to interpreted texts (regardless of their source language) as *pieces of oral discourse,* in relation to comparable texts in the same language. It would also allow us to identify the patterns which single out interpreted texts as distinct oral translational products in a given language irrespective or their source language, through comparisons with comparable written translational products.

Regarding the design of parallel corpora, Shlesinger (1998: 4) notes that three collections of texts would be necessary: source-language texts, the corresponding interpreted versions, and the corresponding written translations, if available. Thus, using parallel corpora in interpreting could shed light on different linguistic and text linguistics features of the interpreted output.

Some studies focus on the design and research of corpora in simultaneous interpreting.[2] The *Centre for Integrated Acoustic Information Research* (*CIAIR*), at Nagoya University, is involved in some studies on corpora and interpreting. Ryu *et al.* (2003) report the development and compilation of a bilingual speech dialogue corpus (English-Japanese) for linguistic and contrastive purposes. This corpus has been constructed by collecting simulated cross-lingual conversations between English and Japanese speeches (manually transcribed with bilingual sentence alignment) through simultaneous interpretation.

---

2   The simultaneous interpreter's utterance begins before the source one finishes, which enables the simultaneous interpreter to reduce the listener's waiting time and make a contribution to natural bilingual conversations.

Focusing also on simultaneous interpreting, Takagi *et al.* (2002) analyse interpreters' speeches using an aligned simultaneous monolingual interpreting corpus in order to investigate different factors, including interpreters' speaking speed, the interpreting unit of simultaneous interpretation and the difference between the beginning time of the lecturers' and interpreters' utterance. The painstaking analysis involves the description of and statistics about significant interpreting features such as recording time, the number of utterance units, the number of morphemes (words), the speaking time and the number of discourse tags. The authors reach conclusions that clearly allow the identification of patterns in simultaneous interpreting and therefore serve as a starting point for future studies.

Other studies apply a corpus-based methodology to the study of interpreting skills. We can take the research by Van Besien (1999) as an example. This author investigates the interpreting skill known as *anticipation*, which he describes as "the simultaneous interpreters' production of a constituent (a word or a group of words) in the target language before the speaker has uttered the corresponding constituent in the source language" (Van Besien 1999: 250). Anticipation in simultaneous interpreting is generally considered as a language-specific phenomenon and the result of the combination of a top-down strategy and a bottom-up strategy. In outline, the study designed by Van Besien (1999) reveals that anticipation is a general strategy used by interpreters, occurring every 85 seconds, and shows that it is mainly a linguistic phenomenon, as the percentage for verb anticipation is very high.

7. Conclusions

Although the overview of spoken corpora presented in this paper is fairly limited and selective, we hope that it will prepare the ground for the in-depth studies included in this volume, which illustrate the variety and productivity of spoken corpora.

The paper has shown the wide range of applications of spoken corpora. Generally speaking, the most fruitful applications seem to be those that have as their main aim to develop teaching and learning strategies oriented towards the fields of (E)LT and English for professional and academic purposes. Researchers in these areas claim for a situation or context-based approach in the use and analysis of spoken genres through corpora. They also advocate that in the use of multimodal corpora lies the future for a more in-depth analysis where all aspects of oral communication, verbal and non-verbal, can be fully understood (see O'Keefe *et al.*'s (2007: 142) discussion of the term "response token"). The multifunctionality of multimodal corpora should be enhanced by means not only of access to different interlinked corpus formats but also of annotation at different linguistic and educational levels.

As more specialised spoken corpora are created, new research interests come into view that provide fresh insights into how language is used in a given context as well as new ideas on how to exploit these corpora. One such case is research carried out by Farr (this volume), who studies a corpus that shows the use of language in professional teaching practices in order to analyse how such practices are performed, how successful they are, and how to improve them when they are not so successful. Regarding corpora for professional teaching practices, O'Keefe *et al.* (2007: 221) rightly point out how "in-house teacher corpora can offer a valuable supplement to published training materials [...] because the practices of teaching must be interpreted within their contexts of realisation". This observation of professional language teaching practice may also be extended to other areas to observe how people communicate in various professional contexts and in different cultures.

Another important issue is the wide variety of different levels of language expertise covered in new corpora. Spoken learner corpora reflecting a number of proficiency language levels are steadily increasing. There is also a growing interest in the compilation, study and comparison of a wide range of expert language users, ranging from native speakers to successful speakers of English (SUE), to speakers of English as Lingua Franca.

Finally, we have also seen that the use of a corpus-based methodology is opening up new avenues of research in interpreting. Different types of corpora can be designed to identify patterns in interpreted texts (Shlesinger, 1998) and their analysis may reveal interesting results about interpreting skills such as anticipation (Van Besien, 1999).

The great variety and usability of spoken corpora discussed in this introductory chapter and illustrated by the papers in this volume brings to the foreground the need for more publications reporting research in this field. We are confident that the studies in this volume will inspire future advances in the field of corpus linguistics.

8. References

Adolphs, Svenja / O'Keeffe, Anne 2005. Using a corpus to look at variational pragmatics: listenership in British and Irish discourse. Paper read at the *9th International Pragmatics Conference*. Riva del Garda, Italy, July 10–15, 2005.

Adolphs, Svenja / Carter, Ronald 2003. And she's like "it's terrible like": Spoken Discourse, Grammar and Corpus Analysis. *International Journal of English Studies*, 3/1, 45-56.

Andersen, Gisle 1997a. Pragmatic markers in teenage and adult conversation. Paper presented at the *18th ICAME Conference*. Chester, May 1997.

Andersen, Gisle 1997b. "They like wanna see like how we talk and all that." The use of "like" as a discourse marker in London teenage speech. In Ljung, Magnus (ed.) *Corpus-based studies in English*. Amsterdam: Rodopi, 37-48.

Beeching, Kate 2001. Repair strategies and social interaction in spontaneous spoken French: the pragmatic particle *enfin*. *Journal of French Language Studies*, 11, 23-40.

Berglund, Ylva 2000. Gonna and Going to in the spoken component of the BNC. In Mair, Christian / Hundt, Marianne (eds) *Corpus Linguistics and Linguistic Theory*. Amsterdam: Rodopi, 35-49.

Biber, Douglas 2006. Stance in spoken and written university registers. *Journal of English for Academic Purposes*, 5, 97-116.

Biber, Douglas 2003. Variation among university spoken and written registers: a new multi-dimensional analysis. In Leistyna, Pepi / Meyer, Charles (eds) *Corpus Analysis. Language Structure and Language Use*. Amsterdam: Rodopi, 47-70.

Biber, Douglas / Conrad, Susan / Cortés, Viviana 2004. *If you look at...:* Lexical bundles in university teaching and textbooks. *Applied Linguistics*, 25/3, 371-405.

Biber, Douglas / Conrad, Susan 1999. Lexical bundles in conversation and academic prose. In Hasselgard, Hilde / Oksefiell, Signe (eds) *Out of Corpora: Studies in Honor of Stig Johansson.* Amsterdam: Rodopi. 181-190.

Braun, Sabine 2006. ELISA: A pedagogically-enriched corpus for language learning purposes. In Braun, Sabine / Khon, Kurt / Joybrato, Mukherjee (eds) *Corpus Technology and Language Pedagogy.* English Corpus Linguistics. 3. Frankfurt: Peter Lang, 25-48.

Buchstaller, Isabelle. 2003. The Co-Occurrence of Quotatives with Mimetic Performances. *Edinburgh Working Papers in Applied Linguistics*, 12, 1-8.

Carter, Ronald / McCarthy, Michael 1995. Grammar and the spoken language. *Applied Linguistics,* 16/2, 141-158.

Carter, Ronald / McCarthy, Michael 1997. *Exploring Spoken English.* Cambridge: Cambridge University Press.

Cheng, Winnie / Warren, Martin 2002. The Functions of Actually in a Corpus of Intercultural Conversations. *International Journal of Corpus Linguistics*, 6/2, 257-280.

Cheng, Winnie 2007. *Sorry to interrupt, but ...:* Pedagogical implications of a spoken corpus. In Campoy, Mari Carmen / Luzón, Maria José 2007. *Spoken Corpora in Applied Linguistics.* Linguistic Insights 51. Peter Lang: Bern. 199-215.

Cook, Guy 1995. Theoretical issues: transcribing the untranscribable. In G. Leech / G. Myers / J. Thomas (eds) *Spoken English on Computer: Transcription, Mark-up and Applications*. London: Longman, 35-53.

Cortés, Viviana / Csomay, Eniko 2007. Positioning lexical boundaries in university lectures. In Campoy, Mari Carmen / Luzón, Maria José 2007. *Spoken Corpora in Applied Linguistics*. Linguistic Insights 51. Peter Lang: Bern. 57-76.

Crawford, Belinda 2004. Interactive discourse structuring in L2 guest lectures: some insights from a comparative corpus-based study. *Journal of English for Academic Purposes*. 3/1, 39-54.

de Cock, Sylvie. 2007. Routinized building blocks in native speaker and learner speech. In Campoy, Mari Carmen / Luzón, Maria José 2007. *Spoken Corpora in Applied Linguistics*. Linguistic Insights 51. Peter Lang: Bern. 217-233.

de Haan, Pieter (2002) The non-nominal character of spoken English. In Breivik, Leiv / Hasselgren, Angela (eds) *From the COLT's mouth ... and others,* Amsterdam, New York: Rodopi. 59-69.

de Klerk, Vivian. 2006. *Corpus Linguistics and World Englishes: An Analysis of Xhosa English.* Continuum Press: London.

Drescher, Nancy 2007. "Linguistic variation in U.S. universities: a multidimensional analysis of spoken language". In Campoy, Mari Carmen / Luzón, Maria José 2007. *Spoken Corpora in Applied Linguistics*. Linguistic Insights 51. Peter Lang: Bern. 77-95.

Farr, Fiona 2003. Engaged Listenership in Spoken Academic Discourse: The Case of Student-Tutor Meetings. *Journal of English for Academic Purposes*, 2/1, 67-85.

Farr, Fiona 2007. Spoken corpus analysis as a tool for reflective practice in language teacher education: quantitative and qualitative insights. In Campoy, Mari Carmen / Luzón, Maria José 2007. *Spoken Corpora in Applied Linguistics*. Linguistic Insights 51. Peter Lang: Bern. 235-258.

Frazier, Stefan 2003. A corpus analysis of "would"-clauses without adjacent "if-clauses". *TESOL Quarterly*, 37/3, 443-466.

García, Paula 2007. Pragmatics in academic contexts: a spoken corpus study. In Campoy, Mari Carmen / Luzón, Maria José 2007. *Spoken Corpora in Applied Linguistics*. Linguistic Insights 51. Peter Lang: Bern. 97-126.

Granger, Sylviane (ed.) 1998. *Learner English on Computer*. London: Longman.

Holmes, Janet 2000. Victoria University's Language in the Workplace Project: An Overview. *Language in the Workplace Occasional Papers 1*. Retrieved 19 May 2007, from: <http://www.vuw.ac.nz/ lals/research/lwp/docs/ops/op1.pdf>.

Knowles, Gerry 1992 Pitch contours and tones in the Lancaster/IBM spoken English corpus. In Leitner, Gerhard (ed.) *New Directions in English Language Corpora. Methodology, Results, Software Development*. Berlin: Mouton de Gruyter. 289-300.

Koester, Almut Josepha 2002. The Performance of Speech Acts in Workplace Conversations and the Teaching of Communicative Functions. *System*. 30/2, 167-184.

Leech, Geoffrey 1998. English Grammar in Conversation. Paper given at the Language Learning and Computers Conference, 20-21 February, 1998. Retrieved 11 May, 2007, from: <http://www.tu-chemnitz.de/phil/english/chairs/linguist/real/independent/llc/Conference1998/Papers/Leech/Leech.htm>.

Leech, Geoffrey 2000 Grammars of Spoken English: New Outcomes of Corpus-Oriented Research. *Language Learning,* 50/4, 675-674.

Lindemann, Stephanie / Mauranen, Anna 2001. "It's Just Real Messy": The Occurrence and Function of "Just" in a Corpus of Academic Speech. *English for Specific Purposes*, 20/1, 459-475.

Mauranen, Anna 2003. "But here's a flawed argument": socialisation into and through metadiscourse. In Leistyna, Pepi / Meyer, Charles F. (eds) *Corpus Analysis: Language Structure and Language Use*. Amsterdam: Rodopi, 19-34.

Mauranen, Anna 2007. Investigating English as a lingua franca with a spoken corpus. In Campoy, Mari Carmen / Luzón, Maria José 2007. *Spoken Corpora in Applied Linguistics*. Linguistic Insights 51. Peter Lang: Bern. 33-56.

Müller, Simone 2004. 'Well you know that type of person': functions of well in the speech of American and German students. *Journal of Pragmatics,* 36/6, 1157-1182.

Nelson, Gerald 2004. Negation of lexical *have* in conversational English. In Nelson, Gerald (ed.) *World English Special Issue on the International Corpus of English*, 23/2, 299-308.

Nesselhauf, Nadja 2004. Learner corpora and their potential for language teaching. In John Sinclair (ed.) *How to Use Corpora in Language Teaching*. Amsterdam: John Benjamins, 125-152.

O'Connell, Daniel / Kowal, Sabine 1993. Some sources of error in the transcription of real time in spoken discourse. *The Jerome Quaterly*, 8/3, 3-11.

O'Connell Daniel / Kowal, Sabine / Dill, Edward 2004. Dialogicality in TV news interviews. *Journal of Pragmatics*, 36/2, 147-374.

O'Keefe, Anne / McCarthy, Michael / Carter, Ron. 2007. *From Corpus to Classroom*. Cambridge University Press.

Osborne, John 2007. Investigating L2 fluency through oral learner corpora. In Campoy, Mari Carmen / Luzón, Maria José 2007. *Spoken Corpora in Applied Linguistics*. Linguistic Insights 51. Peter Lang: Bern. 181-197.

Pérez Guerra, Javier 2007. "When am I more complex, when I speak or when I write?" A corpus-based study on linguistic complexity in spoken and written present-day English. In Campoy, Mari Carmen / Luzón, Maria José 2007. *Spoken Corpora in Applied Linguistics*. Linguistic Insights 51. Peter Lang: Bern. 127-146.

Poos, Deanna / Simpson, Rita 2002. Cross-disciplinary comparisons of hedging: some findings from the Michigan Corpus of academic spoken English. In Reppen, Randi / Fitzmaurice, Susan / Biber, Douglas (eds), *Using Corpora to Explore Linguistic Variation*. Amsterdam / Philadelphia: John Benjamins, 3-23.

Prodromou, Luke 2003. In search of SUE: the successful user of English. *Modern English Teacher*, 12/5-14.

Reder, Stephen / Harris, Kathryn / Setzler, Kristen 2003. The Multimedia Adult Learner Corpus. TESOL Quarterly, 37/3, 546-557.

Römer, Ute. 2005. Progressives, Patterns, Pedagogy. A Corpus Driven Approach to English Progressive Forms, Functions, Contexts and Didactics. Studies in Corpus Linguistics 18. John Benjamins.

Ryu, Koichiro / Matsubara, Shigeki / Kawaguchi, Nobuo / Inagaki, Yasuyoshi 2003. Bilingual speech dialogue corpus for simultaneous machine interpretation research. *Proceedings of Oriental COCOSDA-2003*. Retrieved 2 February, 2007, from: <http://slp. el.itc.nagoya-u.ac.jp/paper_pdf/2003/Oriental_COCOSDA2003_ ryu.pdf>.

Seidlhofer, Barbara 2005. Key concepts in ELT. English as lingua franca. *ELT Journal,* 59/4, 339-341.

Shlesinger, Miriam 1998. Corpus-based interpreting studies as an offshoot of corpus-based Translation Studies. *Meta*, XLIII/4, 486-493.

Sinclair, John / Mauranen, Anna 2006. *Linear Unit Grammar. Integrating Speech and Writing.* Studies in Corpus Linguistics 25. Amsterdam. John Benjamins.

Stenström, Annette B. 2005. *He's well nice – Es mazo majo.* London and Madrid girls' use of intensifiers. In S. Granath / J. Millander / E. Wennö (eds) *The Power of Words. Studies in Honour of Moira Linnarud.* Karlstad: Karlstad University.

Stenström, Annette B. 2006. Taboo words in teenage talk: London and Madrid girls' conversations compared. *Spanish In Context,* 3/1, 115-138.

Stubbe, Maria / Holmes, Janet (1995). "You Know", "Eh", and Other "Exasperating Expressions": An Analysis of Social and Stylistic Variation in the Use of Pragmatic Devices in a Sample of New Zealand English. *Language & Communication*, 15/1, 63-88.

Swales, John / and Burke, Amy 2003. "It's really fascinating work": Differences in Evaluative Adjective across Academic Registers. In Leistyna, Pepi / Meyer, Charles (eds) *Corpus Analysis. Language Structure and Language Use.* Amsterdam: Rodopi, 1-18.

Takagi, A. / Matsubara, Shigeki / Kawaguchi, Nobuo / Inagaki, Yasuyoshi 2002. A corpus-based analysis of simultaneous interpretation. *Proceedings of Joint International Conference of 5th Symposium on Natural Language Processing (SNLP-2002) & Oriental COCOSDA Worskshop 2002* , Hua Hin, Thailand, May, 2002. 167-174. Retrieved 2 February, 2007, from: <http://slp.el.itc.nagoya-u.ac.jp/ paper_pdf/2002/snlp2002_takagi.pdf>.

Tao, Hongyin / McCarthy, Michael 2001. Understanding Non-Restrictive "Which"-Clauses in Spoken English, Which Is Not an Easy Thing. *Language Sciences*, 23/6, 651-77.

Thomas Jenny / Wilson, Andrew 1996. Methodologies for studying a corpus of doctor-patient interaction. In Thomas, Jenny / Short, Mick (eds) *Using Corpora for Language Research.* London: Longman, 92-109.

Tono, Yukio 2007. The roles of oral L2 learner corpora in language teaching: the case of the NICT JLE Corpus. In Campoy, Mari Carmen / Luzón, Maria José 2007. *Spoken Corpora in Applied Linguistics*. Linguistic Insights 51. Peter Lang: Bern. 163-179.

Tottie, Gunnel / Hoffmann, Sebastian 2006. Tag questions in British and American English. *Journal of English Linguistics*. 34/4, 283-311.

Van Besien, Fred. 1999. Anticipation in simultaneous interpretation. *Meta*, 44/2, 250-259.

Webber, Pauline 2005. Interactive Features in Medical Conference Monologue. *English for Specific Purposes*, 24/2, 157-181.

Wichmann, Anne 1991. A study of up-arrows in the Lancaster/IBM Spoken English Corpus. In Johansson, Stig / Stenström, Annette (eds) *English Computer Corpora. Selected Papers and Research Guide*. Berlin: Mouton de Gruyter, 165-178.

Wichmann, Anne 2004. The intonation of please-requests: a corpus-based study. *Journal of Pragmatics*, 36, 1521-1549.

Williams, Marion 1988. Language taught for meetings and language used in meetings: Is there anything in common? *Applied Linguistics*, 9/1, 45-58.

II. The Use of Spoken Corpora for Language Research

ANNA MAURANEN

Investigating English as a Lingua Franca with a Spoken Corpus

1. Introduction

Analysing spoken language as it occurs in natural interaction has provided radically new insights into language: in the last few decades, research traditions with a focus on speaking (discourse analysis, conversation analysis, pragmatics) have revitalised linguistics and challenged the adequacy of sentence-based models, which tend to be based on written language, even invented examples. Spoken discourse has turned out to be much more organised than the imposition of sentence-based models would allow. New categories of linguistic items, such as discourse particles (e.g. Östman 1981, Aijmer 2002), have made their way to linguistic description, redefining the boundaries of pragmatics and semantics; the analysis of dialogues has questioned descriptions of lexical (e.g. Tao 2001) and grammatical items (e.g. Biber et al. 1999, Ford et al.2003, Carter and McCarthy 2006) as well as the role of grammar in the light of unfolding discourse (e.g. Brazil 1995, Du Bois 2003, Selting and Couper-Kuhlen 2001, Hakulinen and Selting 2005, Sinclair and Mauranen 2006). Significant novel departures from conventional descriptions, such as an understanding of collocations, phraseology and basic units of meaning, are based on corpus data, notably in Sinclair's work (e.g. 1991, 1996), which rests on large-scale evidence of language. In all, recent studies of speech as well of corpora have challenged basic linguistic notions in important ways. Nevertheless, corpus work has on the whole been heavily dominated by written language, which has overshadowed the full potential of combining speech and corpus studies. This balance is gradually getting redressed, as more spoken corpus work is emerging in different places and in different languages.

Pedagogic uses of corpora have been equally, if not more, biased towards written language. Of the rich supply of recent work on corpora in language learning, the vast majority take written discourse as their point of departure – for example Aston et al. (2004), Gavioli (2005), Hunston (2002), Sinclair (2004), to name but a few. It is nevertheless clear that the more emphasis is put on spoken skills in the teaching syllabus, the more we require adequate evidence to build this syllabus on. The traditional understanding in academic spoken skills teaching has been that academic discourse is essentially similar across the spoken and written modes; therefore the teaching contents in terms of terminology, vocabulary, phraseology etc. would be more or less identical, only the practical exercises should differ. A case study of the integration of a spoken corpus into an oral skills course a few years ago brought into sharp focus this time-honoured wisdom, which turned out to be one of the biggest obstacles of a smooth integration of corpus data into teaching EAP spoken skills (Mauranen 2004a).

Since late 1990's, research into academic speaking has greatly shaken previous beliefs in the nature of speaking in university contexts. It has turned out – with hindsight perhaps not so surprisingly – that academic speaking is in most respects closer to speaking in general than it is to academic writing. As Biber puts it in his extensive comparison of academic registers in written and spoken language, "spoken university registers are strikingly different in their typical linguistic characteristics from written university registers" (Biber 2006: 228).

Increasingly, employers expect university graduates to have good skills in English, especially as international company fusions continue and more and more large businesses adopt English as their company language even if none of the countries involved may have English as an official language. The demand for English is not in itself new, but the growing emphasis on fluent spoken skills is, as a recent survey of employers' wishes reveals (Karjalainen and Lehtonen 2005). Another new feature is that graduates in working life use English predominantly with other non-native speakers from all over the world, not so much with native speakers (Suviniitty forthcoming).

Since academics themselves also mostly need English for international purposes, for mobility more often than immigration into an English-speaking country, it is vital to take the requirements of English as a lingua franca (ELF) on board. It is not enough to make use of corpora of native speaker academics, but also of ELF corpora, to get a realistic view of what academic speaking is like in today's world.

This paper focuses on English – but unlike the vast majority of English corpora, it addresses English used by non-native speakers. It presents the new speech corpus of *English as a Lingua Franca in Academic Settings* (ELFA, see section 3 below). This is not a learner corpus, because the speakers are not trying to learn English; they use it for ordinary communication in a university setting. It is important to make a distinction between foreign language speakers and foreign language learners. This difference is thrown in to sharp relief by the current role of English in the world, where it is spoken approximately five times more by non-native than native speakers. We cannot reduce the world to a universe of learners, or capture the current developments of the English language by limiting our research to the native speaking minority.

This increasing use of English as a global lingua franca has implications for teaching spoken English. ELF is very heterogeneous, perhaps even more so than native Englishes, with speakers from virtually any language background. ELF speakers' proficiency in English also varies widely. Anyone using ELF must be prepared for a high degree of unpredictability. Spoken interaction in ELF is therefore very demanding, and requires an understanding of the linguistic characteristics of ELF as well as appropriate coping strategies, which are not the same as those required in native – non-native interaction: in ELF situations, neither of the interlocutors has the large language repertoire nor the authoritative say on preferred expressions that natives are normally attributed with. To come to grips with the demands of the situation, we need good databases on which to draw. We need corpora of English as a lingua franca.

2. English at a new stage

English has long been the language which has attracted the most corpus research and which has the widest variety of different kinds of corpora, as well as the largest ones (notably the *Bank of English* and the *British National Corpus* as the best-known examples). Speech data has been included in the large reference corpora from the start (the OSTI project, see Krishnamurthy 2004), but in large reference corpora speech has constituted only a fraction of the amount of written data. A pioneering spoken corpus, much used by scholars to the present day, was the *London-Lund Corpus of Spoken English* (Svartvik 1990). Others followed, and especially the 1990s witnessed a new wave of interest in spoken corpora, with the compilation of corpora like the COLT corpus (Stenström et al. 2002), the CANCODE corpus (e.g. Carter and McCarthy 2006), the *Santa Barbara Corpus* (Du Bois 2000) and the two American academic corpora: MICASE (Simpson et al. 2002), which is entirely spoken, and T2K-SWAL (Biber et al. 2004), which includes both speech and writing, as well as BASE (www.rdg.ac.uk/slals/base) in the UK.

The study of English corpora has sought to capture the intuitions, norms and preferences of the native speaker from all possible angles. With some reluctance, the research community has even accepted the study of nonstandard English – as long as it is the speakers' native language. Yet the largest group of English speakers today, non-native speakers, have been all but forgotten. This is surprising in view of the global role of English. We could hardly imagine international business and politics now without English – it is used everywhere, from shipping and aviation to peacekeeping troops as a normal part of their activities, just as it has become the language of tourism, sport and entertainment. These uses are a crucial element of the picture of English today – and probably even more of its future.

In a recent report, Graddol (2006) predicts an end to English as a foreign language (EFL) as we know it, with native speakers providing the gold standard. He is convinced that the teaching of English will become an integral part of mainstream education worldwide, that is, a basic skill instead of just another foreign language. In our postmodern world, the myth of a uniform standard language becomes less and less relevant and harder to maintain.

As English has made its way to every corner of the world, it has developed a large number of varieties, some of which have institutional status, others not, some fairly established and identifiable, other less so. Varieties indigenised in countries where English has an institutional status, the "outer circle" in Kachru's (1985) terms, such as India, Singapore, or South Africa, have not always been easily accepted as varieties in their own right, but with time they have increasingly become subject to linguistic research and to codification. The research community has been much slower to react in the case of English used as a lingua franca. While English as a foreign language has been studied extensively for a long time as 'learner language', the actual use of the language outside classrooms and learning contexts has been neglected until very recently. Learner English is of interest to practitioners and researchers for many practical and theoretical reasons (see, e.g. Granger et al. 2002), and the study of second-language *use* is not competing with that: it simply has different goals. Many features of learner language are relevant to and shared by 'real-world' second language speakers; conversely, investigating English as a lingua franca opens a new window to understanding a second language in real-world use.

L2 speakers of English are becoming increasingly aware that their most likely interlocutors are other non-native speakers (Suvi-niitty forthcoming), and that this has consequences on the manner of interaction – its problems as well as its facilitating aspects. Learners follow suit: around a third of students in Germany (Erling 2004) and Finland (Ranta 2004) set their future goals on being fluent speakers of an international variety of English rather than a particular native variety.

The global spread of English has been debated a good deal (e.g. Phillipson 1992, Pennycook 1994, Brutt-Griffler 2002), and the process and politics of this spread has been investigated, but these studies have not been primarily interested in the features of the language itself. However, things are changing. Awareness of ELF has also grown rapidly in applied linguistics since 2000. Before the turn of the millennium the significance and ownership of "international English" or non-native English already raised controversy (e.g. Kachru 1985, Widdowson 1994, Quirk 1990). The debate has gained momentum since then, and become a central topic of discussion in English language teaching. A milestone was the publication of Jenkins's (2000) study on ELF phonology, which has been followed by an upsurge in empirical research (for example papers in collected volumes like Knapp and Meierkord 2002, and Mauranen and Metsä-Ketelä 2006). Now corpora will soon be available to the research community. Apart from databases collected for particular individual studies such as Mollin (2006), two larger research projects compiling ELF corpora are currently in progress. The first to finish is the ELFA project, which has compiled a corpus of academic ELF speech, and which will be described in more detail below. The second is the VOICE project in Vienna (Seidlhofer 2001, Breiteneder et al. 2006), which has a wider spectrum of discourses represented, and is also taking shape fast. Currently we thus stand a good chance of accessing large databases of evidence about the new features of English in its use as a global lingua franca, something that represents a relevant experience to large numbers of people in today's world.

3. Academics as ELF speakers

The academic field has used English as a lingua franca (ELF) for a long time: English has superseded the previously dominant Latin, followed by French, then German as the language of science. This long tradition in itself makes it a natural domain for investigating language features emerging in use. But there are other advantages. To begin with, academic discourses exert considerable social influence by educating a wide range of professionals who disseminate the language and rhetoric acquired in their education; typical groups are media journalists, economic experts, teachers and politicians. Academic language norms exert a strong influence on standard varieties, as revealed the commonly used label 'educated' varieties. Universities thus transmit a fair proportion of language norms which enjoy social prestige. The expansion of university education is likely to accelerate its influence, while at the same time resulting in changes in these registers.

Academic speaking is demanding: complex and often highly abstract meanings need to be negotiated while keeping the discourse going. Participants must be able to handle high-level intellectual content simultaneously with real-time speaking. The language use is therefore more sophisticated than in more stereotypical interaction, say, in routine sales transactions or typical tourist encounters. University discourses also include a wide range of variation in degrees of formality and familiarity. In this way, they provide richer and more rewarding research material than simpler exchanges.

Verbal activity is also central to academia, which is essentially constituted by its own specific genres. These genres make up academic communities as discourse communities. The community's shared discourses, genres, rhetoric, in brief, their ways of speaking, contribute to the cohesion of the community and mark its identity as separate from others. They need to be acquired by novices on their way to membership in the community. From this perspective we could argue there are no native speakers of academic English, but the English of academic genres is a new use to all its practitioners at the outset. Although traditionally the research focus on academic discourses has been overwhelmingly on written publications, a closer look reveals that academic institutions depend crucially on spoken discourses: conferences, lectures, seminars, financial negotiations, faculty meetings... These speech genres structure institutional practices, thereby constituting the institutions themselves (cf. Giddens 1984). Talk is also the chief mode for socialising new generations into academia and beyond, through seminars, lectures, supervision, consultations and so on.

Academic discourses have a long history in employing lingua francas in communication within the international research community, as already pointed out above. Since research discourses do not belong exclusively to any national community, they need not follow the norms of a particular national language either, even if they adopt the language for vehicular purposes. Internationalism and academic mobility at all levels, which were fundamental properties of mediaeval

European scholarship, have recently soared again. Not only research publications, but spoken university discourses make use of English worldwide, including countries where English has no official status.

Considerable variation in proficiency seems to typify ELF use: some speakers are fluent and deviate little from Standard English, while others communicate more hesitantly and follow fewer rules of received native speaker grammar. This is the reality of most ELF encounters, but we might assume that university contexts have a narrower range of variation than many others, given its specific demands. However, proficiency level is not decisive in distinguishing speakers from learners. Insofar as people are not engaged in the study of the English language, they use English as an instrument of communication, and are to be regarded as speakers.

Speakers and speaker groups also bring their linguistic backgrounds into their use of English. Some group features are systematic enough to distinguish user groups, as can be seen from corpus studies of learner language (e.g. Granger et al. 2002). While we can, if we want to, group speakers according to linguistic similarity, these groupings are not dialects in the normal sense, because their commonalities do not arise from communication within the community – they are simply L1-induced speaker similarities. But investigating the effects of L1 background is not a first priority in the study of ELF. The distinctive feature of ELF communication is that speakers will have to adapt to the characteristics of other speakers from different language backgrounds, and this is what makes it so interesting to linguistic research: what happens to a language which is in contact with virtually all other languages in the world?

Despite its general affinities with spoken discourse on the whole, academic speaking falls clearly into the domain of "specialised discourses" as opposed to conversation (for the importance of this distinction see, Warren 2006).The pedagogical implication is that 'general conversation skills' would not be a feasible alternative to domain-specific teaching. That would hardly be a major improvement to the previous attempt of practising an ideal 'general academic language' in the spoken mode. When developing relevant pedagogy to meet the increasing demands for teaching fluent speaking skills for academic and professional purposes, it is important to be aware of the characteristics of university discourses as they really are. Corpus evidence has repeatedly shown its strength in shaking our beliefs about our own language use.

4. The ELFA corpus

Corpus data is ideally suited to the discovery of regularities and patterning in language use, and this goes for ELF just as it does for native English. When we seek to capture language patterns in the process of ongoing change, the best data can be expected from spoken corpora rather than written, because speech is more sensitive to new trends. Writing, especially published writing, which is so central to academia, is more controlled and regulated, and lags behind speaking in the acceptance of new uses. Speech corpora tend to be smaller than written corpora because they are far more laborious to compile, and therefore it is harder to establish new regularities than it would be with larger databases. Nevertheless, speech corpora are important in their sensitivity to change and their ability to capture language as it comes out spontaneously in ongoing dialogue. We have seen in the past that even comparatively small spoken corpora, such as the influential London-Lund corpus of half a million words, are able to combine qualitative insights with enough quantity to discover patterns in speech.

The ELFA corpus (English as a Lingua Franca in Academic Settings; www.uta.fi/laitokset/kielet/engf/research/elfa/) is a domain-specific corpus, targeted at spoken academic discourses. In a research field as new as ELF, it is necessary to start out with exploratory questions, and it is a good idea therefore to begin with a restricted domain, to avoid having too many moving parts at once. This is what most ELF studies have done so far (see, for example Mauranen 2006a).

At the outset, ELFA set itself a target of 0.5 million transcribed words (Mauranen 2003). This was regarded as a sufficient size for a speech corpus, in view of the widely used London-Lund corpus which was no larger, and since the size requirements for a specialised corpus are more modest than for general-purpose corpora. After the initial target size had been achieved, an opportunity arose of supplementing the corpus with disciplinary domains only weakly represented or entirely absent. The final target was set at approximately one million words, the size of the corpus now.

The corpus started out at the University of Tampere, and the original idea was to reflect the discourses of one university, along the lines of MICASE or T2K-SWAL. The one-university approach was nevertheless supplemented with technological data from the Tampere University of Technology, because Tampere University does not have a science faculty and it was felt that leaving the hard sciences entirely without representation was not a happy solution. Thus the idea of one university was modified from the start, and as the opportunity of including other disciplinary domains, particularly from the sciences – physical, chemical, biosciences, forestry – were added to make up a better-rounded whole of academic disciplines. The new data comes from the University of Helsinki, with some supplementary data also from the Helsinki University of Technology.

All these universities offer a number of degree programmes run entirely in English. They are available for international as well as Finnish students, and the students come from a wide variety of countries, with over 40 first languages represented. Many among the teaching staff also come from abroad. The majority of the pro-grammes are for the master's level, but some data comes from international doctoral programmes. The recordings do not cover undergraduate studies because these are not normally run in English. As this is a corpus of ELF, it is important that English is in the position of a vehicular language in all events. This means that it is not the object of study and therefore no language teaching classes have been recorded.

All data in the ELFA corpus is authentic in the sense that it is not elicited for research purposes but has been recorded in natural situations where the speakers are engaged in their normal academic activities. The speech events are recorded as 'complete' in that the individual sessions have been recorded in their entire duration, with-out truncating them or sampling mere extracts. Of course, it is typical of academic events to be heavily interlinked, so that the idea of 'completeness' could be questioned in the case of one in a series of lectures or seminars, but most recordings concern single events even though they might be one in a series. Occasionally two sessions of the same seminar series have been recorded at different times; the participants in these cases are the same, but presenter and discussant roles shift, as does the familiarity of the group members with each other. Variation along the familiarity parameter can be estimated by consulting the recording dates: the point of the term at which recordings have been made is a rough indicator of how long the group has been together.

The criteria of compilation have been 'external' all through in the sense that the compilation process has taken socially based definitions of the prominent genres in the discourse community as the point of departure. Conversely, 'internal' criteria would have meant making use of linguistic features of the texts, or what could be called register features. Such a choice would have meant greater homogeneity within the text types, but inevitably lead to a danger of circularity. It is important that if linguistic features are sought across types of texts, the typology cannot itself rest on linguistic features to begin with. External criteria have meant that the corpus is essentially based on 'folk genres', i.e. the distinctions and labels that the university community uses of its own discourses. As a result, the corpus covers a broad range of discourse types such as lectures, seminars, thesis defences, and conference presentations. Since discourse types are prone to some variability across universities (Mauranen 2006c), having four separate universities as the source of such labelling has meant that the classification is more robust than it would be in a single university, but the types contain potentially more internal heterogeneity. The intention has also been to cover as many different kinds of discourses as possible, while maintaining the focus on those which are regarded as prototypical, shared and named by many disciplines.

Another central criterion of compilation is discipline, where range and balance are important considerations. It was strongly felt that the major disciplinary divisions should be represented, even though a 'correct' balance is an elusive idea: in a single-university approach, a balance between different disciplines might involve their proportion of staff, or students, or something else that can be directly measured and derived from its distribution in the university. As soon as we step outside one university, there is no basis for determining how disciplines should relate to each other in quantitative proportions. The only realistic possibility is to seek a reasonable representation from all major discipline areas. The extension of the corpus outside a single university was motivated by this desire for wide coverage; the hard sciences missing from Tampere were felt to be a problem especially as science and medicine have been keen to adopt English as their lingua franca. Disciplinary representation can be considered at different levels: broad disciplinary domain ('arts', 'technology'), a single discipline ('political history', 'electrical engineering'), or sub-disciplines ('organic chemistry', 'educational psychology'). Experience from corpus work suggests that it is best to avoid narrow divisions because they demand large amounts of data: corpus searches may yield very few examples if comparisons are attempted across finely cut category boundaries.

Wide coverage has also been sought in other socially based parameters like participants' relative social position: both symmetrical relations (as in conference presentations or student groups) and asymmetrical relations (as in a lecture, seminar session or thesis defence) have been included. Again, there is no obvious criterion against which to assess a suitable balance here.

The basic unit of sampling is the 'speech event type', following the solution adopted in MICASE. This is a looser concept than 'genre', and preferred for the present purpose, because the discourses represent a variety of events, some of which are much further established as genres (e.g. lectures) than others (e.g. workshops or panels). Thus, many of the event types which are recognised across the board could easily classify as genres, but 'event type' is used as a convenient cover term.

The main selection criteria for event types are related to their importance in one way or another. The criteria employed for establishing importance were (1) typicality, or the extent to which event types are shared and named by many disciplines; for example lectures, seminars, thesis defences, conference presentations (2) influence: types which affect a large number of participants; for example introductory lecture courses; (3) prestige: event types with a high status in the discourse community, such as guest lectures or plenary talks in conferences.

In an ELF corpus, the speaker's mother tongue is an important consideration. To count as ELF, a speech event needs to include speakers with different L1 backgrounds. Events where all speakers share a first language have therefore been excluded. The most likely problem to occur in a Finnish university would of course be an all-Finnish class in an international programme. However, in practice such groups did not use English amongst themselves, but simply switched to Finnish even if the class was originally intended for an international group.

The second important question regarding the speaker's mother tongue is what to do with native speakers of English. The concept of lingua franca can be restricted to communication between non-natives only or it can permit a broader view, with native speakers as possible participants (most on-line encyclopaedias now take the latter view, e.g. the Encyclopaedia Britannica). Traditionally, situations where non-native speakers communicate with native speakers have been typical settings for second-language acquisition research. The non-native speakers have been conceptualised as learners, as is natural from the SLA perspective, and the analyses have been geared towards identifying problems in the learners' repertoires. At the outset, it would therefore seem more appropriate to restrict ELF to situations where natives play no role. It is clear that communication between speakers using a language foreign to both is the prototypical lingua franca situation. It is also linguistically the most interesting, because neither the help nor the ideal target provided by an interlocutor speaking his or her mother tongue is available. However, despite these important considerations, the reality of speaking English internationally is that native speakers mingle with non-natives. This takes place in many different configurations, and in different ways. Linguistic purity is not a feasible target in the search for a seemingly 'impure' language form such as ELF. The solution adopted in the ELFA corpus has therefore not been to exclude native speakers, but to keep their role within limits so as to maintain a clear focus on L2 speakers. Native speakers have been recorded in polylogic situations, that is, as participants in group discussions, but they do not feature in mono-logues as for example lecturers, or in dyadic speech situations such as thesis defences. In this way, their roles have not been dominant. The minority role thus granted to natives compares nicely with recent predominantly native speaker corpora: academic speech corpora compiled in English-speaking countries, MICASE and BASE, although dominated by NSs, are not 'pure' but include NNSs – because it is not possible to engage in such ethno-linguistic cleansing of the data any longer. Most university contexts today are inter-national to the bone.

In ELFA, native speakers' presence has been coded, so that it is possible to recognize their contributions and exclude them from analyses when necessary, although it may not be important to go to the trouble of excluding all their talk for all research designs.

Despite the general orientation to external criteria in ELFA compilation, one language-internal category distinction has been applied: monologic and dialogic speech have been differentiated. The corpus includes both kinds, that is, situations with one and those with more than one active participants. The proportions between the types are not balanced; instead, a deliberate emphasis on dialogic events has been pursued. Most situations involve several participants, thus in more precise terms are polylogic. This solution was adopted because it is in dialogic interaction that language primarily and most naturally gets negotiated.

The transcription is broad, with spelling normalised to Standard (British) English as far as possible, to facilitate computer searches. To offset this normalisation, the sound files will be made available to researchers who wish to consult them along with the corpus. Basic background information such as context, speaker age, gender, and nationality are included along with recording and transcription information.

5. Pedagogical prospects

The EAP world is characteristically oriented to learners' needs, which can be pinpointed in any ESP teaching with greater accuracy than in teaching general language skills. To keep up with its task, EAP now needs to respond to the new challenges it is facing. The academic world, just like the worlds of business, entertainment, and tourism, is increasingly demanding good spoken skills in international encounters. Students, researchers and teaching staff engage in more and more international activities as a normal part of their academic life. Clearly, if we want to prepare learners for the requirements of real-world language use with any efficiency, we need descriptions of the target language which reflect its actual current use. Ideal models of either the language or the user do not meet learners' needs: we should not waste time with models of speaking which have to be unlearned and revised in the face of real-world experience. The revision of language models for all applicational purposes is a never-ending task, insofar as we believe linguistic theory and description make progress and learners' goals change; one of the fundamental challenges right now concerns the modelling of L2 English speech in its real international contexts today.

Understanding the differences between speech and writing for pedagogic purposes is more of a hurdle than it might seem, as came out very clearly in an experiment with a highly experienced EAP oral skills teacher (Mauranen 2004a): the teacher as well as the students assumed that written academic texts would supply them with suitable "difficult items" to look for in a corpus of spoken academic discourse (MICASE), and the surprise, even disappointment, was great when this turned out to be a mistaken assumption. Despite teaching experience and the best intentions, this turned out to be an example of ideal rather than evidence-based models applied in teaching.

English is paving the way to a new conception of foreign language use; in theory the Council of Europe advocates the concept of plurilingualism, and the EU echoes this in its policies. However, a closer look into the actual definitions and requirements of foreign language targets does not show any major difference between English and other foreign languages. Yet English is fundamentally different because it is a global language unlike any other. Its position in plurilingual speakers' repertoires cannot be equated with locally more restricted languages. Skills which are unique to English as a foreign language compared with other foreign languages – such as coping with the unpredictability of interlocutors' linguistic and cultural background – can best be seen in action if we consult corpus data based on ELF. By seeking to understand the regularities and problem spots in real L2 speech, research on ELF benefits classroom applications; the ELFA corpus feeds into EAP courses.

Research on the ELFA corpus aims at discovering linguistic features of complex language contact as well as understanding mechanisms of language change and describing variation in contemporary English. It also seeks to understand situated foreign language use in the real world, outside the confines of the classroom. The corpus has begun to yield research and findings from its early stages. The first results have been concerned with widespread phenomena, so that although they will no doubt be specified in the light of more data from the finished corpus, they retain their validity. Many are undoubtedly useful for pedagogical planning and coursework.

One of the first studies based on ELFA was concerned with the occurrence and prevention of misunderstandings among speakers (Mauranen 2006b). The findings showed that academic ELF discourse contains relatively few misunderstandings and even fewer are primarily language-based; ELF speakers managed to prevent linguistic misunderstandings quite successfully by resorting to explicitation strategies, repetitions, and a number of collaborative tactics. A variety of other explicitation strategies manifest in the data have since been attested (Mauranen 2007).

The success strategies employed by skilful ELF speakers could be utilised in teaching. Many are interactive strategies: some resemble any L1 interaction, like co-construction of expressions, others are more like L1-L2 interaction, such as frequent self-rephrasing, clarification and repetition, or like L2-L2 interaction, for example particularly active signalling of comprehension or orientation to contents (see also Kurhila 2003, Karhukorpi 2006). Rephrasing seems more common than in comparable L1 speech, but is similar in kind, for example in rephrasing the content (*the ethnic people and eh* **minorities Russian minorities)**, lexical choice (*then it will be no* **questions** *eh it will be no* **conflicts)** or pragmatic features, like adding hedges (*will eh at f- maybe at first they will*). Others again, most conspicuously grammatical rephrasing (*main roles eh* **the** *main roles; to have* **a big influence** *to make* **big influence)**, seem rare in native speech. In ELF speech, grammatical corrections do not get constructed interactively; that is, interlocutors do not participate in formulating grammatical form, but orient themselves to the contents of what is being said. Thus, although cooperation and co-construction are vital prerequisites for successful ELF communication, grammatical form is left to the currently active speaker to formulate.

More specific linguistic features studied in ELFA have included syntax, phraseology and discourse. Ranta (2006) questioned the received wisdom of seeing excessive use of the *ing* form by L2 speakers as a problem: she found no evidence of its causing communication breakdown. Instead, it was used to enhance emphasis and explicitness, both useful strategies. Phraseological units are widely used (Mauranen 2005a, 2006c) despite a common belief that they tend to be absent or incorrect. They are used in both conventional and creative ways, in a very similar manner to native speakers. This points to an essentially similar processing mechanisms in L1 and L2 speakers, contrary to Wray's (2002) suggestion based on findings from classroom learning.

Results from the study of discourse features show similarities as well as differences in comparison to native speakers: expressions of vagueness, which have been alternately seen as a problem of underuse or overuse among non-natives, are employed quite appropriately in ELF discourse (Metsä-Ketelä 2006), although ELF speakers also show preferences for functions which are minor or nonexistent in native speech. Discourse reflexivity, or metadiscourse, is also widely used in ELF, even though preferences for certain expressions do not always match those of native speakers (Mauranen 2005a). Disciplinary domain is a powerful factor in determining academic language practices, and again ELF speakers show preferences specific to their own use across first language boundaries (Mauranen 2006c). Rhetorical devices in discourse organisation show mainly similarities between native and ELF lecturers, which suggests that genre conventions are stronger than language barriers (Mauranen in press), and the same is true of organising arguments in spontaneous, dialogic situations (Mauranen 2005b).

Whether successful strategies can be directly taught remains an open question, but an idea of what works in real international communication is helpful to teachers as well as students, as support and encouragement for their own efforts. It is also important to be aware of major recent developments in the language, and currently ELF is a force of change. This is also the kind of speech students are likely to encounter, and therefore this is what we must prepare them for.

A new applicational development of the ELFA corpus is its daughter project SELF (Studying in English as a Lingua Franca) at the University of Helsinki, developing research-based recommendations for practitioners. The target groups are students and staff in international study programmes: how can we help participants avoid and overcome commonly occurring communication problems and ensure the quality of teaching, research and study in English? This project works in cooperation of instructors in English for Academic Purposes at Helsinki.

6. Conclusion

This paper has presented a speech corpus of English as a lingua franca in academic settings (ELFA), arguing that findings from corpora of this type are needed if the English teaching world is to rise to the challenge of today's language teaching needs.

The research on ELFA is currently very active, with more results soon to be published, and new hypotheses emerging on the research. On the whole, ELFA findings lend support to the perception that lingua franca English has its own specific characteristics. At the same time, many affinities to other kinds of nonstandard English, both native and non-native, are clearly emerging as well.

It is important to remember that most learners of English as a foreign language will use the language as a lingua franca with other foreign speakers. Consequently, our teaching should seriously consider successful lingua franca use as providing valuable models for communication strategies. I am not suggesting that ELF data is the only viable linguistic model for learners; what I am suggesting is, first, that data of successful ELF discourse is indispensable for modelling communication strategies – in authentic speech. Secondly, I am suggesting that in order to keep up with current developments in the target language we must complement our existing databases with English in international use. Native speaker English can continue to be described separately by those who wish to do so, and it is of fundamental significance to any description of the language as a whole, but at the same time, we must respond to change.

7. References

Aijmer, Karin 2002. *English Discourse Particles*. Amsterdam: John Benjamins.

Aston, Guy / Bernardini, Silvia / Stewart, Dominic (eds) 2004. *Corpora and Language Learners*. Amsterdam: John Benjamins

BASE corpus. <http.www.rdg.ac.uk/slals/base>.

Biber, Douglas / Conrad, Susan / Reppen, Randi / Byrd, Pat / Helt, Marie / Clark, Victoria / Cortes, Viviana / Csomay, Eniko / Urzua, Alfredo 2004. *Representing Language Use in the University: Analysis of the TOEFL 2000 Spoken and Written Academic Language Corpus*. Princeton, NJ: Educational Testing Service.

Biber, Douglas 2006. *University Language. A Corpus-based Study of Spoken and Written Registers*. Amsterdam: John Benjamins.

Biber, Douglas / Johansson, Stig / Leech, Geoffrey / Conrad, Susan / Finegan, Edward 1999. *The Longman Grammar of Spoken and Written English*. London: Pearson Education.

Brazil, David 1995. *A Grammar of Speech.* Oxford: Oxford University Press.

Breiteneder, Angelika / Pitzl, Marie-Luise / Majewski, Stefan / Klimpfinge, Theresa 2006. VOICE recording – Methodological Challenges in the Compilation of a Corpus of Spoken ELF. 2006. In Mauranen, Anna and Metsä-Ketelä Maria (eds), *English as a Lingua Franca. Special Issue of The Nordic Journal of English Studies*, 161-188.

Brutt-Griffler, Janine 2002. *World English. A Study of its Development.* Clevedon: Multilingual Matters.

Carter, Ronald / McCarthy, Michael 2006. *Cambridge Grammar of English.* Cambridge: Cambridge University Press.

Du Bois, John W. 2000. *Santa Barbara Corpus of Spoken American English.* CD-ROM. Philadelphia: Linguistic Data Consortium.

Du Bois, John W. 2003. Discourse and Grammar. In Tomasello, Michael (ed.) *The New Psychology of Language* [Vol. 2] Mahwah, NJ: Lawrence Erlbaum, 47- 87.

Encyclopaedia Britannica. <http://www.britannica.com/eb/article-9048392/lingua-franca>.

Erling, Elizabeth J. 2004. *Globalization, English and the German University Classroom: A Sociolinguistic Profile of Students of English at the Freie Universität Berlin.* Department of Theoretical and Applied Linguistics, University of Edinburgh.

Ford, Cecilia / Fox, Barbara / Thompson, Sandra 2003. Social Interaction and Grammar. In Tomasello, Michael (ed.) *The New Psychology of Language* [Vol. 2] Mahwah, NJ: Lawrence Erlbaum, 119-143.

Gavioli, Laura 2005. *Exploring Corpora for ESP Learning.* Amsterdam: John Benjamins.

Giddens, Anthony. 1984. *The Constitution of Society. An Outline of Structuration Theory.* Cambridge: Polity Press.

Graddol, David. 2006. *English Next.* London: British Council.

Granger, Sylviane / Hung, Joseph / Petch-Tyson, Stephanie (eds) 2002. *Computer Learner Corpora, Second Language Acquisition and Foreign Language Teaching.* Amsterdam: John Benjamins.

Hakulinen, Auli / Selting, Margret (eds) 2005. *Syntax and Lexis in Conversation.* Amsterdam: John Benjamins.

Hunston, Susan 2002. *Corpora in Applied Linguistics*. Cambridge: Cambridge University Press.

Jenkins, Jennifer 2000. *The Phonology of English as an International Language*. Oxford: Oxford University Press.

Kachru, Braj. 1985. Standards, codification, and sociolinguistic realism: the English language in the outer circle. In Quirk, Randolph / Widdowson, Henry (eds) *English in the World: Teaching and Learning the Language and Literatures*. Cambridge: Cambridge University Press, 11-30.

Karhukorpi, Johanna 2006. *Negotiating Opinions in Lingua Franca email Discussion Groups. Discourse Structure, Hedges and Repair in Online Communication*. Unpublished Licenciate Thesis, University of Turku.

Karjalainen, Sinikka / Lehtonen, Tuula 2005. Työnantajien näkemyksiä akateemisten ammattien kielitaitotarpeesta. In Karjalainen, Sinikka / Lehtonen, Tuula (eds) *Että osaa ja uskaltaa kommunikoida*. Helsinki: Helsinki University Press. 127-162.

Knapp, Karlfried / Meierkord, Christiane (eds) 2002. *Lingua Franca Communication*. Frankfurt: Peter Lang.

Krishnamurthy, Ramesh (ed.) 2004. *English Collocational Studies* [republication of J. Sinclair, S. Jones and R. Daley, 1970, *English Lexical Studies*]. London: Continuum.

Kurhila, Salla 2003. *Co-constructing Understanding in Second Language Conversation*. Helsinki: University of Helsinki.

Mauranen, Anna. 2003. The Corpus of English as Lingua Franca in Academic Settings. *TESOL Quarterly,* 37/3, 513-527.

Mauranen, Anna. 2004a. Speech corpora in the classroom. In Aston, Guy *et al.* (eds) *Corpora and Language Learners*. Amsterdam: John Benjamins, 197-213.

Mauranen, Anna. 2005a. English as a Lingua Franca – an Unknown Language? In Cortese, Giuseppina / Duszak, Anna (eds) *Identity, Community, Discourse: English in Intercultural Settings* Frankfurt: Peter Lang, 269-293.

Mauranen, Anna. 2005b. Speaking Academics. In Bäcklund, Ingegerd *et al.* (eds) *Text i Arbete / Text at Work*. Uppsala: ASLA, 330-339.

Mauranen, Anna. 2006a. A Rich Domain of ELF – the ELFA Corpus of Academic Discourse. In Mauranen, Anna / Metsä-Ketelä Maria (eds), *English as a Lingua Franca. Special Issue of The Nordic Journal of English Studies*, 145-159.

Mauranen, Anna. 2006b. Signalling and preventing misunderstanding in English as lingua franca communication. *International Journal of the Sociology of Language,* 177, 123-150.

Mauranen, Anna. 2006c. Speaking the Discipline. In Hyland, Ken / Bondi, Marina (eds), *Academic Discourse Across Disciplines.* Bern: Peter Lang, 271-294.

Mauranen, Anna. 2007. Hybrid Voices: English as the Lingua Franca of Academics. *Language and discipline perspectives on academic discourse.* In Flottum, Kjersti et al. (eds) Cambridge: Cambridge Scholars Press, 244-259.

Mauranen, Anna. in press. Spoken Rhetoric: How do natives and non-natives fare? In Suomela-Salmi, Eija (ed.) *Proceedings of the Conference on Cross-linguistic and Cross-Cultural Perspectives on Academic Discourse.* Turku: Turku University Press.

Mauranen, Anna / Metsä-Ketelä, Maria (eds) 2006. *English as a Lingua Franca. Special Issue of The Nordic Journal of English Studies.*

Metsä-Ketelä, Maria 2006. "Words are more or less superfluous": the case of *more or less* in academic lingua franca English. In Mauranen, Anna / Metsä-Ketelä Maria (eds), *English as a Lingua Franca. Special Issue of The Nordic Journal of English Studies,* 117-144.

Mollin, Sandra. 2006. *Euro-English. Assessing Variety Status.* Tübingen: Narr.

Östman, Jan-Ola 1981. *You know. A discourse-functional approach.* Amsterdam: John Benjamins.

Pennycook, Alistair. 1994. *The Cultural Politics of English as an International Language.* London: Longman.

Phillipson, Robert. 1992. *Linguistic Imperialism.* Oxford: Oxford University Press.

Quirk, Randolph 1990. Language varieties and standard language. *English Today.* 21, 3-10.

Ranta, Elina. 2004. *International English – a Future Possibility in the Finnish EFL Classroom?* Unpublished MA thesis, University of Tampere.

Ranta, Elina 2006. The 'Attractive' Progressive – Why use the *-ing* Form in English as a Lingua Franca? In Mauranen, Anna / Metsä-Ketelä, Maria (eds), *English as a Lingua Franca. Special Issue of The Nordic Journal of English Studies*, 95-116.

Seidlhofer, Barbara 2001. Closing a conceptual gap: The case for a description of English as a lingua franca. *International Journal of Applied Linguistics,* 11/2, 133-158.

Selting, Margret / Couper-Kuhlen, Elizabeth (eds) 2001. *Studies in Interactional Linguistics.* Amsterdam: John Benjamins.

Simpson, Rita C / L. Briggs, Sarah / Ovens, Janine / Swales, John M. 2002. *The Michigan Corpus of Academic Spoken English.* Ann Arbor, MI: The Regents of the University of Michigan.

Sinclair, John McH. 1991 *Corpus Concordance Collocation.* Oxford: Oxford University Press.

Sinclair, John McH. 1996. The search for units of meaning. *Textus,* 9/1, 75-106.

Sinclair, John McH. (ed.) 2004. *How to Use Corpora in Language Teaching.* Amsterdam: John Benjamins.

Sinclair, John McH. and Anna Mauranen 2006. *Linear Unit Grammar.* Amsterdam: John Benjamins.

Stenström, Anna-Brita / Andersen, Gisle / Hasund, Ingrid Kristine 2002. *Trends in Teenage Talk. Corpus Compilation, Analysis and Findings.* Amsterdam: John Benjamins.

Suviniitty, Jaana Forthcoming. English as a lingua franca – a tool for educating engineers. In *Proceedings of the International Conference of Engineering Education* (ICEE 2007), Coimbra, September 3-7, 2007.

Svartvik, Jan 1990. *The London-Lund Corpus of Spoken English: Description and Research.* Lund: Lund University Press.

Tao, Hongyin 2001. Discovering the usual with corpora: The case of *remember.* In Simpson, Rita / Swales, John (eds) *Corpus Linguistics in North America.* University of Michigan Press, 116-144.

Warren, Martin 2006. *Features of Naturalness in Conversation.* Amsterdam: John Benjamins.

Widdowson, Henry. 1994. The ownership of English. *TESOL Quarterly,* 28: 377-389.

Wray, Alison 2002. *Formulaic Language and the Lexicon.* Cambridge University Press.

VIVIANA CORTES / ENIKO CSOMAY

Positioning Lexical Bundles in University Lectures

1. Introduction

Describing discourse in the academic context has populated the applied linguistics literature extensively for multiple decades now. While researchers mostly focused on written discourse, from the 1990s, a few studies analyzed spoken academic discourse as well. Since then, researchers have taken multiple approaches and applied varied analytical tools to characterize classroom discourse from a linguistic point of view.

Studies looking at spoken academic discourse took particular lexical items to investigate their role in the discourse structure. For example, lexical phrases (Nattinger and De Carrico 1992) were identified as signals to the micro- and macro-structure of discourse, discourse markers were reported to be the best signals for topic shifts (Hansen 1994), or lexical repetition was investigated for its relationship to coherence in lectures (Tyler 1995). Other scholars took a functional approach to segment classroom discourse into smaller units in order to see how these units are sequenced and lead to the hierarchical organization of discourse. These units were called different names, depending on the function they filled or the researcher that described them. For example, initial units were called "openings" or final units were called "closings" depending on where they were in the stretch of discourse (Sinclair and Coulthard 1975). Young (1994) simply called them "phases" as she investigated how disciplines differ in their discourse organization based on these smaller units. In all of these studies, where the units began or where they ended depended on the researcher's close reading and interpretation of the transcribed text. Although invaluable to building our knowledge about academic lectures, this earlier work lacked generalizable findings as to how the units themselves, e.g., openings and closings, are different in terms of their lexico-grammatical characteristics.

Most recently, corpus-based methodologies have been used to investigate lexical patterns and discourse structure, especially in university classroom talk (Swales 2001, Swales and Malczewski 2001, Mauranen 2001, 2003, Swales and Burke 2003, Simpson and Mendis 2003, Fortanet 2004, Csomay 2005a, Csomay 2005b, Biber 2006). Many of these studies use such methodologies to describe specific word functions in university classroom talk, or list frequent collocations of particular words, and to describe the use of idioms and recurrent word combinations in spoken academic discourse. Among others, the analysis of extended collocations has become the topic of many studies of spoken academic discourse (Biber, Conrad and Cortes 2004, Schmitt 2004, Biber, 2006). In a recent study, Nesi and Basturkmen (2006) investigated the use of a special type of recurrent word combination, lexical bundles (Biber, Johansson, Leech, Conrad and Finegan 1999), as cohesive devices in classroom teaching. Their findings showed that several lexical bundles played a signaling role in academic lectures. This role is very important for students, particularly non-native speakers of English, to become aware of, as it is "intended to help the listener predict the nature of upcoming ideas and information" (p. 301). When students can't recognize these signals, they are faced with more demanding cognitive processing in order to decipher intrinsic propositional meanings.

Corpus-based methods are applied in identifying smaller units of analysis as well. A specially designed computer program was developed (Csomay 2002, Biber, Csomay, Jones and Keck 2004) to automatically identify smaller units of analysis, called "Vocabulary-based Discourse Units" (VBDUs, henceforth) in university lectures. Briefly, this program signals the introduction of newly occurring vocabulary into the discourse, and tracks the vocabulary that is recycled in a stretch. As we move along the discourse, this pattern of old and new vocabulary results in chunks and in the automatic identification of lexically coherent units (lexical episodes). In this study, we rely on the VBDUs identified with this methodology in previous work (Csomay 2005b). That is, no close reading is given to the text a priori, but the existing vocabulary patterns in a stretch of discourse is the basis of determining where the units start and where they end. What is relevant to this study from earlier work applying this methodology is that the first three units' linguistic characteristics are very different from that of the subsequent units. Based on the linguistic characteristics of these units, earlier work in this area (Csomay 2005b) concluded that, indeed, the first three units identified in this way functioned as 'openings' in a university classroom setting. This served as justification to choose the first three VBDUs as our corpus to find the most frequently occurring lexical bundles in them. This study extends earlier work by examining the lexical bundles appearing in the first three units, and by looking at how they might be aligned with earlier linguistic characterizations of these units.

The primary aim of the present study is to investigate which lexical bundles previously identified as frequently occurring in classroom talk (Biber, Conrad and Cortes 2004) appear in the initial discourse units of university lectures (Csomay 2005b). A second aim is to see the relationship between that position and the functions that the bundles are performing in discourse. This positioning of the lexical bundles in the first few VBDUs in a university lecture could provide further lexical information of the units and can relate to their discourse functions. The following research questions have guided our study: (i) What are the lexical bundles that occur in the first three VBDUs?, (ii) What functions do those bundles perform?

In section two, we will provide an extended definition and examples of lexical bundles and a brief description of the procedure used for the identification of VBDUs. Section three will introduce the research methodology used for the identification of bundles in the initial VBDUs in university lectures and the functional classification used for the analysis of these bundles in context. Section four will present the results of the study together with a discussion of the most important findings. Finally, section five will include some recommendations for further research.

2. Lexical bundles and discourse units

As the purpose of our study was to analyze the position of lexical bundles in the first three VBDUs in university lectures, we consider it important to carefully describe and exemplify these constructs before presenting the methodology we used in the study.

2.1. A closer look at lexical bundles

Biber et al. (1999) defined lexical bundles as the most frequent recurring lexical sequences in a register. They are not structural units or fixed expressions. Even though lexical bundles are word combinations of three or more words, only four word sequences are considered in the present study, drawing on previous studies of lexical bundles in academic discourse (Cortes 2004). Examples of these expressions in every day conversation are *what do you mean, I don't know why;* in academic prose *as a result of, in the case of, on the other hand;* and in university lectures *if you look at, nothing to do with, I want you to,* among many others.

Lexical bundles are identified with a computer program that stores every 4-word sequence in the corpus. The program goes through each text in the corpus, storing every sequence in a database, beginning with the first word of the text and advancing one word at a time. Each time a sequence is identified, it is checked against the database. A frequency count is kept to show how often each sequence was repeated. In order to be considered a lexical bundle, a 4-word combination must repeat at least 20 times in a million words and it must occur in at least five different texts, to avoid idiosyncrasies. Bundles are classified according to two criteria: their structural correlates and the discourse functions they perform. Regarding their structural correlation, although lexical bundles are not structurally complete units, they do have strong structural associations. For example, bundles like *you want me to* are constructed from verbs and clause components, while bundles like *in the case of* are constructed from noun phrase and prepositional phrase components. In addition, lexical bundles perform various discourse function such as expressing different types of stance (as in *I don't think so, if you want to,* and *it is important to),* organizing discourse (in bundles such as *on the other hand,* and *let's have a look),* and expressing reference (e.g., *the rest of the, in the case of,* and *at the same time).* Because of these characteristics, their structural constituency and the functions they perform, lexical bundles have been considered "important textual building blocks used in spoken and written discourse" (Tracy-Ventura, Cortes and Biber, in press).

2.2. Identifying Vocabulary-Based Discourse Units

The VBDUs are lexically coherent units (lexical episodes) automatically identified in the discourse by means of a specially designed computer program, a modified version of Text Tiler (Hearst 1994). This program (Biber, Csomay, Jones and Keck 2004) compares vocabulary items (i.e., orthographic words in transcribed classroom texts) in nearby segments of a text. The text is processed via a "sliding window" of 100 words, and the program compares the first 50 words in that window to the second 50 words. That is, at the start, the window is positioned at the beginning of the text and contains words 1-50 in the first half of the window and 51-100 in the second half. Then the window "slides" one position and contains words 2-51 in the first half and 52-101 in the second half. The window continues to slide one position at a time, allowing the comparison of two 50-word chunks of the target text, until the end of the text is reached. In the meantime, at each word, a similarity value is calculated that indicates the extent to which the words in the first half of the window are identical within those in the second half. If the two halves use the same vocabulary to a large extent, they are considered to belong to a single VBDU, and are interpreted as lexically coherent units (Biber, Csomay, Jones and Keck 2004). In contrast, when the two segments are maximally different in their vocabulary, they are considered to mark the boundaries between two VBDUs. The accumulation of new vocabulary into the discourse is claimed to introduce new topics (Prince 1981, Youmans 1991). Tracking the alternating new and recycled vocabulary would lead to lexically coherent units also considered topical units.

We combine the two perspectives on university classroom talk outlined above, one looking at frequent word combinations and the other segmenting discourse based on lexical patterns in our present research.

3. Methodology

For the analysis reported in this chapter we used the lexical bundles previously identified in the lectures of the T2KSWAL (TOEFL 2000 Spoken and Written Academic Language Corpus) (see Biber, Conrad, Reppen, Byrd and Helt 2002) corpus (Biber, Conrad and Cortes 2004, Biber 2006). The lectures section of the T2KSWAL corpus is a collection of university lectures in Business, Education, Engineering, Humanities, Natural Science, and Social Science from different academic levels in four American universities. For the present study, the researchers decided to hold a very conservative position and established the lexical bundle frequency cut-off point at 40 times in a million words and 5 or more texts in order to reduce the number of tokens for a more reliable analysis. Appendix A presents a list of the lexical bundles identified in the T2KSWAL corpus grouped by function (Biber, Conrad and Cortes 2004), which have been used as target bundles to analyze their position in the first discourse units of university lectures.

Using a specially designed computer program, the bundles on this list were identified in the first three VBDUs of classroom lectures. The computer also registered the number of times each bundle appeared in each of the first three units. The data were then transferred to an Excel file in order to be sorted by frequency. Then, total frequencies per bundle and per unit were manually computed. Finally, the bundles were compared across units and they were grouped following the functional taxonomy designed by Biber, Conrad and Cortes (2004). For this task, lexical bundle tokens were analyzed in their contexts using concordancing software, Monconc Pro 2.2 (Barlow 2002).

4. Results and discussion

Of the 84 most frequently occurring bundles in class sessions identified by Biber, Conrad and Cortes (2004), 65 bundles (77.4% of the
total) appeared at least once in the first three VBDUs and 19 bundles
(22.6% of the total) did not occur at all in this segment of the class. In
this section, first we report on those bundles that could not be found in
the initial VBDUs. Then, we will discuss the frequency of those lexical bundles that did appear in those first units and those that appeared
exclusively in one unit. Finally, we relate the functions of these
bundles to the discourse functions of the VBDUs in the structure of
class sessions.

4.1. Missing bundles

As pointed out above, about 23% of the bundles found in class
sessions did not appear in the start of the class. These "missing"
bundles belong mainly to two functional categories: stance markers
(14 bundles or 16.6%) and referential bundles (4 or 4.8%), with only
one discourse organizer (1.2%).

First, the stance markers not found in the initial units of these
lectures correspond to expressions of personal epistemic stance (such
as *I don't know if, I don't know what,* and *I don't know how*) and
expressions of attitudinal/modality stance indicating personal desire (*I
don't want to*), personal obligation or directive (*you don't have to, you
don't want to*), personal intention/prediction (as in *I'm not going to,
we're going to do,* and *what we're going to*) and impersonal
intention/prediction (*it's going to be*). It can be noted that most of
these expressions can be classified into two groups. One group is
made up of expressions in the negative and mostly with a first person
subject, while the other group includes expressions that use the in-
clusive "we" subject and an affirmative verb. All those lexical bundles
have been identified as frequently occurring in university lectures.
However, they don't seem to belong to the opening stages. Instead,
instructors favor positive stance expressions and the use of first and

second person pronouns in these units. The absence of these bundles may indicate that at the beginning of the lesson, instructors emphasize certainty and the use of direct instructions leaving stance markers that could imply uncertainty (as in the case of those lexical bundles starting with *I don't know*) or counter instructions (as in *you don't have to* and *you don't want to*) for later stages in the class.

Second, the small group of referential bundles that were not found in the first VBDUs belong to different subcategories such as identification/focus (*that's one of the*), imprecision (*and things like that*), and specification of attributes, particularly of quantity (*there's a lot of*). Many other bundles in each of these functional subcategories did appear frequently in these first VBDUs. Through further research the starting position of those bundles not found in these units in the thread of discourse could be located.

Finally, the only discourse organizer not found (*want to talk about*) is mainly used by instructors to introduce content materials, which explains its absence at this stage of the classroom discourse.

4.2. Most frequent lexical bundles in the first three VBDUs

From the lexical bundles tracked in the initial VBDUs, a group of 13 bundles occurred at least ten times in the three units overall. Among these bundles, we can find 5 referential expressions, 5 discourse organizers, and 3 stance markers, as displayed in Table 1 below (see Appendix A for a complete list of the lexical bundles found in these units).

The referential expressions found within the most frequent lexical bundles in these units belong to many different subcategories, such as those used for identification or focus, time reference or multi-functional reference and those which refer to certain attribute specifications such as quantity.

Lexical bundles	Function	unit1	unit2	unit3	units 1+2+3
if you want to	attitudinal stance	6	11	2	19
I want to do	discourse organizer	7	9	2	18
going to talk about	discourse organizer	5	4	8	17
the end of the	referential	7	7	3	17

a little bit of	referential	10	5	2	17
at the end of	referential	6	6	4	16
one of the things	referential	1	7	7	15
want to do is	discourse organizer	3	5	5	13
what I want to	discourse organizer	6	6	1	13
is going to be	attitudinal stance	4	4	4	12
to be able to	attitudinal stance	4	4	2	10
take a look at	discourse organizer	4	2	4	10
at the same time	referential	2	4	4	10

Table 1. Most frequent lexical bundles in the first three VBDUs.

Prior research describing the linguistic characteristics of VBDUs in the discourse structure (Csomay 2005b) found that the first three VBDUs are very different in their linguistic profile from the fourth, and other immediately following subsequent units. This finding suggests that in terms of instructional purpose, the first three units would have a different function from those following them, and based on the linguistic characteristics, they are considered to function as an opening, as if contextualizing the given class session. Thus, the most frequent discourse organizers found in these units are mainly introducing topics or stressing the importance of the succeeding discourse as in the following example:

Topic introduction or focus

(1)   OK what *I want to do* is pick up with what uh, pick up where I hope you left off with it last week and maybe even take a, a bit of time to revisit that, and, uh, that exercise that you did. (engceleudmi103)

The most frequent stance markers (one of which was in fact the most frequent lexical bundle in the three units) were functioning as attitudinal stance markers. *To be able to* was used to indicate ability as in the following example:

(2)   … and do a critical review, the rest of the class, you know… they're gonna read some better than they read others Um, but it's uh they have to be, written up and you have *to be able to* carry on a discussion because uh that's a part of your grade so, it's a cool course, we read cool stuff… (socanleudli118)

Bundles that contained forms of *going to* were used to indicate intention or prediction while other varied bundles were used to express desire, ability, or obligation as illustrated in these utterances:

Intention

(3)   Uh thermodynamics is not something we look at a whole lot except, in so much as how it relates to, uh, equilibrium in reversible reactions. We've done a little bit of that but that's *not going to be* a big part of this course (engceleudli100)

Personal desire

(4)   Uh, you know actually the best way to show me the results would be to show me the chart with the date column with the start date and finish date column. Uh, *if you want to* put it in the form of the node diagram and put the put the right data in the right boxes, that's fine (busmgleudmg114)

Obligation

(5)   OK what we're *going to have to* do is uh... have this due Wednesday but you've got the exam Wednesday it won't do you any good to have the homework due next Friday with the exam on Wednedsay... (engeeleldmn261)

4.3. Lexical bundles identified in only one of the first three VBDUs

Very few of the lexical bundles identified in the first three units belonged exclusively to only one unit. The bundle *I mean you know* used as a discourse organizer for topic elaboration was found once overall in the first three units and only in unit 1. It was used by a student as shown in the following example:

(6)   You know it was really hard for me. I went to [xxx] and I was really trying to find, a book in the book, not the bookstore but the library but this is the only one I came up with. *I mean you know*, from, um, this had in the book review tonight and some of the other books that the other students had, you know I mean, I want it to have all. (edubelegrhn161)

The lexical bundles *and one of the* used as a referential expression for identification and *you need to know* used as a stance marker indicating personal obligation or as a personal directive were used only once over-all in the first three units and only in unit 2 as shown in this utterance:

(7)   … but you certainly need to be aware of what are your pitfalls… one of the things that stay between you and getting a paper written *and one of the* things between between you and getting a paper in press… you want to think about that… (socpolegrmn206)

Finally, only unit 3 presented two instances of *and this is the* function-ing as a referential expressions for identification, three examples of *in a lot of* used in reference to quantity, and four tokens of *greater than or equal* and *than or equal to* also used as referential expression specifying quantity. Examples:

(8)   …it will matter and the main reason is if you're not a member of the elite you get ignored. *And this is the* danger of society. Now do we think, and I've heard this argument over and over again particularly in places like Arizona. (socpoleldmn178.txt)

(9)   X three *greater than or equal to*[1] zero. I've written them under the columns as I said just to make a point which is the rows of this thing are going to be the constraints (busatlegrmg084.txt)

It is important to point out that while all these lexical bundles occurred in the body of each of the corresponding units, *greater than or equal to* was used in the limit of unit 3 with unit 4, which makes it less similar to the contextualized expressions that frequently occurred in the first three VBDUs and more similar to expressions used in the discussion of content materials.

4. 4. Discourse structure and bundles: the case of the first three VBDUs

The list of lexical bundles tracked in the first three units of these classroom discourse samples undoubtedly reflects the type of func-tions linked to the beginning of university lectures. As pointed out

---

1   Two bundles, *greater than or equal* and *than or equal to* together formed a 5-word bundle used four times.

earlier, the beginning of the class sessions are considered "openings" (Sinclair and Coulthard 1975). The linguistic characteristics of these initial units supported this function (Csomay 2005b) with empirical measures, and locating frequent lexical bundles and their functions (Biber, Conrad and Cortes 2004) in these units also empirically supports the initial claim but from a different perspective.

The expressions found through this study are used mainly as discourse organizers to introduce a topic or to emphasize the forthcoming discourse as well as referential expressions used to identify information or to focus certain prominence on this information. Among the stance expressions found, those indicating obligation or closely related to directions need to be emphasized. These types of expressions have been intuitively linked to classroom talk, particularly to teacher talk. The evidence presented here supports those intuitions. Expressions such as *what I want to, want to do is,* and *I want to do* indicate volition and are used at this stage to guide students toward the organization of the class that is about to start, and the framing of the content about to follow. Other expression such as *take a look at, if we look at, if you look at, to look at the* follow a directive function. Example:

(10)   But I, I was instructed that I must have you, and I assume you are familiar with this exercise go through and initial, uh, your presence. Uh, today, uh I assume today's the fourth. OK *what I want to do is* pick up with what uh, pick up where I hope you left off with it last week and maybe even take a, a bit of time to revisit that, and, uh, that exercise that you did (engceleudmi103)

There is also a wide variety of stance markers used in these early stages of the lecture. These expressions are used mainly to stress desire or to tentatively provide directions or special information to students as in the following example:

(11)   And I'll pass this around so that you can take a look at, especially the lectures. *You might want to* go to Tuesday the tenth at seven, and then Wednesday the eleventh at twelve thirty. One for the university one for our department (humenlegrhi003)

Finally, the last big group of expressions of stance corresponds to those that express impersonal intention or prediction. These expressions are used to anticipate what that day's class is going to deal with or what the current course is going to deal with. This is one example of one of those lexical bundles:

(12)   uh as far as the kinds of questions that could be asked uh *they are going to be* since they are short answer questions, they're going to be the kind of answers that will only take about at best ideally would take only about a paragraph (socanleudmi116.txt)

5. Conclusions and future directions

All in all, our first exploratory study into the lexical bundles used in the first three Vocabulary-based Discourse Units of university lectures provided us with new insights to classroom talk. These units made extensive use of lexical bundles for the functions that are commonly perceived to introduce a class session. This section or "phase" (Young 1994) in the class sets students and instructors in the organization of the class about to start, contextualizing the content to be delivered or discussed further – all supported by evidence of lexical patterns as well.

Our intention is to continue exploring the use of lexical bundles in other sections of university lectures as represented in subsequent Vocabulary-based Discourse Units in order to obtain further information on classroom talk, benefiting both instructors and students in different academic communities.

6. References

Barlow, Michael 2002. *MonoConc Pro.* (Version 2.0.) [Computer Software]. Houston, TX: Athelstan.

Biber, Douglas 2006. *University Language: A Corpus-Based Study of Spoken and Written Registers.* Amsterdam and Philadelphia: John Benjamins.

Biber, Douglas / Conrad, Susan / Cortes, Viviana 2004. 'If you look at...': Lexical bundles in university teaching and textbooks. *Applied Linguistics. 25,* 371-405.

Biber, Douglas / Csomay, Eniko / Jones, Kirk James / Keck, Casey 2004. A corpus linguistic investigation of vocabulary-based discourse units in university registers. In Connor, Ulla / Upton, Tom (eds) *Applied Corpus Linguistics: A Multidimensional Perspective.* Amsterdam: Rodopi, 53-72.

Biber, Douglas / Conrad, Susan / Reppen, Randi / Byrd, Patricia / Helt, Marie 2002. Speaking and writing in the university: A multi-dimensional comparison. *TESOL Quarterly. 36,* 9-48.

Biber, Douglas / Johansson, Stig / Leech, Geoffrey / Conrad, Susan / Finegan, Edward 1999. *The Longman Grammar of Spoken and Written English.* London: Longman.

Cortes, Viviana 2004. Lexical bundles in published and student disciplinary writing: Examples from history and biology. *English for Specific Purposes.* 23, 397-423.

Csomay, Eniko 2002. *Episodes in University Classrooms: A Corpus-Linguistic Investigation.* Unpublished Ph.D. Dissertation. Flagstaff, AZ: Northern Arizona University.

Csomay, Eniko 2005a. Linguistic variation in the lexical episodes of university classroom talk. In Tyler, Andrea / Marie Takada / Yiyoung Kim / Diana Marinova. (eds) *Language in use. Cognitive and discourse perspectives on language and language learning. Georgetown University Round Table on Languages and Linguistics.* Georgetown: Georgetown University Press, 150-162.

Csomay, Eniko 2005b. Linguistic variation within university classroom talk: A corpus-based perspective. *Linguistics and Education. 15*, 243-274.

Fortanet, Inmaculada 2004. The use of "we" in university lectures: Reference and function. *English for Specific Purposes.* 23, 45-66.

Hansen, Christa 1994. Topic Identification in Lecture Discourse. In Flowerdew, John (ed.) *Academic Listening: Research Perspectives*. New York: Cambridge University Press, 131-145.

Hearst, Martin 1997. TextTiling: Segmenting text into multi-paragraph subtopic passages. *Computational Linguistics*. 23, 33-64.

Mauranen, Anna 2001. Reflexive academic talk: Observations from MICASE. In Simpson, Rita / Swales, John (eds) *Corpus Linguistics in North America: Selection from the 1999 Symposium*. Ann Arbor: The University of Michigan Press, 165-178.

Mauranen, Anna 2003. "A good question." Expressing evaluation in academic speech. In Cortese, Giuseppina / Riley, Philip (eds) *Domain-Specific English: Textual Patterns across Communities and Classrooms*. New York: Peter Lang, 115-140.

Nattinger, James / DeCarrico, Janette 1992. *Lexical Phrases and Language Teaching*. Oxford: Oxford University Press.

Nesi, Hilary / Basturkmen, Helen 2006. Lexical bundles and discourse signalling in academic lectures. *International Journal of Corpus Linguistics*. 11, 147-168.

Prince, Ellen 1981. Toward a taxonomy of given-new information. In Cole, Peter (ed.) *Radical Pragmatics*. New York: Academic Press, 223-256.

Simpson, Rita / Mendis, Dushyanthi 2003. A corpus-based study of idioms in academic speech. *TESOL Quarterly*. 37, 419-441.

Sinclair, John / Coulthard, Malcolm 1975. *Towards an Analysis of Discourse*. Oxford: Oxford University Press.

Schmitt, Norbert 2004. *Formulaic Sequences*. Amsterdam: John Benjamins.

Swales, John 2001. Metatalk in American academic talk. *Journal of English Linguistics*. 29, 34-54.

Swales, John / Malczewski, Bonnie 2001. Discourse management and new-episode flags in MICASE. In Simpson, Rita / Swales, John (eds) *Corpus Linguistics in North America: Selection from the 1999 Symposium*. Ann Arbor: University of Michigan Press, 145-164.

Swales, John / Burke, Amy 2003. "It's really fascinating work": Differences in evaluative adjectives across academic registers. In

Leistyna, Pepi and Meyer, Charles (eds) *Corpus Analysis: Language Structure and Language use.* New York: Rodopi, 1-18.

Tracy-Ventura, Nicole / Cortes, Viviana / Biber, Douglas (in press). Lexical bundles in speech and writing. In Giovanni Parodi (ed.) *Researching Spanish across Corpora: A Corpus Linguistics Approach.* New York: Continuum.

Tyler, Andrea 1995. Patterns of Lexis: How Much Can Repetition Tell Us about Discourse Coherence? In Alatis, James / Straehle, Carolyn / Gallenberger, Brent / Maggie Ronkin (eds) *Linguistics and the Education of Language Teachers: Ethnolinguistic, Psycholinguistic, and Sociolinguistic Aspects. Georgetown University Round Table on Languages and Linguistics.* Georgetown University Press: Georgetown.

Youmans, Gilbert 1991. 'A new tool for discourse analysis: The Vocabulary Management Profile.' *Language.* 67, 763-89.

Young, Lynne 1994. University Lectures – Macro-structure and Micro-features. In Flowerdew, John. (ed.) *Academic Listening: Research Perspectives.* New York: Cambridge University Press, 159-176.

Appendix A. Lexical bundles identified in the first three VBD units grouped according to their functions

Functions – bundles	unit1	unit2	unit3	units 1 2 3
1. Stance Markers				
A. Epistemic Stance				
Personal				
and I think that**	0	3	1	4
I think it was**	2	1	1	4
you know what I**	1	1	2	4
I don't know if**	0	0	0	0
I don't know what**	0	0	0	0
I don't know how**	0	0	0	0
I don't know I**	·0	0	0	0
and I don't know**	0	0	0	0
B. Attitudinal/Modality Stance				
b.1. desire – personal				
if you want to***	6	11	2	19
I don't want to**	0	0	0	0
do you want to**	0	0	0	0
you want to go**	0	0	0	0
do you want a**	0	0	0	0
what do you want**	0	0	0	0
b.2. obligation/directive – personal				
going to have to**	1	7	1	9
and you have to**	1	3	1	5
you have to do**	1	1	2	4
you look at the**	1	2	1	4
you might want to**	0	1	3	4
I want you to***	1	2	0	3
you have to be**	1	2	0	3
you need to know**	0	1	0	1
you don't have to**	0	0	0	0
you don't want to**	0	0	0	0
you might want to**	0	0	0	0

b.3.a. intention/prediction – Personal				
I'm not going to**	0	0	0	0
we're going to do**	0	0	0	0
we're going to have**	0	0	0	0
and we're going to**	0	0	0	0
what we're going to**	0	0	0	0
b.3.b. intention/prediction – Impersonal				
is going to be***	4	4	4	12
not going to be**	1	4	4	9
going to be a**	4	3	1	8
are going to be**	3	2	1	6
going to be the**	1	0	2	3
it's going to be**	0	0	0	0
b.4. ability – Personal				
to be able to***	4	4	2	10
to come up with**	1	2	3	6
2. Discourse Organizers				
A. Topic Introduction/focus				
I want to do**	7	9	2	18
going to talk about**	5	4	8	17
want to do is**	3	5	5	13
what I want to**	6	6	1	13
take a look at**	4	2	4	10
what do you think**	1	5	3	9
a little bit about**	2	2	2	6
if we look at**	3	2	1	6
if you look at**	1	2	3	6
if you have a**	0	1	2	3
to go ahead and**	1	0	1	2
to look at the**	1	0	1	2
you know if you**	1	1	0	2
want to talk about**	0	0	0	0

B. Topic elaboration/clarification				
on the other hand**	4	3	2	9
has to do with**	2	1	2	5
you know I mean**	1	1	2	4
to do with the**	1	0	2	3
I mean you know**	1	0	0	1
3. Referential Expressions				
A. Identification/focus				
one of the things***	1	7	7	15
those of you who**	3	2	4	9
of the things that***	0	3	5	8
and this is a**	0	3	2	5
is one of the**	1	4	0	5
was one of the**	1	2	1	4
and this is the**	0	0	2	2
and one of the**	0	1	0	1
that's one of the**	0	0	0	0
and stuff like that**	2	2	2	6
or something like that**	1	4	1	6
and things like that**	0	0	0	0
C. Specification of attributes				
C.1. Quantity				
a little bit of**	10	5	2	17
a lot of people**	0	4	4	8
have a lot of**	0	2	5	7
and a lot of**	1	2	3	6
a little bit more**	3	2	0	5
a lot of the**	2	2	1	5
how many of you**	1	2	2	5
the rest of the**	2	0	3	5
greater than or equal**	0	0	4	4
than or equal to**	0	0	4	4
in a lot of**	0	0	3	3
there's a lot of**	0	0	0	0
a lot of times**	0	0	0	0

C.2. Intangible framing attributes				
in the case of**	3	3	2	8
in terms of the**	2	0	3	5
D. Time/place/text reference				
D.1. Time				
at the same time**	2	4	4	10
D.2. Place				
in the united states**	2	2	1	5
D.3. Multi-functional reference				
the end of the**	7	7	3	17
at the end of**	6	6	4	16
in the middle of**	1	2	1	4

Key to symbols:
From the functional classification of common lexical bundles in university lectures (adapted from Biber, Conrad, & Cortes, 2004)
   ** = 40-99 per million words
*** = over a hundred per million words

Nancy L. Drescher

A Multi-dimensional Examination of Spoken Language in U.S. Universities

1. Introduction

A great deal of sociolinguistic research has been done in the areas of gender, power, register, and language. Many previous studies (e.g., Bergvall 1999, Holmes 1984, Tannen 1994) have associated a wide variety of linguistic and pragmatic features with a smaller set of communicative functions and further associated those communicative functions with the linguistic construction of identity. A primary goal of this study is to find patterns in the use of those linguistic features in order to provide a broader window into the communicative functions associated with identity. By performing a factor analysis, the variables that cluster together in the data can be examined as units with communicative purposes that provide a framework for further analysis of gendered language. The focus of this paper is to examine the way that features work together within spoken texts. The terms "male" and "female", in this article, refer to the sex of speakers/addressees, rather than an attempt to interpret male as masculine or female as feminine.

2. Methods

After reviewing relevant literature to determine an initial set of linguistic and pragmatic variables, a computer program was created to count those specific features within a corpus of language according to speaker and addressee(s) identities. Those features were then analyzed using a multidimensional approach in order to discover patterns in the use of those features across speakers and registers. The following sections will describe the corpus used in the study as well as the methods used to determine and interpret the five dimensions of gender-associated linguistic markers.

2.1. Description of Corpus

This research was carried out using part of the spoken portion of the Test of English as a Foreign Language (TOEFL) 2000 Spoken and Written Academic Language (T2K-SWAL) Corpus. Without including the classroom lecture portion of the corpus, the spoken portion includes approximately 400,000 words from office hours, study groups, service encounters, labs, and classroom management sessions. The T2K-SWAL corpus (see Biber et al. 2002) was designed to represent academic language used by professors, service providers, and students of various levels (undergraduate and graduate) from six major disciplines (business, education, engineering, humanities, natural science, and social science) from four public universities in different parts of the United States. While the corpus does not come from a community in its most restricted sense, it does represent a group of people who interact around common goals defined by that social group (Eckert and McConnell-Ginet 1992) and is, in that sense, a community of practice. Because this corpus is representative of dozens of adult participants who interact within varied, but specified contexts in university settings, it can be assumed to reflect typical language use among the members of an academic community in the United States.

2.2. Factor Analysis

Because of the exploratory nature of this study, a principal factor analysis, which attempts to account for shared variance, was used. The initial solution was rotated for interpretation with the Promax method because it was assumed that the original structure was oblique, i.e., there were minor correlations among the factors, as tends to be the case with linguistic data (Biber 1988). An examination of the Scree Plot of Eigenvalues for this analysis showed that breaks occur between factors 3 and 4, and between 5 and 6 (see figure 1).

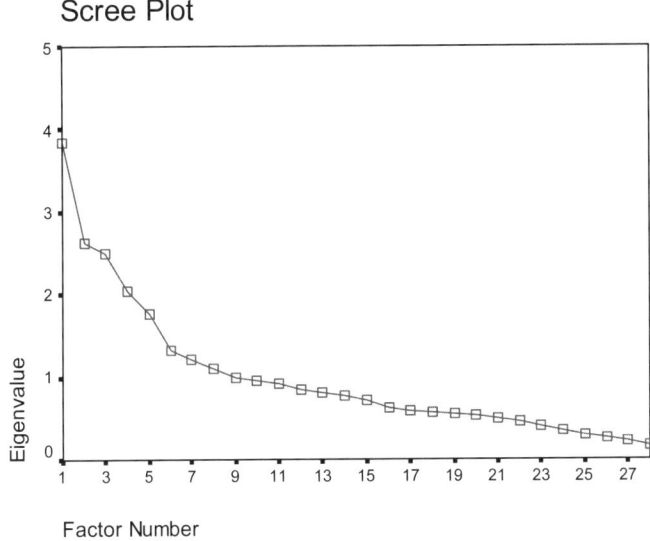

Figure 1. Scree Plot of Eigenvalues.

In the process of determining how many factors to include, solutions around 3 through 6 factor solutions were examined to determine the most interpretable solution. With more than 5 factors in the solution, many of the individual factors had too few variables loading on them to be interpretable and reliable, and the data was, thus, considered over-factored. With 3 and 4 factor solutions, the multiple constructs seemed to be collapsed, thus information was lost. For these reasons, a 5 factor solution was chosen for interpretation. With the 5 factor solution, several of the variables did not yield high enough loadings (at least .30) on any factor to be considered. Those variables (*Direct Disagreement, Elevated Structures, Compliments, Quantity Markers, Indirect Disagreement, Indirect Suggestions,* and *Apologies*) were then discarded. The discarding of variables in this study does not mean that these variables are uninteresting or unconnected with language differences; it simply means that they are not working with other variables as part of any of the factors that will be examined here.

The final set of factors with their loadings can be seen in Table 1 below. As can be seen in this table, the greatest number of variables overall were found in the first factor. This fact is a function of factor analysis and is to be expected. These issues will be examined in more depth in the next section when the interpretation of factors is presented.

Factor 1	
Syntactic Questions	0.53
Negation	0.44
Expletives/interjections	0.35
Tag Questions	0.34
WH Clause Heads	-0.40
Prepositions	-0.46
Amount of Talk	-0.53
Hesitation	-0.54
That Clause Heads	-0.54
Factor 2	
Adverbs Begin Turn	0.95
Minimal Response	0.74
Conjunctions Begin Turns	0.57
Fillers	0.52
Factor 3	
That Deletion	0.80
Private Verbs	0.79
Pronoun to Noun Ratio	0.47
1st and 2nd person Pronouns	0.45
Factor 4	
Empty Adjectives	0.45
Politeness Markers	0.43
Non-standard Forms	0.36
Doubt Markers	0.30
Certainty Markers	0.30
Pro Forms (do and so)	-0.34
Attitude/Affect Markers	-0.35

Factor 5	
Direct Directives	0.51
Modals of Possibility	0.50
Imperatives	0.49
Indirect Directives	0.41

Extraction Method: Principal Axis Factoring.
Rotation Method: Promax with Kaiser Normalization.

Table 1. Final Factorial Structure.

3. Interpretations of the Underlying Dimensions

The interpretation of the factors for this study involved an extensive qualitative examination of language samples with both high and low factor scores (Drescher 2005). Examples and explanations of each factor are provided in the following sections to illustrate and interpret each of the five dimensions.

Dimension 1: Interactional Relationship Building
vs. Information Providing.

Dimension 1 includes 4 positive features (syntactic questions, negation, expletives/interjections, and tag questions) and 5 negative features (WH Clause heads, Prepositions, Amount of Talk, Hesitations, and That clause heads). These negative features have been variously associated with informational exchanges. The WH and that clause heads indicate referentially explicit language, which has been linked to informational elaboration, particularly in unplanned interaction (Biber 1988). The fact that hesitations tend to occur in this type of language is not surprising because the function of hesitations is often attributed to discourse planning in on-line spoken contexts. Informational language has been associated with masculine language in previous studies (e.g., Biber and Burges 2000, Cameron 1992, Tannen 1990, Wodak 1981), while hesitations have been associated with a feminine style of speaking (Maltz and Borker 1982, McFadyen 1997). The positive features on Dimension 1, on the other hand, have been associated with feminine language (Lakoff 1975, Maltz and Borker 1982, McFadyen 1997, Mulac, et al. 1988). These features contribute to the function of relationship building rather than the relaying of information as is the case for the negative features. This first dimension, then, was titled Interactional Relationship Building vs. Information Providing. The following excerpts of data exemplify Dimension 1. Each underlined segment is labeled with a number to indicate which feature it is. In the first example, which provides insights into the high end of that dimension, the features that combine to create a high interactional relationship building score include tag questions [1], negation [2], syntactic questions [3], and expletives/ interjections [4]. The underlined segments in the excerpt all work together to create a sense of interaction and relationship building.

Example of High Dimension 1 Score

Female Server and Male Servee (both high scores) in Service Encounter (Dorm Front Desk)

> Male Servee: Hey
> Female Server: What are you up to, [3] going to the library?
> Male Servee: Actually I'm going to get something to eat, I uh
> Female Server: Well you can always come back and color. I have more things to color.
> Male Servee: I would but I have this huge paper that is due Monday
> Female Server: OK
> Male Servee: and I haven't [2] even started writing it
> Female Server: OK go now
> Male Servee: [laughing] OK fine, uh yeah it's really actually it's pretty evil but, so I'll be doing that for like the next three days
> Female Server: Well sounds like fun
> Male Servee: Or four days yeah it'll it'll be [unclear] it'll be a big joy for me
> Female Server: I bet
> Male Servee: Yeah
> Female Server: What class is it for? [3]
> Male Servee: Uh advanced international relations
> Female Server: Wow [4]

Male Servee: I'm doing it on uh the new Medievalism political structures of the future, doesn't it sound fun? [2, 3] [laughs] The demise of the nation state and the rise of non-governmental organizations and super national orders
Female Server: OK
Male Servee: [laughs]
Female Server: So how bout them, Cardinals? [3].. oh football seasons over
Male Servee: Uh no [2] football season isn't [2] over
Female Server: Well, it's just starting
Male Servee: Yeah exactly
Female Server: I know
Male Servee: Yeah what's your problem, [3] dammit [4]?
Female Server: Hey, We don't need no bad language around here
Male Servee: We don't need no bad language.. we don't need no bad grammar neither
Female Server: That's what they learned me here
Male Servee: That's the sad thing, you know, it's probably true
Female Server: So what are you up to this weekend? [3]
Male Servee: Uh writing my paper will probably cover it
Female Server: Oh really I thought [unclear] how long does it have to be? [3]
Male Servee: Uh eight to ten pages
Female Server: Ooh when is it due? [3]
Male Servee: Uh Monday
Female Server: Cool [4]
Male Servee: Yeah, yeah it's going to be fun very analytical, huh? [1]

The following example shows a male professor using more of the features found on the informational side of the dimension including prepositions [1], a higher percentage of the total words spoken than language samples with low dimension scores [not labeled], that clause heads [2], WH clause heads [none in example], and hesitations [4].

Example of Low Dimension 1 Score

(Male Professor to Class in Classroom Management Session)

Student: Dr. J.?
Male Professor: yes.
Student: is there any chance that um .. if you wanted us to do more smaller essays, we would not do the term paper? Or did you consider that...
Male Professor: no, no.
Whole class: [laughter]

Male Professor: the term paper is essential_. The term the term paper allows for [1] a demonstration that [2] you can do research aside from [1] a textbook [incomplete word] and the essays basically are things that [2] you could answer simply by [1] consulting textbooks. Um, [4] the term paper, I suppose could be based on [1] textbooks but probably it would be an inadequate term paper, with [1], if [1] you just used textbooks [....] Ah so, we have a division of [1] labor here and it works out that [2] ah [4] [clears throat] if [clears throat] you judge that [2] you are being unfairly evaluated as a result of [1] this shift in points, come and talk with [1] me. I I will try to assure you that [2] it is not going [clears throat] [few unclear syllables]. This distribution of [1] points is not so very different from [1] what I had proposed initially that [2] you're going to be, your grade is going to be changed at least not very dramatically, if at [1] all.

It can be seen in the previous excerpt that the professor was explaining why the class assignment was important and would not be changed. In order to accomplish his goal, he used many more words (319 words spoken by the professor compared to 30 words spoken by the students) and packed more information into his utterances (using prepositional phrases, subordinate that clauses, and hesitation markers) than either of the interactants in example 1, who were primarily focused on relationship building.

Dimension 2: Cooperative Interaction

The second set of features involved only positive features (Adverbs Beginning Turns, Minimal Response, Conjunctions Beginning Turns, and Fillers) which have been associated with the co-construction of conversation (Fishman 1978, Mulac et al. 1988, Edlesky and Adams 1990, Hirschman 1994, Cameron 1998). Because this dimension does not have any negative features, the low end of the dimension was interpreted from a lack of the positive features and from a thorough qualitative examination of samples with low dimension 2 scores. Thus, this dimension was titled Cooperative Interaction. The samples with low dimension 2 scores are highly informational in nature in addition to being primarily focused on advising, directing, and explaining. The language samples with both high and low dimension scores, in fact, seem to be specifically related to the receiving and giving of advice. The cooperative interaction dimension focuses on various types of discourse markers, or phatic items, and features which connect a speaker's language to what has been said before. This combination of features primarily indicates interlocutors' acknowledgement of the other participant's turns.

The first excerpt that follows provides an example of language between two speakers with high cooperative interaction scores. The underlined features work together to create a sense of cooperation between participants and include such features as adverbs [1] and conjunctions [2] beginning turns, minimal response [3], and fillers [4].

Example of High Dimension 2 Scores

(Female Tutor and Male Student in Study Group)

> Female Tutor: Just [1] make sure… just remember these groups are alike.
> Male Student: Right.[3]
> Female Tutor: OK,[4] so try that one.
> Male Student: All right.[3]
> Female Tutor: OK,[4] so how many stereo centers do you have?
> Male Student: Get three, right?
> Female Tutor: Mhm, three?
> Male Student: Or [2] you've got, five.
> Female Tutor: Stereo centers?
> Male Student: yeah. [3]
> Female Tutor: OK [4] a stereo center has, four different groups.
> Male Student: Oh OK [4] so this one doesn't count.
> Female Tutor: Does it have four different groups?
> Male Student: No. This one?

The following example is of a Female professor speaking to a class. It is her language that is low on the 2nd dimension and is more informational in nature than that of the participants in the example above. This informational nature can be understood by observing the fact that she uses only 1 feature from this dimension, OK, and that the rest of her language simply provides information without focusing on interactive language features such as minimal response, other fillers, or other linguistic and pragmatic features associated with cooperative interaction.

Example of Low Dimension 2 Score

(Female Professor to Class in Classroom Management)

> Any Student: What's, what's the info card? Info card, from the library? What is that? There's some computers that said please insert your info card.
> Any Student: <u>Oh</u> [5] that's the for the
> Any Student: That's just to copy
> Female Professor: Copying card
> Student: <u>Oh</u>,[5] for copies?
> Female Professor: If you want to print you just put that card in.
> Any Student: <u>And</u> [2] it's a pre-paid card for your copies?
> Female Professor: It's a pre-paid copy-card that you can purchase on the second floor of the library. <u>OK,</u> [5] we're actually going to special collections now….

In this negative end of dimension 2 (as is the case with 3 and 5), it is the lack of features associated with cooperative interaction that provide a unifying communicative function, in this case informing, that can be seen in the example above.

Dimension 3: Hedged Opinion

The third dimension was titled Hedged Opinion for the fact that the features comprising it (that deletion [1], private verbs [2], high pronoun to noun ratios [not labeled], and first and second person pronouns [3]) seem to be working together to hedge opinion statements rather than stating those same opinions as factual or informative. As can be seen in the next example, the students are working together to complete an assignment. They both use a great deal of this feature combination with the effect of sounding more cautious and careful than they would if they presented the same opinions without these leads.

Example of High Dimension 3 Score

(Female Students in Study Group)

> Student 1: <u>I</u> [3]don't <u>know</u> [2] <u>I</u> [3]don't <u>think</u> [2] <u>[that deletion]</u> [1] she has a scanner though. how to get it onto the computer.

Student 2: I [3] don't know [2] . well [unclear words]
Student 1: because we[3] we[3]'ll have to find it on the internet.
Student 2: oh could we do that?
Student 1: I [3] think [2] so. I[3]'ll, C. and I [3] can figure [2] that out
Student 2: OK
Student 1: see, I [3] mean [2] I [3] don't know [2] what it's capable of doing.
Student 2: yeah
Student 1: as far as that goes. organize the index page. so this is what we [3]'re doing right now is the index page.
Student 2: OK. now we [3] need to have good, we [3] basically in the index page is where you [3] just kind of decide which area you [3] want to go into.
Student 1: mhm
Student 2: now,
Student 1: like I [3] wonder [2] if you [3] would leave like an abstract in that even. You [3] know [2] like just something that basically says what this whole thing focuses on? Or
Student 2: yeah that would be actually I [3] think [2] [that deletion] [1] that would be a good idea. just to kind of explain

A specific example pulled from the more complete example above is the statement "I don't think she has a scanner." The speaker uses a first person pronoun (I), a third person pronoun (she), a private verb (think), and deletes the "that" in her subordinate clause. An alternative way of stating this same information in a less hedged way would be "She doesn't have a scanner", in which case the first person pronoun, the that deletion, and the private verb are not used.

In the next example, the student has a low hedged opinion score. He states many of his opinions in a way that have the effect of informing the professor rather than stating his opinion about something. In many of the cases it would be difficult to imagine how he could have used these features (e.g., it would not make sense to say, "I think [that deletion] I've contacted a number of people at Scripps"), but in other cases he might have added a hedge (e.g., he could have said "I think that's looking good", but chose instead to say "That's looking good"), which would have created a less informational effect. In still other places, he uses a variety of other features that create a hedged effect (e.g., I'd appreciate it, if you could, write a um, letter of recommendation for me), and even uses the features of this dimension on occasion (e.g., I'm totally glad [that deletion] you asked) though not necessarily with the same effect.

Example of Low Dimension 3 Score

(Male Student to Male Professor in Office Hours)

> Male Professor: Have you [3] done any more on your [3] grad school?
> Male Student: Yes, uh, I [3]'ve contacted a, number of people at Scripps.
> Male Professor: Mhm.
> Male Student: And uh, gotten some responses back.
> Male Professor: Good.
> Male Student: From some, positive responses too.
> Male Professor: Good.
> Male Student: That's looking good. Um, my application is almost off.
> Male Professor: OK.
> Male Student: And, that reminded me [3] , I [3]'m totally glad you [3] asked because I [3] would have felt quite stupid, um, if, if you [3] wouldn't mind, I [3]'d appreciate it, if you [3] could, write a um, letter of recommendation for me [3] .
> Male Professor: Mhm. Yeah just be sure to give me at least two weeks' notice.
> Male Student: Yeah. Got plenty of time.
> Male Professor: OK. So what's the deadline?
> Male Student: Uh, January sixth.

Dimension 4: Formally Polite Interaction vs. Person Oriented Stance

Dimension 4 includes 5 positive features (empty adjectives, politeness markers, non-standard forms, and certainty and doubt markers) and 2 negative features (Stance Markers of Affect/Attitude and pro forms, do and so). The positive features on Dimension 4 have been associated with polite interaction and phatic communication, particularly among strangers, and have typically been connected to feminine language (e.g., Fishman 1978, Cameron 1992, Hirschman 1994, Biber and Burges 2000). The negative features are both related to the construction of stance, which can be defined as "the lexical and grammatical expression of attitudes, feelings, judgments, or commitment concerning the propositional content of a message" (Biber and Finegan 1989). Proforms (do and so) stand for entire verbal clauses and tend to be used in situations concerned more with personal matters than with the providing of information (Biber 1988). It seems in these samples, that these forms are functioning to reduce the informational load because of the on-line spoken delivery, but the language itself seems to be quite information focused. This 4th dimension, then, was titled *Formally Polite Interaction vs. Person Oriented Stance*. The person oriented stance end of this dimension is reflective of Precht's 5th stance factor, for which she argues that the opinionated affect/person-oriented stance uses words like "afraid" and "wrong" to express opinions in "emotional ways" (Precht 2000: 128).

The following excerpts of data exemplify Dimension 4. In the first example, which provides insights into the high end of that dimension, the features that add together for a high polite interaction score include empty adjectives [1], politeness markers [2], non-standard forms [none shown in example], and certainty [4] and doubt markers [5]. The underlined segments in the excerpt all work together to create a sense of polite interaction.

Example of High Dimension 4 Score
(Two Women in Service Encounter – business services)

> Female Server: please [2] and if you'll put your student I. D. number on it.
> Female Servee: I think [5] you might [5] have the wrong name in there. you know I came in a couple weeks
> [12 turns deleted]
> Female Server: I would definitely [4] check at student accounts
> Female Servee: OK, thank you. [2] yeah I don't want now [unclear words] maybe [5] not but everything else I've gotten in the mail has been
> Female Server: probably [5] sent this to [married name]
> Female Servee: yeah and it all came out like that last Summer and I don't know what why. before it had the right name so I'm guessing [5] I filled it out wrong. oops. yeah on this my I. D. it was all right.
> Female Server: that's really odd or very inconvenient
> Female Servee: so just go [unclear words]
> Female Server: yes student accounts counter on the left. let me give you a receipt.
> Female Servee: so every class I go in they call me [married name]
> Female Server: oh whoopee
> Female Servee: [laughs] [unclear words] thank you. [2] Have a nice [1] day.
> Female Server: thank you. [2] [maiden name] [laughs]?

Much of the excerpt above is formulaic and involves the use of phatic communication devices such as please, thank you, and have a good day which work together to create a polite conversation with a stranger. This example, in fact, has much more other content than many of the interactions in this dimension. Because these conversations are short and the formulas are repeated continually, the scores add up quickly. It also can be seen in this example that the participants are using many doubt hedges such as "probably", "maybe", "guess" and emphatics or certainty markers (definitely), which taken together also serve to keep the interaction between strangers feeling very friendly and informal. The tone, for example, would have been very different, indeed, had the servee said, "You have the wrong name on there" and the server replied, "Check at student accounts". The following example shows a Male professor using more of the negative features (Stance Markers of Affect/Attitude [1] and pro forms (do and so) [2]).

Example of Low Dimension 4 Score

Male Professor to Male Student During Office Hours (both low scores)

> Male Student: Could there also be like a factor like the creation story being a factor with it being like, Male is, the, the, the world was made from Male and Male was, can conquer you know. And so they thought just like, I mean like, some of the, Indians were like you know like you said were powerful, uh, like, population cities whatever, and they didn't, like push, what they believed, on other Indians around them as long as they weren't bothered, whereas, in the Europeans they really pushed it on, others because they believe what they were doing was the right [1] thing to do. [2]
> Male Professor: Yeah and, the problem [1] with, the problem [1] with that argument not that it's wrong [1] but the problem [1] the problem [1] with that argument in, in trying to, make sense of it is, just, um, it's always hard to know what's causing what's effect which is that, you're successful and so you create a kind of, culture that rationalizes what you do, [2] or you have a culture and that affects then what you do [2] because, your argument, I mean your argument's a good [1] one

It can be seen in the previous excerpt that the professor was explaining why he felt the student's point was inadequate (using Stance Markers of Affect/Attitude and the pro verb do) just as the student used some of these same constructions to make his point.

Dimension 5: Directive

The features that load on this final dimension include direct directives, imperatives, modals of possibility, and indirect directives. This dimension suggests that, in contrast to the assumption that some speakers are more direct when giving directives and others are less direct, the same speakers are actually using all of the various forms of directives in combination. Perhaps this interplay is a function of the "correction" that takes place during spoken interactions. For example a speaker might offer an indirect suggestion that is not taken up and then follow up with a more explicit directive. Conversely, a speaker might give a direct directive and upon seeing a negative reaction, follow with a more hedged version of the directive.

In the following example, the professor (a man) was explaining how the student (also a man) should approach his homework assignment. While there are other features in this example, the professor is primarily using direct directives such as "you'll need to" and imperatives such as "make sure…" in order to tell the student how to find articles. Again, the underlined forms work together to create a sense of providing direction or directive: direct directives [1], imperatives [2], modals of possibility [3], indirect directives [4].

Example of High Directive Score

(Male professor to Male student in office hours)

> Male Professor: You put Ethiopia [typing] how did you spell it? There we go and Eritrea uh I think so
> Male Student: oh OK
> Male Professor: [mumbling]
> Male Student: that's that's how I spelled it
> Male Professor: that's the other thing make sure you spell things properly [1] cuz if you've got them misspelled nothing is gonna come up. um let's see, a hundred and ninety one documents. there you go [laughing]
> Male Student: [laughing]
> Male Professor: so so pick a dozen [2] and you're fine yeah so then and you'll find lots of stuff here, Eritrea faces mass attack, Ethiopia snubs European Union peace envoys, uh, who cares who shot first, Eritreans wait in fear for Goliath's air strikes. um what you'll need to do is you'll need to [1] look

through these and <u>make certain</u> [2]that you <u>can</u> [3] find an article that really explains it to you

In contrast to the example above where the male professor has a high directive score while providing advice to the student, the following example is of a male student addressing a male professor. It is the student, in this case, who has the low score. He is explaining how he did the work on a problem and what he was thinking while he did that work. This act is typical of low directive scores. These language samples are also highly interactive as is illustrated in the following excerpt.

Example of Low Directive Score

(Male Student to Male Professor in Office Hours)

> Male Student: well what I kinda did is jump down to here thinking "OK I know the the uh the uh figure under row zero under my slide variable X seven..."
> Male Professor: right
> Male Student: "is gonna be that number", so I just started
> Male Professor: [many unclear syllables] right
> Male Student: doing the (simplex)
> Male Professor: right right, so
> Male Student: instead of realizing that if everything else is zero it cuts em out, a lot of your work [few unclear syllables].
> Male Professor: yeah that's, and that's what they're after on this. It's is that you recognize that if if exponents five are the basic variables then you can figure out what the values are
> Male Student: right
> Male Professor: without going through anything else
> Male Student: OK
> Male Professor: because in effect everything else can be dropped out, of the problem.
> Male Student: right.

The directive continuum seems to be from a high end of telling someone what to do in the future to a low end of telling someone what has already been done, and particularly what someone was thinking in the past. This view of the negative end of the continuum was achieved through an extensive qualitative analysis (Drescher 2005). Unlike the negative end of the first four dimensions, this negative end actually seems to have many more interactive features (such as minimal response, fillers, and conjunctions beginning turns) than the high end of the directive dimension.

4. Conclusion

While further studies will need to be conducted in order to substantiate the results of this study (as is the case with any exploratory analysis), the patterns among the variables have resulted in five dimensions: *Interactional Relationship Building vs. Information Providing, Cooperative Interaction, Hedged Opinion, Formally Polite Interaction vs. Person Oriented Stance*, and *Directive.* These dimensions are plainly interpretable and understandable as sets of features within the context of previous research and analysis. Furthermore, these dimensions provide a productive theoretical framework from which to view the construction of identity across registers in future research.

One final note that should be made clear is that while this factor analysis has provided a great deal of insight into the ways in which many of these variables work together, it in no way suggests that the variables that have been excluded through this process are not important or interesting. The fact that a variable is not working together with other features in a dimension does not suggest that the variable in itself is not worth examining. While not explored in the confines of this study, examination of the remaining variables could in and of itself be a fruitful direction for future research.

5. References

Bergvall, Victoria. L. 1999. Toward a comprehensive theory of language and gender. *Language in Society,* 28, 273-293.

Biber, Douglas / Burges, Jena 2000. Historical Change in the Language Use of Women and Men: Gender Differences in Dramatic Dialogue. *Journal of English Linguistics,* 28/1, 21-37.

Biber, Douglas / Conrad, Susan / Reppen, Randi / Byrd, Patricia / Helt, Marie 2002. Speaking and Writing in the University: A Multidimensional Comparison. *TESOL Quarterly,* 36/1, 9-48.

Biber, Douglas 1988. *Variation across Speech and Writing.* Cambridge: Cambridge University Press.

Biber, Douglas / Finegan, Edward 1989. Styles of stance in English: Lexical and grammatical marking of evidentiality and affect. *Text,* 9/1, 93-124.

Cameron, Deborah 1992. Review of Tannen 1991. *Feminism and Psychology,* 2-3, 465-89.

Cameron, Deborah 1998. Performing gender identity: Young men's talk and the construction of heterosexual masculinity. In Coates, Jennifer (ed.) *Language and Gender: A Reader.* Oxford: Blackwell Publishing, 270-284.

Drescher, Nancy 2005. *Sex, Roles, and Register: A Corpus-Based Investigation of Sex-Linked Linguistic and Pragmatic Features.* PhD Dissertation. Northern Arizona University.

Eckert, Pennelope / McConnell-Ginet, Sally 1998. Communities of practice: Where language, gender and power all live. In Coates, Jennifer (ed.) *Language and Gender: A Reader.* Oxford: Blackwell Publishing, 484-494.

Edelsky, Carole / Adams, Karen 1990. Creating inequality: Breaking rules in debates. *Journal of Language and Social Psychology,* 9/3, 171-190.

Fishman, Pamela 1978. Interaction: The work women do. *Social Problem.* 25, 397-406.

Hirschman, Linette 1994. Female-male differences in conversational interaction. *Language in Society,* 23, 427-442. (Originally from 1973 LSA conference presentation).

Holmes, Janet 1984. Hedging your bets and sitting on the fence: Some evidence for hedges as support structures. *Te Reo,* 27, 47-62.

Lakoff, Robin 1975. *Language and Woman's Place.* New York: Harper & Row.

Maltz, Daniel N. / Borker, Ruth A. 1982. A cultural approach to male-female miscommunications. In J.J. Gumperz, (ed.) *Language and Social Identity.* New York: Cambridge University Press, 196-216.

McFadyen, Ruth G. 1997. The relationship between powerless speech, agentic behavior, and amount of talk. *The Journal of Social Psychology,* 137, 470-479.

Mulac, Anthony / Wiemann, John M. / Widenmann, Sally J. / Gibson, Toni W. 1988. Male/female language differences and effects in same-sex and mixed-sex dyads: The gender-linked language effect. *Communication Monographs*, 55, 315-335.

Precht, Kristen 2000. *Patterns of Stance in English.* PhD Dissertation. Northern Arizona University.

Tannen, Deborah 1990. Gender differences in conversational coherence: Physical alignment and topical cohesion. In Dorval, Brucw (ed.) *Conversational Organization and its Development.* Norwood, N.J.: Ablex, 167-206.

Tannen, Deborah 1994. *Gender and Discourse.* New York: Oxford University Press.

Wodak, Ruth 1981. Women Relate, Men Report: Sex Differences in Language Behaviour in a Therapeutic Group. *Journal of Pragmatics,* 5/2-3, 261-285.

PAULA GARCÍA

Pragmatics in Academic Contexts: A Spoken Corpus Study

1. Introduction: The context of pragmatic meaning

The past thirty years have seen the pragmatic dimension of language use develop from a philosophical concept to an area of linguistic research with important implications for language learning and teaching. With the growing acknowledgement of the role of pragmatic competence in second language (L2) learning, researchers and theorists have been attempting to define, describe, and investigate this important aspect of communicative competence. Despite research exploring some areas of cross-cultural differences and interlanguage development (e.g., Blum-Kulka, House and Kasper 1989, Rose 2000), the question of what constitutes the nature of pragmatic competence remains unanswered. In other words, very little is known about how native English speakers use language pragmatically. The study described here is an attempt to fill this knowledge gap by describing how native English speakers use pragmatic function. It takes a corpus-based approach to investigate how speakers occupying various social roles and situational contexts use language pragmatically to accomplish their communicative goals.

Using several computer programs, including one that was written specifically for this study, natural language collected from a corpus of conversations within university settings were analyzed along multiple contextual and linguistic variables. Contextual variables included situation types, such as office hours, service encounters, and study groups, and speaker roles, such as students, professors, and service providers. The corpus samples were analyzed for linguistic features that are used by native English speakers in the formulation of pragmatic function. These linguistic features included stance markers, such as modals, hedges, and amplifiers; syntactic structure, such as statements, interrogatives, and imperatives; agency, such as first person, second person, or third person; and length of utterance. Some of these features have been found to contribute to the realization of pragmatic meaning (e.g., Aijmer 1996, Blum-Kulka, House and Kasper 1989, Blum-Kulka and Levenston 1987, Blum-Kulka and Olshtain 1986, Garcia 2004a, He 1998), and some have only been theorized to do so (Levinson 1983).

This study utilized a taxonomy based on theoretical frame-works, namely Searle's (1969) pragmatic categories of directives, commissives, expressives, and representatives. The taxonomy was augmented with an element of participation (Hancher 1979), which specifies whether the utterances identify an act to be accomplished by the speaker, by the hearer, or both; or, for the benefit of the speaker, of the hearer, or both. Applying the taxonomy to the coding of utterances in the corpus sample involved making judgments about the intentions of speakers. These judgments were based on the situation and co-text in order to determine pragmatic function and degree of participation. Because of this subjective aspect, the taxonomy was validated empirically in a sub-study in which two independent raters coded a sub-sample of the corpus conversations. The raters' levels of agreement with the researcher were sufficient for determining the usefulness of the taxonomy.

The results of this study show how pragmatic utterances were realized linguistically in different ways in different situation types and by different speakers. Each pragmatic category was analyzed to see how acts are realized by speakers in different roles and in different situations. For instance, when students in office hours use directives, are they formulated differently than when they are used by students in service encounters or study groups? This part of the investigation provides evidence of the effects of contextual variables in the realization of pragmatic functions.

2. Methodology

2.1. Variables and computerized data collection

The corpus files came from the spoken language component of the TOEFL 2000 Spoken and Written Academic Language Corpus (see Biber, Conrad, Reppen, Bird and Helt 2002). Fourteen corpus files, totaling 43,000 words, from office hours, study groups, and service encounters were analyzed. Corpus files were marked for utterance breaks (as the unit of analysis), syntactic type (fragment, statement, question, or command), agency (none, I/we, you, third person, and multiple), and pragmatic function using a process called hard-coding. The hard-coding process involved listening to the audiocassettes and reading the printed transcripts simultaneously in order to determine pragmatic function. This required repeatedly reviewing the conversations and becoming familiar with them because determining exactly what a speaker was trying to do with a particular utterance was usually not immediately discernable.

Each utterance in all of the corpus conversations was coded according to 9 variables falling into three major categories: contextual, linguistic, and pragmatic. The contextual variables were 1) situation type: service encounter, office hour, or study group; and 2) speaker role: student, service provider, or professor. The linguistic variables were modals, hedges, such as *maybe*, *kind of*, and *I think*, amplifiers, such as *really* and *so*. These linguistic features have been linked to pragmatic meaning by Poos and Simpson (2002), Precht (2003), and Scott (2002).

Utterances were also coded for grammatical features, namely, syntactic type and agency. For syntactic type, each utterance in the files was coded as being a fragment, a statement, an interrogative, or an imperative, according to the syntactic structure of the utterance. This feature might have been identified by the computer program, but it likely would have included a great deal of error. Agency depended on whether the operator of the main proposition was the speaker or speaker and hearer (1st person singular or plural), the hearer (2nd person), someone or something other than the speaker or hearer (3rd person), or if there was no discernable or specified agent. This also could have been coded by the customized computer program but with great risk of error because spoken language often contains a lot of embedded clauses and verb phrases, often with a different agent from the main clause. Length of utterance, found to contribute to pragmatic competence by Blum-Kulka and Olshtain (1986), was calculated by a customized computer program, which counted each word in each utterance.

Pragmatic function was hard-coded for each utterance using a taxonomy of pragmatic functions developed specifically for this study based on observations from a sample of the corpus files. The taxonomy was modeled on Searle's (1969, 1979) categories (i.e., directives, commissives, expressives, and representatives) with an added dimension of speaker-hearer involvement (Hancher 1979) described by the "degree of participation" column in Table 1 below. This taxonomy was piloted with two inter-rater agreement studies (see García 2004b) and found to be a thorough and complete tool appropriate for analyzing the academic conversations from the corpus.

In the case of directives, speaker-gain directives are utterances in which the speaker tries to get the hearer to do something for the benefit of the *speaker*. Hearer-gain directives are utterances in which the speaker tries to get the hearer to do something for the benefit of the *hearer*. In the commissives category, speaker-action commissives are utterances in which the speaker identifies something he or she will do. Joint-action commissives describe what the speaker wants the hearer *and* the speaker to do, emphasizing the intention that speaker and hearer commit the act jointly. The expressives category refers to a speakers' expression of feelings and opinions. Personal expressives reflect what the speaker thinks or feels about him or herself. Inter-personal expressives reflect what the speaker thinks of the hearer. The final category of representatives includes personal representatives in which the speaker provides his or her knowledge about something, and interpersonal representatives in which the speaker comments on the hearer's knowledge, for instance, in disagreeing or contradicting.

	Examples of pragmatic acts	Searlean category	Degree of participation
1	Request a service, assistance, or favor, put on hold	Directives	Speaker-gain
2	Suggest, advise, warn, command, grant permission	Directives	Hearer-gain
3	Offer, promise, refuse	Commissives	Speaker-action
4	Plan, invite	Commissives	Joint-action
5	Apologize, express affect or opinion	Expressives	Personal
6	Complain, criticize, admonish, compliment	Expressives	Interpersonal
7	Explain, give directions, report, identify	Representatives	Personal
8	Correct, contradict, disagree, agree	Representatives	Interpersonal

Table 1. Classification scheme used in this study.

Utterances described as conventional expressives (e.g., greet, thank, exclaim) were not included in the analysis in this study because they have been addressed extensively in previous literature. In addition, utterances classified as minimal responses and backchannels (simple representatives according to Searle's taxonomy) were also not included in the analysis. These types of utterances, such as *mhmm*, *Ok*, and *yeah*, have been analyzed in previous research (e.g., Farr 2003) as indicators of involved interaction among interlocutors. Pragmatically, they can be viewed as having the function of indicating involvement, but because of their brevity, they do not include sufficient linguistic evidence (e.g., lexical items) to determine the exact nature of their function. Therefore, they were not analyzed in the study, and the results of their frequencies are not reported in the results.

Corpus files were processed through three different computer programs: a grammatical tagging program, a customized program developed by the researcher, and Monoconc Pro. The tagging program, developed by Biber (1988), tagged corpus files for grammatical categories, such as verb, noun, adverb, etc. The tagger allowed for several linguistic variables to be recorded, including use of modal, hedges, and amplifiers. Files were then read by a second customized computer program that compiled the variables for each observation, i.e., each utterance in terms of contextual, linguistics, and pragmatic function code. The third program used was the commercially-available Monoconc Pro. This program was used to search and compile sets of utterances with the same pragmatic function thus facilitating searches for specific utterances with the larger text files. For example, it could collect all the interpersonal commissives that had interrogative syntactic structure that occurred in office hours.

2.2. Normalizing counts

The data was analyzed in terms of the two contextual variables: speaker role and situation type. Different groups of speakers varied in the amount of talk they produced. For instance, students in office hours produced a total of 292 utterances, whereas professors produced 419. Therefore, normalization was used to provide a standard basis on which utterance frequencies could be compared (cf. Biber et al. 1998). Normalization is calculated by dividing the raw frequency by the word count for the category, and multiplying the result by a number that is a suitable basis for comparison given the size of the corpus. In most corpus studies, such standardization of frequency counts is based on word count; however, since this study used the utterance as the unit of analysis, I standardized counts based on the number of utterances produced by each speaker role in each situation, which became the denominator of the normalizing equation. The normalized count for linguistic features was calculated with the following equation:

$$\frac{\text{raw frequency}}{\text{utterance count per role \& situation}} \times 100 = \text{normed count}$$

3. Results

The corpus samples yielded a total of 2,045 utterances reflecting pragmatic functions of interest to this study. One question of interest is: what types of pragmatic utterances are produced by the various speaker roles in various academic situations? Table 2 presents the use of pragmatic utterances by speakers in different roles and in different situation types.

	OFFICE HOURS		SERVICE ENCOUNTERS		STUDY GROUPS
Pragmatic Category	Students (292 utterances)	Professors (419 utterances)	Students (285 utteranc.)	Service Providers (431 utter.)	Students (617 utteranc.)
Speaker-gain Directives	7	2	28	9	3
Hearer-gain Directives	0.3	39	5	37	9
Speaker-action Commissives	21	4	10	13	7
Joint-action Commissives	0.7	3	0.7	0.2	15
Personal Expressives	24	8	18	8	21
Interpersonal Expressives	7	9	4	1	2
Personal Representatives	26	22	27	28	32
Interpersonal Representatives	14	13	8	4	11

Table 2. Pragmatic utterances per speaker role and situation type (N= 2045).

The table shows that categories of pragmatic utterances were used with varying degree according to the role of the speaker and the situation type. For instance, speaker-gain directives (e.g., requests) were used in 28 out of 100 utterances produced by students in service encounters, but they were used with much less frequency (fewer than

10) by students in any other situation type. Hearer-gain directives
(e.g., suggestions, advice) were used more often by professors and
service providers than by students in any situations. Speaker-action
commissives (e.g., promises, refusals) were used most frequently by
students in office hours, and joint-action commissives (e.g., plans,
invitations) were used most often by students in study groups.

Personal expressives (e.g., feelings, opinions) were used mostly
by students in all three situation types, with a frequency of 24 per 100
utterances in office hours, 18 in service encounters, and 21 in study
groups. Interpersonal expressives (e.g., criticisms, compliments) were
used with relatively low frequency across speaker roles and situations,
with fewer than 10 per 100 utterances reflecting their use. In contrast,
personal representatives (e.g., reports, explanations) were used with
relatively high frequencies across all speaker groups, ranging from 22
per 100 utterances produced by professors to 32 produced by students
in study groups. Interpersonal representatives (e.g., corrections,
disagreements) were used most often by students and professors in
office hours and by students in study groups.

Another question of interest addressed by the results of this
study is: Are pragmatic utterances realized linguistically in different
ways in different situation types and by different speakers? This
question will be addressed for each of the eight pragmatic categories.

Speaker-gain directives

The speaker-gain directives category (e.g., requests) shows some
interesting trends in different speakers' use of linguistic features (see
Table 3). These types of utterances are used by speakers to ask the
hearer to do something for the benefit of the speaker. They would
therefore include linguistic strategies that vary depending on how
direct or indirect the speaker wants to be in bidding the hearer to carry
out some kind of action. Linguistic features that are likely to facilitate
this kind of goal would logically be imperative structure and second
person agency for direct utterances, and hedges and modals for more
indirect utterances. The table below shows that speakers used all of

these linguistic features in realizing speaker-gain directives; however, the situation and speaker role determined which features were used.

	OFFICE HOURS		SERVICE ENCOUNTERS		STUDY GROUPS
	Students	Professors	Students	Servers	Students
Stance Markers					
Modals	32	-	47	22	20
Hedges	32	-	13	17	20
Amplifiers	11	-	10	31	15
Syntactic Structure					
Fragments	11	-	5	11	10
Statements	84	-	54	17	10
Interrogatives	5	-	37	11	25
Imperatives	0	-	4	61	55
Agency					
None/unknown	26	-	17	25	30
1st person	63	-	54	47	5
2nd person	5	-	10	14	65
3rd person	5	-	19	14	0
Utterance Length					
Mean	14	-	10	8	7

Table 3. Linguistic realizations of speaker-gain directives (N=161).

Modals were used in 32 out of 100 utterances when they were produced by students in office hours, 47 per 100 by students in service encounters, and only 20 per 100 by students in study groups. Given that modals are seen as markers of hesitancy and indirectness, the lower use of modals in study groups reflects students' use of more direct language while conversing in study groups. Another piece of evidence that students are more direct in study groups is a much higher use of imperatives than when they conversed in office hours and service encounters. Students in study groups also exhibited use of shorter utterances in the expression of speaker-gain directives. Students' mean utterance length in study groups is 7, while in office hours it is 14, and in service encounters it is 10. The combination of these three features of directness (i.e., few stance markers, high imperatives, and low mean utterance length) indicates that students realize speaker-gain directives in a very direct manner when communicating in study groups.

Hearer-gain directives

	OFFICE HOURS		SERVICE ENCOUNTERS		STUDY GROUPS
	Students	Professors	Students	Servers	Students
Stance Markers					
Modals	-	48	31	33	29
Hedges	-	35	8	9	20
Amplifiers	-	15	23	16	13
Syntactic Structure					
Fragments	-	4	0	16	5
Statements	-	56	23	56	46
Interrogatives	-	6	8	3	9
Imperatives	-	35	69	25	40
Agency					
None/unknown	-	13	15	20	7
1st person	-	8	8	10	4
2nd person	-	75	69	46	77
3rd person	-	4	8	24	12
Utterance Length					
Mean	-	18	8	10	10

Table 4. Linguistic realizations of hearer-gain directives (N=393).

As acts of suggestion, advice, command, and warning, hearer-gain directives have the potential to cause threats to the hearer's face. They would therefore be expected to include a high number of stance markers, particularly hedges, to mitigate or soften the possible threats to the hearer's face. However, in order to be effective, they would also be expected to include high use of second person agency, and, possibly, imperatives.

Table 4 shows that hearer-gain directives include high use of modals and hedges, but not noticeably more frequently than in speaker-gain directives. They also include high use of imperatives and second person agency as would be expected of utterances used to direct the hearer to do something. Imperatives are used with much greater frequency than in any other pragmatic category by all speakers across the board (with the exception of students in office hours, who did not produce enough of these utterances for comparison). Second person agency is also used with markedly greater frequency in hearer-gain directives than in any other pragmatic category.

Interestingly, service providers exhibited a low use of hedges and a relatively low mean utterance length in their realizations of hearer-gain directives. They also showed a fairly high use of second person agency. Servers' use of these linguistic features can be interpreted as more direct expression of hearer-gain directives. Take for example the extract below, which is from a conversation in which a student is seeking assistance with dropping a class and getting a refund.

> Extract 1
> Service Provider: Ok *you* need to drop your class first.
> Student: Ok.
> …[later in same conversation]
> Service Provider: Ok *go* ahead and just *fill* this out and *turn* it back to me.
> Student: Ok.

In this extract, the service provider uses imperative forms and a clear second person agent to direct the student (in bold). The server's utterances are precise in their directions and do not provide a lot of follow-up explanation for why the student should do as the server orders. The service provider's utterances were taken up by the student, who responds with *Ok*.

Professors' use of hearer-gain directives (e.g., suggestions, advice, warnings, grants of permission) is characterized by a high use of modals and hedges, and a high use of second person agency. This linguistic pattern indicates that professors are fairly stanced in their realizations of hearer-gain directives, which may be interpreted as a politeness strategy. They also use relatively long utterances, meaning that professors include explanations justifying their suggestions in contrast to servers. Extract 2 is from a conversation in which a professor and student are reviewing the student's academic transcript in order to determine whether she will be able to graduate:

> Extract 2
> Professor: Now here's what *you should* do if you want me to go over your graduation papers, *you gotta* do it this semester because if you wait until the summer or the fall...
> Student: Uh huh...
> Professor: then *you'll have to* go through somebody else and it'll just take longer.
> Student: Yeah...

In extract 2, the professor is providing advice to the student so that she can graduate on time. He accomplishes this goal through a sequence of utterances that are a combination of pragmatic acts: advice (*here's what you should do if...*), command (*you gotta do it this semester...*), and warning (*if you wait until the summer or the fall... then you'll have to go through somebody else and it'll just take longer*). These utterances are realized through heavy use of modals of obligation (*gotta, should*) and the second person pronoun as agent (in bold). The use of modals and second person agency allows the professor to be very explicit about directing the student to follow his orders, while the use of long utterances allows him to explain the reasons why the student should do as he is advising.

Speaker-action commissives

Speaker-action commissives, where speakers say what they intend to do or not to do, reflect a high use of modals and first person agents across speaker roles and situation types (see Table 5).

	OFFICE HOURS		SERVICE ENCOUNTERS		STUDY GROUPS
	Students	Professors	Students	Servers	Students
Stance Markers					
Modals	74	76	70	70	70
Hedges	19	12	20	83	18
Amplifiers	15	18	10	11	23
Syntactic Structure					
Fragments	6	6	7	0	0
Statements	90	70	93	75	90
Interrogatives	3	0	0	18	0
Imperatives	0	24	0	7	10
Agency					
None/unknown	3	12	3	7	3
1st person	97	88	97	77	94
2nd person	0	0	0	12	3
3rd person	0	0	0	4	0
Utterance Length					
Mean	13	16	10	8	14

Table 5. Linguistic realizations of speaker-action commissives (N=206).

Extensive use of modals is characteristic of speaker-action commissives. Extracts 3 and 4 are examples of how servers employ speaker-action commissives to offer assistance to students. Extract 3 is from a conversation that took place in a student business office; and, 4 is from a conversation in the campus bookstore.

> Extract 3
> Service Provider: Oh if you if it's like an emergency *I can* do it for you.

> Extract 4
> Service Provider: Did you want to come back? 'Cause *I can* hold onto your stuff.

Both of these extracts show how service providers offer to perform a service for student customers. In both utterances, the server uses first person agency to identify herself as the person who will perform the service. She also uses the modal *can* to indicate her willingness to perform the tasks. These examples reveal the application of *I can* as a formula for offering to do things.

Speaker-action commissives were also defined as refusals. The following extract is an example of how service providers employ modals to express speaker-action commissives of refusal. In extract 5, the student customer has asked the service provider for information about another student. Because the information is confidential, the service provider cannot disclose it, and she refuses the student's request.

> Extract 5
> Student: Ok what is his social security number?
> Service Provider: *I can't* release that.
> Student: Ok.
> Service Provider: I'm sorry.
> Student: Ok.
> Service Provider: *That's just* for confidentiality.

In this extract, the service provider shows an interesting pattern of linguistic feature use as she refuses the student's query for information through a sequence of utterances, all of which perform the act of refusing. And, all of the server's refusal utterances are taken up by the student, who responds with *Ok*. In the first utterance, the server uses the modal *can* in the negative to express her refusal. In the second utterance, she says that she is sorry. In the third utterance, it seems as if she is trying to explain why she is refusing. She does this by employing a third person agent (*That*), which has no explicit referent, but it could be inferred that the referent is the university policy forbidding the release of student information (i.e., social security numbers). She also uses a hedge (*just*) that serves to minimize the effect of her refusal. The shift from first person agency in the first and second utterances to third person agency in the final utterance reflects a shift of responsibility from the server to university policy in general. Accordingly, the server releases herself from the blame, and places it instead on a non-individual, i.e., the university. This shift of blame also has the effect of mitigating the negative force of the refusal. The use of third person agency to accomplish this effect reflects an interesting linguistic behavior unique to servers' realization of speaker-action commissives. The role of service provider was the only role that used third person agency in this pragmatic category with frequency.

Joint-action commissives

Joint-action commissives (e.g., offers, invitations) showed interesting results in that they were used with frequency by two speaker roles only (see Table 6): professors in office hours and students in study groups. Both speaker roles showed high frequencies of first person agency, high frequencies of modal and hedge stance markers, and high mean utterance lengths.

	OFFICE HOURS		SERVICE ENCOUNTERS		STUDY GROUPS
	Students	Professors	Students	Servers	Students
Stance Markers					
Modals	-	55	-	-	52
Hedges	-	73	-	-	41
Amplifiers	-	9	-	-	22
Syntactic Structure					
Fragments	-	0	-	-	18
Statements	-	82	-	-	70
Interrogatives	-	0	-	-	7
Imperatives	-	18	-	-	5
Agency					
None/unknown	-	0	-	-	23
1st person	-	82	-	-	63
2nd person	-	9	-	-	10
3rd person	-	9	-	-	4
Utterance Length					
Mean	-	18	-	-	16

Table 6. Linguistic realizations of joint-action commissives (N=111).

Joint-action commissives in office hour conversations provide interesting examples of linguistic realization. These types of utterances were used to make joint plans or to extend invitations. Extract 6 shows two instances of a professor using joint-action commissives to make future plans with his student.

> Extract 6
> Professor: So *we'll* try to link up and you guys *could* all sit in a room and then I *could* link up with you in a conference call, *maybe we could* chat about that stuff.
> Student: Ok, that sounds good.
> Professor: And then *maybe we can* schedule that conference call next week.

In extract 6, the professor uses several linguistic features that interact to express a planning function (in bold). He uses stance markers such as the modals *will* and *could*, and he uses the hedge *maybe*. This use of stance markers reflects tentativeness, showing that the professor is perhaps thinking aloud, or suggesting this plan to the student. The professor also uses a first person agent in his utterances, specifically the first person plural pronoun *we*. This feature reflects the professor's intention to project a joint plan, something that the student and professor will accomplish together. The student acknowledges the plan with *Ok, that sounds good*.

Students used joint-action commissives rarely in office hours. To contrast professors' use of these types of utterances with students' use, an example from a student is presented below. Extract 7 shows a student using a joint-action commissive to invite a professor to view a project that he and another student have been working on.

> Extract 7
> Student: Hi.
> Professor: Hey.
> Student: *If you want to come down and look at these slides.*
> Professor: Oh. Where are you set up?

The student's joint-action commissive in extract 7 (in bold) is fairly different from the professor's utterances in 6. The student does not use any of the modals or hedges that were used in 6. Instead, the student uses a fragmented *if* statement, which is a dependent clause that is never completed. The utterance is taken up by the professor nevertheless, who responds with a question about where he should go to see the work.

The differences between the professor's joint-action commissives in 6 and the student's in 7 may be due to differences associated with the speaker role. The professor, who holds the higher status role, uses modals and hedges to express a suggestive tone, and first person agency signaled by singular and plural first person subject pronouns, to express the collaborative nature of what he is suggesting. The student, on the other hand, holds a lower status, and is therefore much more indirect in inviting the professor. The use of second person agency (underlined) demonstrates the student's realization that it is the decision of the professor to view the slides. The student's invitation is worded in a way that yields to the professor, rather than assuming that he and the professor are about to engage in a joint activity.

As acts that speakers use to plan joint activities, joint-action commissives were used with great frequency in study groups. Linguistically, students' realizations of joint-action commissives differed little from professors' realizations. Students' realizations include much greater uses of amplifiers, fragments, and interrogatives than professors, and a diminished use of imperatives in comparison to professors. The following extract shows how two students working on a website for a class project employ some of these linguistic features to collaborate on a joint project.

Extract 8
Student 1: Like *I wonder* if you would leave like an abstract in that even. You know like *just* something that *basically* says what this whole thing focuses on or?
Student 2: Yeah that would be *actually I think* that would be a good idea. *Just* to *kind of* explain
Student 1: So…
Student 2: Um …now *I don't know* if you *would* leave an abstract after each point that you *could* go into. Do you know what I mean?
Student 1: That's true, like *I mean* you have a little box that says …
Student 2: Yeah, that says what's *going to* be in there.

In 8, student 1 suggests including abstracts in their website on research articles about child development (*leave like an abstract in that even*). She presents her suggestion with several stance markers (in bold) that show either hesitancy or that she is thinking aloud. Student 2 takes up her suggestion and agrees (*yeah...*). Student 2 continues the idea with a reason for including abstracts (*just to kind of explain*). Student 2 also uses stance markers, particularly hedges, to present her suggestion. Student 2 then goes on to present another suggestion about how they will link the abstracts to their website, again using modals and hedges (*I don't know*) to express her hesitancy. Student 1 agrees, and seems to explain what student 2 was trying to say by suggesting the use of a box. Student 2 completes student 1's fragment, thereby completing the suggestion of what purpose the box will serve.

Throughout these utterances, the ideas of student 1 and student 2 interlock into a single cohesive plan for their joint activity. Both students use fragments, hedges, and modals to express a desire to be cooperative; neither student used language that make the speaker appear dominant or definite. This extract exemplifies the linguistic behavior commonly used for planning purposes in the collaborative types of study groups.

Personal expressives

Personal expressives are used to express feelings, opinions, and apologies. As such, they would be expected to be realized with a high frequency of stance markers and first person agency. According to Table 7, personal expressives are realized through the high use of amplifiers by all speaker roles with the exception of professors. Syntactically, they are structured as statements almost to the exclusion of any other syntactic structure. And, they are characterized by high use of first person agency except when used by students in study groups, who used third person agency with equal frequency.

	OFFICE HOURS		SERVICE ENCOUNTERS		STUDY GROUPS
	Students	Professors	Students	Servers	Students
Stance Markers					
Modals	27	37	22	21	23
Hedges	41	43	28	62	39
Amplifiers	25	11	22	27	27
Syntactic Structure					
Fragments	1	6	6	6	1
Statements	97	94	92	91	97
Interrogatives	0	0	2	3	2
Imperatives	1	0	0	0	0
Agency					
None/unknown	1	6	6	6	11
1st person	79	60	70	71	43
2nd person	1	0	0	0	3
3rd person	19	34	24	23	43
Utterance Length					
Mean	13	19	12	13	14

Table 7. Linguistic realizations of personal expressives (N=319).

Hedges also tended to be used in the realization of personal expressives except when used by students in service encounters. Students' lack of hedges and relatively low mean utterance length indicate that students are quite direct in uttering personal expressives in service encounters. The next extract is a typical example of how personal expressives were used by students in service encounters. The extract is from an interaction in which a student customer expresses her preferences and opinions while explaining why she wants to drop a class.

> Extract 9
> Student: I don't like that computer class. I checked into it. I don't like *just* sitting there.
> Service Provider: Which one is that? Sociology 101?
> Student: Uh huh. I'd rather have a person speak… talking to me and stuff.

In 9, the student customer is very blunt in describing how she feels about an on-line course that she had been registered for and is trying to drop. She uses plain statements with first person agency, such as *I don't like* and *I'd rather have*. These types of phrases are strong indicators of stance, but they were not included in the computerized searches used in this study. This omission points out a shortcoming of the study, as well as pointing out the diversity of linguistic features in the realization of pragmatic meaning. Although these types of phrases were not counted as stance markers in the data set, they can still be informative in the descriptive analysis of linguistic realization. In her first utterance, the student describes her participation as *just sitting there*. The word *just* has been coded in this study as a hedge; however, here it seems to be functioning differently. In this instance of use, *just* is used to diminish the activity of taking the on-line course. This particular instance of *just* is certainly marking stance in that its use reflects the speaker's perception and attitude, but it should not be interpreted as a downtoner or as a mark of tentativeness. It may be more accurate to interpret it as an amplifier in this case because it amplifies the student's meaning in describing how she feels about the on-line course.

Interpersonal expressives

Defined as the speaker's evaluation of the hearer, interpersonal expressives is a category that has great potential to cause threats to the hearer's face. Interpersonal expressives are utterances used by speakers to complain, criticize, admonish, or compliment the hearer, which are acts that place the hearer at a marked disadvantage or advantage in a communicative setting. Linguistically, they are realized differently by speakers in different roles and situations, particularly in the use of hedges and agency (see Table 8).

	OFFICE HOURS		SERVICE ENCOUNTERS		STUDY GROUPS
	Students	Professors	Students	Servers	Students
Stance Markers					
Modals	26	32	33	-	47
Hedges	53	16	50	-	0
Amplifiers	16	13	0	-	20
Syntactic Structure					
Fragments	5	3	17	-	0
Statements	95	94	83	-	93
Interrogatives	0	3	0	-	0
Imperatives	0	0	0	-	7
Agency					
None/unknown	11	7	25	-	0
1st person	31	11	17	-	27
2nd person	11	66	0	-	46
3rd person	47	16	58	-	27
Utterance Length					
Mean	20	12	17	-	9

Table 8. Linguistic realizations of interpersonal expressives (N=88).

Professors' linguistic pattern of interpersonal expressives reflects a direct approach. Professors used second person agency and relatively few hedges in their realizations. In the corpus examples, professors were found to use interpersonal expressives to articulate their evaluations of students; however, students use them too, but to express their dissatisfaction with the course or their grade. Students' use of these pragmatic acts reflects how students assert themselves as consumers in pursuit of the educational commodity. Extract 10, from a conversation in which the student has gone to her geology professor to discuss her performance on an exam, is an example of a student employing an interpersonal expressive directed at her professor. Throughout the extract, the student uses hedges, third person agency, and long utterances in the realizations of interpersonal expressives. However, she also uses some linguistic strategies to make her complaint clear.

Extract 10
Student: Ok, I have more questions.
Professor: Mhm.
Student: Um, *I feel* like *my answer* answered your question and *you* were looking for more. Like the well efficiency, and *I feel* my answer answered the corner depression.
Professor: Let's see, so you're talking about uh…
Student: *I guess you* were *just* looking for more, but *I* didn't read that in the question, what *you* were looking for.
Professor: Yeah so the difficulty here is on your sketch, uh you show here's the well um…

In her second turn, the student uses expressions of stance (*I feel*) to convey her complaint to the professor, and the third person agent (*my answer*) to remove blame from the professor directly. Yet, she also employs second person agency (*you were looking for more*), which has the effect of focusing blame on the professor. She repeats this statement in her third turn, again using hedges (*I guess, just*) to mitigate the complaint, while at the same time, using second person agency (*you were looking for*) to direct blame at the professor. She also uses first person agency (*I didn't read that*) to remove the blame from herself. (Note: The word *well* in this conversation refers to a physical structure; it is not a stance marker).

This example shows that in order to use pragmatic utterances that may have the effect of threatening the hearer's face, such as interpersonal expressives, speakers have at their disposal linguistic strategies that soften their utterances, such as hedges and third person agency, as well as strategies that make their complaints explicit, such as second person agency. Students who find themselves in situations in which they are expressing face-threatening acts to hearers who are in positions of respect, such as professors, must be adept at using all of the linguistic strategies at their disposal in order to achieve their communicative goals.

Personal representatives

Personal representatives are utterances that serve the pragmatic function of supplying information, explanations, and directions. Speakers in different situations use personal representatives to serve different communicative purposes; however, linguistically, they seem to be fairly uniform according to the results in Table 9.

Use of statement syntactic structure ranged from 94 to 97 per 100 utterances, indicating that personal representatives were realized as statements in almost all cases. Also of note is the high use of third person agency across all speaker roles, and the high utterance length. The high use of these two features is characteristic of the explanatory nature of personal representatives. Speakers need to describe and explain things outside of the speaker-hearer relationship, hence the high third person agency use. They also need to explain and describe explicitly to make their points clear, hence the high utterance length.

	OFFICE HOURS		SERVICE ENCOUNTERS		STUDY GROUPS
	Students	Professors	Students	Servers	Students
Stance Markers					
Modals	17	46	18	23	27
Hedges	32	27	20	39	26
Amplifiers	21	16	9	11	13
Syntactic Structure					
Fragments	5	4	3	2	4
Statements	95	94	96	97	96
Interrogatives	0	0	1	0	0
Imperatives	0	2	0	1	0
Agency					
None/unknown	11	29	9	7	8
1st person	26	15	50	18	19
2nd person	3	8	1	8	6
3rd person	60	48	40	67	67
Utterance Length					
Mean	15	20	12	16	17

Table 9. Linguistic realizations of personal representatives (N=564).

The extract below, from an office hour conversation in which a student has gone to her history professor to get advice on her paper topic, shows how professors used long statements with third person agency to explain course content.

Extract 11
Professor: Yesterday we were talking about the Washington Naval Conference...
Student: Navel Conference, that's the one where we were just getting rid of...
Professor: Yeah, it was *basically* because during World War One there had been this great escalation of of arms of navy ships and all this stuff and so *because we* didn't join the League of Nations we were...which Wilson's League of Nations *was gonna* be all encompassing and take care of all these things...
Student: Ok.
Professor: And *since we* didn't join that, then *we* had to go piece by piece and start thinking, well, what's important to *us*...

Extract 11 shows lengthy utterances used by the professor to explain the context of World War One. He used few stance markers: one amplifier (*basically*) and one modal, reflecting that he is expressing his knowledge in a straightforward and non-hesitant manner. He used the words *because* and *since* as signals that he is explaining reasons and justifications. One interesting trend in this extract, which was characteristic of this particular office hour file, is the professor's use of the first person pronouns *we* and *us* for agency. He does this throughout his explanations of the American's actions and reactions leading up to the war. This may be used as a strategy to put the war in the context that the student can understand, a kind of *us versus them* explanation for why the United States entered the war. This use of first person agency in professors' realizations of personal representatives was unique to this particular office hour conversation, probably due to the professor's placement of events in a historical context that the student can relate to; and using first person agency was an effective strategy for doing so.

Interpersonal representatives

Interpersonal representatives are used by speakers to express information in relation to the hearer's information, such as correcting, contradicting, disagreeing, and conceding. It is considered a category that can cause face threats, and therefore would logically include high use of stance markers, particularly hedges. Because they are statements inherently against the hearer, high use of second person agency would also be expected.

According to the normalized counts in Table 10, different speakers employ different linguistic features when expressing inter-personal representatives. Students show a high use of hedges when using them in office hours, but a relatively low use when using them in service encounters. This shows that students were willing to be more direct when expressing interpersonal representatives towards servers, but not when expressing them towards professors. Servers also showed a relatively high use of hedges, indicating that they tended to soften utterances that function as corrections and contradictions.

	OFFICE HOURS		SERVICE ENCOUNTERS		STUDY GROUPS
	Students	Professors	Students	Servers	Students
Stance Markers					
Modals	26	27	17	16	25
Hedges	43	22	13	32	22
Amplifiers	7	22	9	16	13
Syntactic Structure					
Fragments	19	4	22	11	14
Statements	76	88	69	89	81
Interrogatives	5	4	9	0	5
Imperatives	0	4	0	0	0
Agency					
None/unknown	15	13	17	26	22
1st person	38	16	52	16	17
2nd person	9	27	5	16	19
3rd person	38	44	26	42	42
Utterance Length					
Mean	15	16	11	10	11

Table 10. Linguistic realizations of interpersonal representatives (N=203).

In terms of agency, speakers employed agency strategically depending on their roles and the situation. For example, students used very few second person agents in office hours and in service encounters, but they used more of them in study groups. In office hours, students preferred to use first or third person agents; and in service encounters, they preferred to use first person agents. Professors showed the highest use of second person agents, but they tended to use third person agents even more. Even students in study groups preferred to use third person agency more so than the more direct second person. The trends in agency use show that because interpersonal representatives have the potential to threaten the hearer's face, speakers prefer to use first and third person agency to express interpersonal representatives indirectly, thus mitigating the face threat, no matter what situation they are in.

Students in office hours were found to use interesting linguistic strategies when realizing interpersonal representatives. Extract 12 is from an office hour in which the professor and student are discussing internship possibilities for the student. The student is arguing that he is not eligible for a specific internship.

Extract 12
Student: OK. Yeah *I'm not sure* if I'm eligible for that uh Woods Hole, uh, project either 'cause I found some information *I I'm not sure* if it was the same, uh opportunity or not but uh, one of them *at least* was for minorities only.
Professor: Oh really? OK.
Student: So.
Professor: OK yeah 'cause *I know* we have…*I know* some of them aren't though 'cause we've had uh, some students who aren't minorities participate in some of these.
Student: Right. Sure.
Professor: Mhm.
Student: Ok.

In the preceding talk, the professor had suggested several intern opportunities for the student to look into. In 12, the student presents information about not being eligible for a specific internship (i.e., that it is open to minorities only). He uses hedges (*I'm not sure, at least*) to frame his disagreement as uncertainty. The professor returns with a strong argument that supports his own viewpoint (*we've had uh, some students who aren't minorities participate*). He uses *I know*, which was coded as a hedge by the computer program; however, in this instance the phrase enforces his point, and should therefore be interpreted as a stance marker that strengthens his statement, rather than one that minimizes it. This extract is counterintuitive to what we assume about disagreements because both speakers are using positive language (*yeah, right, sure*) while disagreeing. This characteristic may be indicative of how speakers of different social roles (e.g., professor and student) use linguistic strategies to express disagreement while, on the surface, give the appearance of agreement through their use of positive language.

4. Conclusion

The results and examples from this study demonstrate the complex intersection of linguistic features and speaker roles in the realization of pragmatic functions. Pragmatic functions require speakers to be direct in some situations, and indirect in others. Features that contribute to indirectness include hedges, fragments, and high mean utterance length. Features that contribute to directness include second person agency and low mean utterance length. Depending on who the interlocutor is, speakers strategically use different combinations of these linguistic features to express pragmatic functions in ways that are effective for achieving their communicative goals.

Conclusions about which linguistic features are commonly used in specific pragmatic functions cannot be made without the concomitant consideration of speaker role and situation. Past literature that has tried to associate specific linguistic features with certain pragmatic acts (e.g., Blum-Kulka, House and Kasper 1989) must be readdressed and questioned. As early speech act theorists tried to emphasize, context plays a heightened role in pragmatic language use (Levinson 1983). More research on pragmatic functions across different contexts (i.e., speaker roles and situations) is needed so that linguistic profiles for different functions in different situations can be added to our knowledge of pragmatic competence.

The purpose of this study was to fill the gap in what is known about how native English speakers use language pragmatically. Previous applied linguistics studies on pragmatics have focused on a limited set of speech acts (e.g., Blum-Kulka, et al. 1989) or a limited set of lexical items (e.g., Aijmer 1996). This study diverged from previous studies because it took a broad approach to investigate pragmatic functions. It did this by exploring whole categories of pragmatic meaning, as well as lexical and grammatical features, namely stance markers, syntactic structure, agency, and length of utterance.

This study has also shown that how people construct pragmatic utterances may reveal some patterns, but, in the case of native speaker use, there is more variability than consistency. Pragmatic language use can be predicted more in terms of which pragmatic categories are used in which situations, but less in terms of which linguistic features are used. Perhaps it is the intersection of context and role with pragmatic function that should steer the direction of future research on pragmatic language use.

5. References

Aijmer, Karin 1996. *Conversational Routines in English: Convention and Creativity*. London: Longman.

Bardovi-Harlig, Kathleen / Hartford, Beverly 1990. Congruence in native and nonnative conversations: Status balance in the academic advising session. *Language Learning,* 40, 467-501.

Biber, Douglas 1988. *Variation across Speech and Writing*. Cambridge: Cambridge University Press.

Biber, Douglas 2002. Tagger. [computer program]. Flagstaff, AZ.

Biber, Douglas / Conrad, Susan / Reppen, Randi 1998. *Corpus Linguistics: Investigating Language Structure and Use*. Cambridge: Cambridge University Press.

Biber, Douglas / Conrad, Susan / Reppen, Randi / Byrd, Pat / Helt, Marie 2002. Speaking and writing in the university: A multi-dimensional comparison. *TESOL Quarterly.* 36, 9-48.

Blum-Kulka, Shoshana / House, Juliane / Kasper, Gabriele. Eds. 1989. *Cross-cultural Pragmatics: Requests and Apologies.* Norwood, NJ: Ablex.

Blum-Kulka, Shoshana / Levenston, Edward A. 1987. Lexical-grammatical pragmatic indicators. *Studies in Second Language Acquisition.* 9, 155-170.

Blum-Kulka, Shoshana / Olshtain, Elite 1986. Too many words: Length of utterance and pragmatic failure. *Studies in Second Language Acquisition,* 8, 165-180.

Farr, Fiona 2003. Engaged listenership in spoken academic discourse: The case of student-tutor meetings. *Journal of English for Academic Purposes*, 2, 67-85.

Garcia, Paula 2004a. Developmental differences in speech act re-cognition: A pragmatic awareness study. *Language Awareness*, 96-115.

Garcia, Paula 2004b. *Meaning in Academic Contexts: A Corpus-based Study of Pragmatic Utterances.* Unpublished doctoral dissertation, Northern Arizona University.

Hancher, Michael 1979. The classification of cooperative illocutionary acts. *Language in Society.* 8, 1-14.

He, Agnes Weiyun 1998. *Reconstructing Institutions: Language Use in Academic Counseling Encounters.* Stamford, CT: Ablex.

Kidwell, Mardi 2000. Common ground in cross-cultural communication: Sequential and institutional contexts in front desk service encounters. *Issues in Applied Linguistics*, 11, 17-37.

Levinson, Stephen 1983. *Pragmatics.* Cambridge: Cambridge University Press.

Poos, Deanna / Simpson, Rita 2002. Cross-disciplinary comparisons of hedging: Some findings from the Michigan Corpus of Academic Spoken Language. In R. Reppen, S. Fitzmaurice, and D. Biber (eds) *Using Corpora to Explore Linguistic Variation.* Amsterdam: John Benjamins, 3-23.

Precht, Kristen 2003. Stance moods in spoken English: Evidentiality and affect in British and American conversation. *Text,* 23/2, 239-257.

Rose, Kenneth R. 2000. An exploratory cross-sectional study of inter-language pragmatic development. *Studies in Second Language Acquisition,* 22, 27-67.

Scott, Susan 2002. Linguistic feature variation within disagreements: An empirical investigation. *Text*, 22/2, 301-328.

Searle, John 1969. *Speech Acts.* Cambridge: Cambridge University Press.

Searle, John 1979. *Expression and Meaning: Studies in the Theory of Speech Acts.* Cambridge: Cambridge University Press.

JAVIER PÉREZ-GUERRA

"Am I more complex when I speak or when I write?" A Corpus-based Study on Linguistic Complexity in Spoken and Written Present-day English [1]

1. Introduction

The concept of linguistic complexity has been approached from different perspectives (cognitive, informative, syntactic, lexical) both cross- and intra-linguistically. While I do not deny McWhorter's (2001: 127) claim that "it is a truism in linguistics in general that all languages are equally complex" and the corollary that one cannot compare languages according to their linguistic complexity, I favour the view that certain (linguistic) aspects within a given language can exhibit different degrees of (linguistic) complexity. Such an intra-linguistic perspective can lead to the study of the linguistic complexity of different clausal constituents, different genres or different periods of the history of the language under investigation. Where elsewhere I have tackled the analysis of complexity in the recent history of the English language (Pérez-Guerra and Martínez Insua 2006, 2007), in this chapter I concentrate on textual variation in Present-day English and, more specifically, on the measurement of the structural and

1   The research reported has been funded by the Spanish Ministry of Education and Science, grant number HUM2005-02351/FILO, which is hereby gratefully acknowledged. This investigation is couched in a larger project on the degree of variation experienced by the English language in its recent history as far as the syntactic complexity of clausal constituents is concerned. Standard corpora of Modern and Contemporary (British) English such as ARCHER (*A Representative Corpus of Historical English Registers*) and the BNC provide the empirical data on different text types, which will be analysed according to the syntactic complexity of the core clausal constituents.

syntactic complexity of the subjects in declarative clauses found in both written-to-be-read and spoken texts. In section 2 I describe the corpus from which the data have been retrieved and justify the rationale of investigating specifically subject complexity in such varieties of English. Section 3 is devoted to the exploration of the metrics which will be used as indicators of linguistic complexity. Finally, section 4 discusses the results of the application of the metrics to the corpus material.

2. The corpus

This pilot study investigates the structure of the categories fulfilling the function subject in three Present-day English text types, namely academic writings, newspapers and spoken language.[2] The data are retrieved from the *Baby* version of the *British National Corpus* or *BNC Baby* (<http://www.natcorp.ox.ac.uk>; see Burnard 1995 for the reference guide). Whereas the BNC contains 100 million words of contemporary spoken and written English, in this *Baby*-version each of the textual families subject to our analysis comprise approximately one million words, of which I have selected a representative sample of circa 100,000 words. The details are given in Table 1.

dimension		BNC Baby	sample	% of whole corpus
written	academic	1,037,877	100,346	9.66
	newspapers	1,001,821	100,462	10.02
	Subtotal		200,808	
spoken		935,414	100,199	10.71
Total			301,007	

Table 1. Word totals.

---

2   The *BNC Baby* also contains imaginative writing (fiction) which has not been considered in this study in an attempt to warrant that the data are not stylistically marked.

As regards the text types chosen in this study, I contend that written and spoken English are taken as two textual variants of the same language. Since text types are here understood as codifications of linguistic features (Taavitsainen 2001: 141), one can characterise a given text type by exploring its linguistic characteristics. That stated, this chapter investigates complexity in two such text variants by quantifying several linguistic factors which, according to the relevant literature, are determinants of complexity. As already mentioned in the introduction, the working hypothesis is that text types (or variants) differ in complexity or, in other words, that text types can be graded in terms of complexity.

The two text types selected in this study, namely spoken and written Present-day English, will be subjected to the same experiment, that is, the description of the unmarked subjects in unmarked or kernel clauses. I have focused on these core functional components of the clause since the structure of subjects has been claimed to have important consequences for the syntactic (and cognitive) processing of a sentence (see, for example, Ferreira 1991, who investigates sentential complexity based exclusively on the syntactic complexity of the subjects). As an illustration of this, Davison and Lutz (1985: 60) maintain that "the high load of processing would occur in subject position of the target sentence [...]. The syntactic element in this position is what matches or fails to match with information in the context sentence". Furthermore, in connection with his Syntactic Prediction Locality Theory, Gibson (1998: 27) emphasises the relevance of subjects (or external arguments) to the determination of the processing cost of a sentence; in his words, "modifying the subject should cause an increase in the memory cost for predicting the matrix verb, whereas modifying the object should not cause such an increment".

Table 2 gives the raw figures and the proportions of the 33,198 subjects investigated and classifies them categorically:

	non-pron.	pronominal						Total
		pers.	*Ø*	*there*	*wh*	*other*	*Subtot.*	
written acad.	4,827 56.73%	2,413	268	219	658	123	3,681 43.26%	8,508
written news	5,758 64.16%	2,069	202	292	539	114	3,216 35.83%	8,974
Subtot.	10,585 60.54%	4,482	470	511	1,197	237	6,897 39.45%	17,482
spoken	1,740 11.07%	11,558	877	338	338	865	13,976 88.92%	15,716
Total	12,325 37.12%	16,040	1,347	849	1,535	1,102	20,873 62.87%	33,198

Table 2: Distribution of subjects.

Some clarifying remarks seem in order here with respect to the categories in which the subjects have been divided in Table 2. First, the 'non-pron(ominal)' category includes clauses, coordinative structures, prepositional phrases, multi-word noun phrases and one-word noun phrases whose heads are not pronouns. Second, the 'pers(onal)' column embraces personal pronouns and all the occurrences of *it*, be they pronominal or expletive. Third, 'Ø' classifies clauses which are subjectless, normally because of the ellipsis of an anaphoric subject. Fourth, '*there*' groups altogether the examples with expletive *there* functioning as the grammatical subject in existential sentences. Fifth, '*wh*' has been used in order to keep track of unbound relative clauses which have relativisers as their subjects. Finally, in the 'other' class I include other pronouns (demonstrative, indefinite, etc).

Table 2 shows that approximately 9 out of 10 subjects in the spoken material are pronominal, the vast majority of them being the first- and second-person personal pronouns *I* and *you*. By contrast, the proportions of pronominal subjects in the written text types amount to approximately 40 percent of all the subjects, the difference between the academic writings and the newspaper materials also being statistically significant (χ^2=100.886, p ≤ 0.001). Even though these results by themselves lead to the conclusion that the subjects in the spoken texts are radically less elaborated than those in the written material and, in consequence, the strategies of subject complexification are more productive in the written text types, in what follows I shall undertake the task of examining linguistic complexity in exclusively non-pronominal subjects in order that such an analysis can either corroborate or refute the conclusion resulting from the observation of pronominal and non-pronominal subjects.

3. Linguistic complexity

In a nutshell, linguistic complexity is here interpreted as a theoretical concept connected with both syntactic expansion and phrase-marker configuration, in which the size (Wasow 1997: 94), the weight (Arnold *et al.* 2000: 35) and the 'depth' (Ferreira 1991: 226, Sampson 2001: 47) of the constituents under examination play a significant role. Since this study is based not on sentence structure but exclusively on the syntactic organisation of the subjects, the analysis of syntactic relations such as embedding or subordination will be restricted to the scope of the subjects constituents. On the other hand, in this chapter I do not intend to address complexity relativity among constituents, that is, on parsing differences depending on positioning since the methodology is applied only to the structure of the grammatical subjects occurring in the corpus.

The theoretical assumptions on which this study is based are as follows. First, I contend that the process of decoding and interpreting a message is unambiguous on the hearer/reader's part. In other words, I assume that the human parser is able to interpret correctly the linguistic input, thus discarding any sort of processing ambiguity. As Carlson (2002: 8) points out, this assumption fits a 'garden-path' approach to language, rather than a constraint-satisfaction theory which subsumes the existence of parallel processings of the same utterance, to which an optimality model has to be applied. When I analyse a database subject, I shall stick to only one syntactic interpretation of the constituent under study, which will be regarded as the optimal one.

Second, complexity is understood as a relational notion; put differently, 'something is always less/more complex THAN something else' and, in consequence, one can compare, for example, textual variants in a given language in terms of complexity. That stated, the hypothesis is that texts can be graded in terms of complexity and, to that end, I have selected in this pilot study three representative text types of the written and the spoken dimensions, which will be confronted to the same experiment.

Third, complexity is a relative concept. As Frazier (1988: 204) puts it, "there is no general unit of complexity (defined either in terms of time or number of computational operations) which would permit us to predict in 'absolute' terms the complexity of a sentence". My account of complexity, which will be based not on one but on several metrics, will inevitably be partial.

Fourth, syntactic or structural complexity is not associated to linguistic richness or McWhorter's (2001) 'ornamentation'. McWhorter's concept of 'ornamentation' is only valid on cross-linguistic grounds and has no consequences for a study of linguistic complexity within a given language.[3] Such a notion of complexity as functional richness is often coupled with linguistic explicitness or transparency. In this respect, Rohdenburg (1996: 151) claims that "[i]n the case of more or less explicit grammatical options the more explicit one(s) will tend to be favored in cognitively more complex environments".[4] That stated, grammatical systems with many overt functional options will be more complex since, on the one hand, they will comprise more

---

3   In McWhorter's (2001: 135) words, "an area of grammar is more complex than the same area in another grammar to the extent that it encompasses more overt distinctions and/or rules than another grammar". Such a concept of 'ornamentation', in line with Hawkins' (2004: 38) 'Minimize Forms' principle, also based on the reduction not only of linguistic forms but also of the functional properties associated to them, does not necessarily coincide with Dahl's (2004: 43) when the latter maintains that, for instance, more vocabulary and less phonetic reduction, that is, more phonetic weight, implies more complexity, independently of whether such lexical and phonetic richness is functional in the language.

4   To give an example of complexity as linguistic explicitness, Rohdenburg (1996) maintains that (i) is more explicit, and thus more complex, than (ii) since the infinitival particle *to* in (i) marks *write the paper* as an embedded nonfinite clause: (i) I help him to write the paper.
                                      (ii) I help him write the paper.

ornamentation and, on the other, they are more transparent because the different functional meanings are overtly materialised in those languages.

Fifth, syntactic or structural complexity is not linked to conceptual and/or informative complexity. Conceptual complexity is strongly tied to the referentiality of the entities conveyed by the referring categories (mainly nouns). This issue, together with syntactic complexity, is covered by, for example, Gibson's (1998, 2000) Dependency Locality Theory, according to which the measure of the so-called 'integration cost' of a constituent involves counting, in broad outline, the number of new discourse referents which have to be processed so that the constituent under examination can be integrated in the syntactic structure (see Warren and Gibson 2002: 86ff for an experiment on this issue). Informative and/or semantic complexity will not play a role in this study either. Since the concern of this chapter is the investigation of complexity in strictly unmarked subjects, rather than in the whole sentence, I cannot assess the influence which informative factors such as givenness and/or newness (see Arnold et al. 2000: §1) or semantic determinants such as animacy (see Rosenbach 2005), among others, have on complexity.

Finally, complexity is regarded as a synonym of processing difficulty or cost, either for the speaker or for the hearer: Whereas I agree with McWhorter (2001: 134) when he says that "all languages [in all periods] are acquired with ease by native learners" and, in consequence, languages cannot be graded on a scale of processing difficulty, I contend that, within a given language, certain syntactic structures are particularly 'demanding' (Dahl 2004: 40) in terms of processing cost and, with no doubt, 'more' demanding than others. Put differently, structures can be graded in terms of processing cost. The relationship between processing cost and syntactic apparatus is not one-to-one since a sentence which is apparently complex from the point of view of its syntactic organisation does not have to be difficult to process (see Gayraud and Martinie 2005). The measurement of the processing cost of a subject will not be based on derivational mechanisms which explain the emergence of a given structure.

Two comments seem in order here as regards the nature of the syntactic analysis undertaken in this study. On the one hand, the basic

formal representation to which I have stuck in this chapter does not
utilise empty nodes and simply combines the different constituents in
a syntactically hierarchical structure based on the notion of dependency. As a consequence, the related complexity metrics (metrics 5 and 6;
see section 4) will not encompass processes of syntactic derivation or,
in Dahl's (2004: 44) terminology, 'steps', and will have no validity in
order to prove whether a given (Externalised) manifestation of a
language is due to a more primitive/elaborated version of Internalised-
language or Universal Grammar.[5] On the other hand, since I have
avoided null terminal nodes in this (basic) analysis, I have not made
any distinction between dependents which are subcategorised by the
heads and those which are adjoined to some sort of intermediate, let us
say, X' projection. Such an approach has been left for further research
(see, in this respect, Shapiro et al. 1992 or Gayraud and Martinie
2005, who claim that such a distinction has consequences for the
processing cost of an utterance).

    In this section I have favoured a concept of complexity based
on an objective analysis of the surface structure of core clausal
components, which permits the scaling of the constituents in terms of
syntactic processing cost. I have avoided any sort of connection
between complexity and systemic functionality, semantic content or
referentiality in the external world, cognitive processing or derivational intricacies.

4. The metrics

Since this experiment relies on the scaling of subjects in different text
types according to their syntactic or structural complexity, it requires a
set of objective quantitative metrics which somehow evaluate objec-

---

5   Since syntactic derivation lies beyond the scope this paper, my measures for
     complexity will not shed any light on, for example, McWhorter's (2001: 136)
     notion of syntactic complexity, which is based on the number of derivational
     rules which are necessary in order to process an utterance.

tively the complexity of the surface appearance of the constituents, independently of uses and users. In what follows I describe the metrics which will be used in the analysis of the data in section 5.

4.1. Metrics 1 and 2 (size)

Metrics 1 and 2 measure the size or length of the constituent, by counting the number of words of the subject (metric 1) and the number of words up to (and including) what I call 'marker' of the last immediate constituent of the subject (used in metric 2). Length is commonly associated with complexity in the literature; among others, Wasow (1997: 81) maintains that grammatical weight implies "size of complexity", Yaruss (1999: 330) claims that "attempts to separate length and complexity are somewhat artificial" and Hawkins (2004: 9) argues that "[c]omplexity increases with the number of linguistic forms".

Whereas counting all the words of the subject (metric 1) provides us with the objective length of the subject, the computation of the number of words from the first word to the syntactic 'marker' of the last constituent (metric 2) offers the empirical value of the length of the subject which the hearer/reader has to process syntactically in order to grasp the syntactic structure of the whole subject and, in consequence, of the amount of the construction which has to be memorised so that the parsing of the whole subject can be correct.[6] Metric 2 relativises the effect of metric 1 since the former focuses on the length of the minimal segment in the construction which is capable of informing about the overall syntactic structure independently of the length of the final constituent (see Wasow 1997: 102 on the felicitousness of relativising weight).

The portion of lexical structure up to what we are calling the 'marker' of the last immediate constituent is similar to Hawkins

---

6   Awareness of the overall syntactic structure of the subject, that is, of the identification of its main constituents via the recognition of their syntactic markers is particularly relevant to processing time since, as maintained by Davison and Lutz (1985: 60), "the processing time for a given sentence includes identification of syntactic constituent".

(2004: 32) 'Constituent Recognition Domain', defined as follows: "[t]he [Constituent Recognition Domain] for a phrasal mother node M consists of the smallest set of terminal and non-terminal nodes that must be parsed in order to recognize M and all [Immediate Constituents] of M". My concept of syntactic marker (a preposition in a prepositional phrase, a determiner or a possessive specifier in a noun phrase, a participle in a participial phrase, a coordinating conjunction in a coordinative structure, a subordinator (or complementiser) in a subordinate clause (or CP), a *wh*-proform in a relative clause, etc.) relies on Prideaux and Baker's (1986: 32) 'bracketing', according to which, "[t]he language user assumes that when a new unit for processing is encountered or initiated, it will be marked as such". Examples (1) to (9) illustrate the most frequent types of markers (underlined) in the subjects (italics) found in the corpus:

(1)   *THE Conservatives* sought last night to force the election debate back on to Mr Kinnock's fitness to govern (ahf) [determiner as the marker of the noun/determiner phrase]

(2)   *his report* had been grossly misrepresented (e9s) [possessive specifier as the marker of the noun/determiner phrase]

(3)   *Last night's Conservative election broadcast* questioned whether the electorate could 'trust' Mr Kinnock after he had changed his mind on na-tionalisation, Europe, Scottish devolution and unilateral nuclear disarmament. (ahf) [possessive marker *'s* as the marker of the noun/determiner phrase]

(4)   *Groups* have put tremendous efforts into past projects and we always see a high standard of work. (39s) [noun as the marker of a determiner-less noun phrase]

(5)   To understand the behaviour of polymers in solution more fully, *a knowledge of the enthalpic and entropic contributions to ΔG M* is essential (hrg) [preposition as the marker of the postmodifying prepositional phrase]

(6)   *Cambridge, who have won only one Boat Race in 16 years,* believe they can end Oxford's run today. (ahf) [relativiser as the marker of the *wh* relative clause]

(7)   *That environmentalism may be superseded in schools, as it appears largely to have been in universities,* by the locational analysis school is no guarantee of a

more appropriate form of explanation. (clw) [complementiser as the marker of the *that*-clause]

(8) *Flory and Huggins* considered that formation of the solution depends on... (hrg) [coordinating conjunction as the marker of the coordinative construction]

(9) *The campaign aimed at the general population* had been right at a time when there was ignorance about AIDS (e9s) [*ed*-participle as the marker of the participial clause]

After calculating the number of words up to the marker, metric 2 reports the ratio of such a figure and the number of words of the subject, already measured by metric 1. As accorded in the literature, the higher the ratio in metric 2, the more complex the constituent under discussion. In Hawkins' (2004: 9) words, "efficiency is increased by selecting and arranging linguistic forms so as to provide the earliest possible access to as much of the ultimate syntactic and semantic representation as possible".

4.2. Metrics 3 and 4 (syntactic density)

Inspired by Hawkins' (1994) IC-to-non-IC ratio,[7] metrics 3 and 4 have been designed in order to computerise syntactic density (in Smith's 1988: 272 terminology). Metric 3 measures the number of basic immediate constituents and metric 4 gives the ratio of words per immediate constituent.

4.3. Metrics 5 and 6 (syntactic depth)

The syntactic depth of the subjects has been measured by way of the number of abstract (non-terminal) nodes in a simple syntactic structure of the subject (in metric 5) and the ratio of non-terminal-to-

---

7   Hawkins' IC-to-non-IC ratio links the ratio in (my) metric 3 not to the total number of words, that is, of terminal nodes, but to the total number of non-terminal plus terminal nodes up to the marker.

terminal nodes (my metric 6). As suggested in Frazier (1985: 156, based on Miller and Chomsky 1963), "the complexity of a [author: constituent] may be determined by simply dividing the number of nonterminals [author: intermediate nodes] in the sentence by the number of terminals [author: minimal nodes]". The figure in metric 5 gives an idea of the amount of structure that is associated with the words of a constituent.

Metrics 5 and 6 receive support from the relevant literature; among others, Beaman (1984: 45) declares that "[i]t has generally been accepted that syntactic complexity in language is related to the number, type, and depth of embedding in a text"; Sampson (2001: 47) maintains that the depth of a word or constituent is the "total number of those nonterminal nodes in the word's lienagee which have at least one younger sister"; Warren and Gibson (2002: 79-80) claim that "*nested* [...] syntactic structures are more difficult to process than non-nested structures. Increasing the number of nestings[8] makes a sentence unprocessable"; finally, Dahl (2004: 44) says that "'structural complexity' [is] a general term for complexity measures that pertain to the structure of expressions, at some level of description".

4.4. Metrics 7 and 8 (syntactic efficiency)

Hawkins' (1994) measures the degree of syntactic efficiency by way of his IC[Immediate Constituent]-to-word (similar to my metric 7) and his on-line IC-to-word ratios (comparable to my metric 8). The former consists of the division of the number of immediate constituents by the number of words up to the marker of the last immediate constituent. By contrast, Hawkins' on-line IC-to-word ratio is the aggregate of the division of the number of immediate constituents by the number of words which belong to it up to the marker, as illustrated in (10):

---

8   Gibson's nesting does not coincide with my notion of embedding. For Gibson
     (2000: 96), the definition of nesting is as follows: "[a] syntactic category *A* is
     said to be nested within another category *B* if *B* contains *A*, a constituent to the
     left of *A*, and a constituent to the right of *A*". The defining factor of embedding
     in this chapter is simply inclusion, with no attention to subcategorisation.

(10)   The first detachment of the Austrian reinforcement, amounting to 24,000 men.

[*The first detachment*]	[*of the Austrian reinforcement,*]	[*amounting to 24,000 men*]	
Immediate Constituent 1	Immediate Constituent 2	Immediate Constituent 3	
3 words	4 words => 7 words up to here	1 word up to and including the marker => 8 words up to the marker	
1/3 = 33.33%	2/7 = 28.57%	3/8 = 37.5%	aggregate 33.13%

As Hawkins (2004:33) declares, "[t]he higher these ratios, the more minimal is the Constituent Recognition Domain"; "[t]he human parser prefers linear order that minimize [Constituent Recognition Domains] (by maximizing their IC-to-non-IC [or IC-to-word] ratios" (Hawkins, 2004:32). So that all the metrics can lead positively to the measurement of complexity of the subjects, I have opted for changing the order of the terms of the division of Hawkins' ratios, the resulting ones being word-to-IC (my metric 7) and on-line word-to-IC (metric 8). Such ratios will thus describe lack of (or negative) syntactic efficiency.

5. Analysis of the data

Table 3 shows the values of the metrics described in section 4, summarised as follows:
- metric 1: total number of words of the subject
- metric 2: ratio 'words up to the marker'/'total number of words'
- metric 3: number of immediate constituents
- metric 4: ratio 'total number of words'/ 'number of immediate constituents (up to the marker)'
- metric 5: number of non-terminal nodes
- metric 6: non-terminal-to-terminal-node ratio
- metric 7: word(up to the marker)-to-IC ratio
- metric 8: on-line word-to-IC ratio

	\complexity \metric	size [1]	[2]	density [3]	[4]	depth [5]	[6]	lack of efficiency [7]	[8]
written	academic	4.25	2.42	1.46	2.64	3.43	0.74	1.44	60.19
	Newspap.	4.1	2.57	1.44	2.65	3.22	0.71	1.69	52.18
	mean	4.17	2.49	1.45	2.64	3.32	0.72	1.56	56.18
spoken		2.3	1.46	1.18	1.86	1.69	0.76	1.17	79.42
mean		3.23	1.97	1.31	2.25	2.5	0.74	1.36	67.8

Table 3. Metrics.

The following conclusions can be drawn from Table 3.

First, as regards size, metric 1 shows that the subjects in the written samples are considerably longer than those in the spoken texts, even after the exclusion of the pronominal subjects. This accords with O'Donnell's (1974) conclusion that the average length of syntactic units in written language is greater than in spoken language. On the other hand, the differences evinced by metric 2, which relativises the findings of metric 1 by taking into account the influence of the right-most immediate constituent, are also sounding in the two text variants. The fact that the total number of words is greater in the written texts, coupled with the importance of the ratio of words up to the markers with respect to overall size of the subjects, suggests that the length of the material previous to the syntactic marker of the rightmost constituent is responsible for the greater size of the written passages. If this concluding remark is correct, then processing the unmarked larger subjects of the written samples is more costly since they contain more material before the syntactic marker of the last immediate constituent. It must be pointed out that the differences between academic texts and newspapers are statistically non-significant.

Second, as far as the density of the subjects is concerned, both the number and the size of the immediate constituents resulting from the basic syntactic analysis of the subjects are higher in the written texts, according to metrics 3 and 4 – the figures for the academic and the newspaper samples are practically identical. However, a remark seems in order here with respect to metrics 3 and 4: whereas metric 4 shows that the constituents conforming the spoken subjects are considerably smaller than those into which the written subjects can be analysed, the figures reported by metric 3 are not so divergent, which indicates that the number of constituents of the subjects in the written subjects is not radically higher than that of the spoken subjects.

Third, with respect to the syntactic depth of the subjects, metric 5 corroborates that more non-terminal nodes, that is, intermediate groupings of syntactic categories, are found in the written subjects. This observation accords with the fact that the written subjects are bigger, as shown by metrics 1, 2, 3 and, to a lesser extent, 4. Thus, the lexical material of the subjects in the written texts is organised in a larger number of syntactic layers or, in other words, a higher number of strategies of complementation and adjunction are found in the written subjects. The figures for metric 6, which report the ratio of non-terminal to terminal nodes, that is to say, the number of inter-mediate abstract syntactic categories per word, are not statistically different among text variants. In fact, the difference between the spoken and the academic figures are comparable to that between the academic and the newspaper values. Since the results of metric 6 are considerably similar in all the text types, one can only conclude that the higher degree of syntactic depth of the written registers, evinced by metric 5, is justified not by a specific increase of the grammar in the written samples but simply by the size of the subjects in the written text types. Providing that the overall size of the subjects is larger in the written texts and that metric 6 shows that the proportion of (non-terminal) nodes per word (terminal nodes) is statistically comparable in both variants, one must lend support to the hypothesis that the increase in the number of (non-terminal) nodes is simply the consequence of the increase in the number of words.

Fourth, metrics 7 and 8 instance the mirror image of Hawkins' (1994, 2004) IC-to word and on-line IC-to word ratios. Whereas metric 7 coincides with metric 4 since it also relativises the number of words per the number of immediate constituents, the former differs from the latter in the count of words: all the words in metric 4 and only the words up to the marker in metric 7. The value of complexi-fication given by metric 7 pictures the proportion of text which the reader/hearer has to process in order to grasp the overall syntactic structure of the sentence or, in Hawkins' (2004: 33) words, the Consti-tuent Recognition Domain. On the basis of metrics 4 and 7, both the immediate constituents and the immediate constituents up to the marker are longer in the written texts. Given that the higher number of immediate constituents in the written material is a consequence of the size of the subjects, metric 7[9] emphasises that the portion of text previous to the marker, that is, the material which has to be processed in order to grasp the syntactic structure of the whole subject, is organised in more immediate constituents in the written than in the spoken subjects. In conclusion, the material up to the marker has been shown to be syntactically more complex in the subjects found in the written samples. In its turn, metric 8 measures the average degree of complexification of each of the immediate constituents in the subjects. This is lower in the written subjects, which means that, on average, the constituents appear to be more complex in the spoken texts. As I have shown that the constituents previous to the marker are more complex in the written subjects, one is obliged to conclude that it is specifically the material after the marker that is larger in the spoken subjects since such subject-final constituents are lexically heavier than the preceding immediate constituents. This finding suggests that, as far as the production of the post-marker constituents is concerned, the spoken subjects are lexically heavier than the written subjects, which accords with end-weight premises, although linguistically less complex since their pre-marker constituents are (syntactically) lighter.

6. Concluding remarks and further research

The ensuing remarks are focused on a tiny aspect of linguistic complexity in the English language, namely, the syntactic arrangement of the unmarked subjects, and, in consequence, cannot lead to conclusive judgements on complexity variation in the language.

---

9   Metric 7 does not tell us whether the segment previous to the marker is longer or not – the ratio is identical with 8 words and 4 immediate constituents, and with 12 words and 6 immediate constituents.

The main (tentative) conclusions reached in this paper are the following. First, the proportion of pronominal subjects in the spoken texts is far greater than the rate in the written material. This fact, according to Gibson and Thomas (1999: 232), is interpreted as a signal of low complexity. Second, there are minor differences of complexity between the academic and the newspaper samples. Third, the non-pronominal subjects in the written passages are considerably longer than those in the spoken corpus. Fourth, and most important, even though the number and the size of the immediate constituents is larger in the written subjects as a consequence of the overall length of the subjects, the metrics have shown that the material previous to the marker is greater in the written texts and that the constituents following the marker are lexically richer in the spoken material. This has been interpreted as a signal of higher *syntactic* complexity in the written complexity in the written subjects.

I have left for further research the analysis of non-preverbal (marked) subjects and the application of a fine-grained syntactic analysis which reflects the differences of both the integration of subcategorised versus adjoined constituents and of left- and right-adjunction in the tree diagrams (see Liiv and Tuldava 1996: 182, based on Yngve 1960).

7. References

Arnold, Jennifer / Wasow, Thomas / Losongco, Anthony / Ginstrom, Ryan 2000. Heaviness vs. Newness: The Effects of Structural Complexity and Discourse Status on Constituent Ordering. *Language.* 76/1, 28-55.

Beaman, Karen 1984. Coordination and Subordination Revisited: Syntactic Complexity in Spoken and Written Narrative Discourse. In Tannen, Deborah (ed.) *Coherence in Spoken and Written Discourse.* Norwood, NJ.: Ablex, 45-80.

Burnard, Lou 1995. *User Reference Guide for the British National Corpus*. Oxford: Oxford University Computing Services.

Carlson, Katy 2002. *Parallelism and Prosody in the Processing of Ellipsis Sentences*. New York: Routledge.

Dahl, Östen 2004. *The Growth and Maintenance of Linguistic Complexity*. Amsterdam: John Benjamins.

Davison, Alice / Lutz, Richard 1985. Measuring Syntactic Complexity Relative to Discourse Context. In Dowty, David R. / Karttunen, Lauri / Zwicky, Arnold M. (eds) *Natural Language Parsing. Psychological, Computational, and Theoretical Perspectives*. Cambridge: Cambridge University Press, 26-66.

Ferreira, Fernanda 1991. Effects of Length and Syntactic Complexity on Initiation Times for Prepared Sentences. *Journal of Memory and Language*. 30/2, 210-233.

Frazier, Lyn 1985. Syntactic Complexity. In Dowty, David R. / Karttunen, Lauri / Zwicky, Arnold M. (eds) *Natural Language Parsing. Psychological, Computational, and Theoretical Perspectives*. Cambridge: Cambridge University Press, 129-189.

Frazier, Lyn 1988. The Study of Linguistic Complexity. In Davison, Alice / Green, Georgia M. (eds) *Linguistic Complexity and Text Comprehension. Readability Issues Reconsidered*. Hillsdale, NJ: Lawrence Erlbaum, 193-221.

Gayraud, Frédérique / Martinie, Bruno 2005. Does Structural Complexity (Defined as Sentential Subordination) Necessarily Involve Processing Difficulty (Measured in Term of Time of Planning)? Paper delivered at the Symposium 'Approaches to Complexity in Language', University of Helsinki, August 24-26.

Gibson, Edward 1998. Linguistic Complexity: Locality of Syntactic Dependencies. *Cognition*. 68/1, 1-76.

Gibson, Edward 2000. The Dependency Locality Theory: A Distance-based Theory of Linguistic Complexity. In Marantz, Alec / Miyashita, Yasush / O'Neil, Wayne (eds) *Image, Language, Brain. Papers from the First Mind Articulation Symposium*. Cambridge, MA.: MIT, 95-126.

Gibson, Edward / Thomas, James 1999. Memory Limitations and Structural Forgetting: The Perception of Complex Ungrammatical Sentences as Grammatical. *Language and Cognitive Processes.* 14/3, 225-248.

Hawkins, John A. 1994. *A Performance Theory of Order and Constituency.* Cambridge: Cambridge University Press.

Hawkins, John A. 2004. *Efficiency and Complexity in Grammars.* Oxford: Oxford University Press.

Liiv, Heino / Tuldava, Juhan 1996. Syntactical Structures of a Text and Its Readability. In Sajavaara, Kari / Fairweather, Courtney (eds) *Approaches to Second Language Acquisition.* Jyväskylä: University of Jyväskylä, 179-186.

McWhorter, John H. 2001. The World's Simplest Grammars are Creole Grammars. *Linguistic Typology.* 5, 125-166.

Miller, George A. / Chomsky, Noam 1963. Finitary Models of Language Users. In Duncan Luce, R. / Bush, Robert R. / Galanter, Eugene (eds) *Handbook of Mathematical Psychology. Vol. 2.* New York: Wiley, 419-492.

O'Donnell, Roy 1974. Syntactic Differences between Speech and Writing. *American Speech.* 49, 102-110.

Pérez-Guerra, Javier / Martínez Insua, Ana E. 2006. Subjects and Complexity in the Recent History of English. Paper delivered at DELS, University of Manchester, April.

Pérez-Guerra, Javier / Martínez Insua, Ana E. 2007. Do some Genres Become more 'Complex' than Others? Paper delivered at DGFS, University of Siegen, February.

Prideaux, Gary D. / Baker, William J. 1986. *Strategies and Structures: The Processing of Relative Clauses.* Amsterdam: John Benjamins.

Rohdenburg, Günter 1996. Cognitive Complexity and Increased Grammatical Explicitness in English. *Cognitive Linguistics.* 1/2, 149-182.

Rosenbach, Anette 2005. Animacy versus Weight as Determinants of Grammatical Variation in English. *Language.* 81/3, 613-644.

Sampson, Geoffrey. 2001. *Empirical Linguistics.* London: Continuum.

Shapiro, Lewis P. / McNamara, Patric / Zurif, Edgar / Lanzoni, Susan / Cermak, Laird 1992. Processing Complexity and Sentence Memory: Evidence from Amnesia. *Brain and Language.* 42/4, 431-453.

Smith, Carlota S. 1988. Factors of Linguistic Complexity and Performance. In Davison, Alice / Green, Georgia M. (eds) *Linguistic Complexity and Text Comprehension. Readability Issues Reconsidered.* Hillsdale, NJ: Lawrence Erlbaum, 247-279.

Taavitsainen, Irma 2001. Changing Conventions of Writing: The Dynamics of Genres, Text Types, and Text Traditions. *EJES.* 5/2, 139-150.

Warren, Tessa / Gibson, Edward 2002. The Influence of Referential Processing on Sentence Complexity. *Cognition.* 85, 79-112.

Wasow, Thomas 1997. Remarks on Grammatical Weight. *Language Variation and Change.* 9/1, 81-105.

Yaruss, J. Scott 1999. Utterance Length, Syntactic Complexity, and Childhood Stuttering. *Journal of Speech, Language, and Hearing Research.* 42/2, 329-344.

Yngve, Victor H.A. 1960. A Model and an Hypothesis for Language Structure. *Proceedings of the American Philosophical Society.* 104, 444-466.

AMÁLIA MENDES
MARIA FERNANDA BACELAR DO NASCIMENTO

Grammaticalization Processes in a Spoken Portuguese Corpus: Space, Time and Discourse

This paper presents an analysis of the grammaticalization process undergone by *daí* "from there" in European Portuguese, based on real occurrences extracted from a spoken subcorpus of the *Reference Corpus of Contemporary Portuguese* (330M),[1] compiled at the Centre of Linguistics of the University of Lisbon (CLUL). The spoken corpus is 1,2 million words, both less formal and more formal (in this case, radio and television), with two main characteristics: the spontaneous nature of the spoken discourse and the diversity of themes and situations included.

We define grammaticalization as a process where, due to pragmatic and cognitive factors, linguistic units undergo a progressive evolution from less grammatical to more grammatical, involving a gradual loss of semantic autonomy and a pragmatic enrichment, and, in some cases, a more constrained syntax as well as morphological and phonological changes.

We will focus on the morphological, semantic and pragmatic properties associated to the progression of *daí*, contraction of the preposition *de* "from" + the adverb *aí* "there", from a deictic form to a discourse marker.

---

1   CRPC is a monitor corpus developed at the Centro de Linguística da Universidade de Lisboa and containing, at present, 334 million words, taken by sampling from several types of written and spoken text. These samplings pertain to national and regional varieties of Portuguese, including European, Brazilian, African (Angola, Cape Verde, Guinea-Bissau, Mozambique and Sao Tome and Principe) and Asiatic Portuguese (Macao, Goa and East-Timor) and they cover the second half of the XIX century up until 2006, mostly after 1970.

1. Space

The word form *daí* is the result of the contraction of preposition *de*, indicating movement from [a place], and adverb *aí*, a locative adverb that points to a place near the interlocutor (the adverb *aqui* points to a place near the locator, and the adverb *ali* to a more distant place) and, thus, it has prototypically a deictic function, like in (1), this meaning its reference is dependent on the properties of the communicative occurrence, namely time, place and interlocutors. Although the deictic function is listed first in dictionaries and assumed by native speakers as the cognitive primary meaning of the adverb *aí* "there" (and, consequently, of the contraction *daí*), its frequency is significantly low in the corpus.

(1)   a senhora sai *daí* e senta-se *acolá* (PF)
       "could you move from *there* and sit down *over there*"

The locative element *daí* is more frequently used in the corpus with anaphoric function, where reference is not established through the deixis, but is rather dependent on the existence of an antecedent in the sentence.

(2)   perto ali de Felgueiras São Caidé e Vizela. portanto, *daí* para Felgueiras há
       camionete (PF)[2]
       "near Felgueiras(LOC) São Caidé(LOC) and Vizela(LOC). So, *from there* to
       Felgueiras(LOC) there is a bus"

---

2   The 1,2M word corpus used contains spoken corpora compiled at CLUL for 3
     different projects: *Português Fundamental* (PF), the first spoken corpus com-
     piled for the *Reference Corpus of Contemporary Portuguese* (the PF corpus
     can be downloaded at CLUL's website: www.clul.ul.pt); *REDIP*, a spoken
     media corpus compiled by CLUL and ILTEC; *C-ORAL-ROM*, a EU-funded
     project for the compilation and annotation of spoken corpora for 4 romance
     languages: French, Italian, Portuguese and Spanish. Since the corpora were
     compiled for different projects, there is variation in what concerns the conven-
     tions for prosodic tagging. We indicate in brackets the source of our examples.

2. Time

The spatial element *daí* (just as the adverb *aí*) can assume temporal meaning in larger expressions that identify a temporal moment in the nearby future, like *daí a (um) bocado* "in a while" (3), *daí a pouco* "in a little while" (4), *daí a dois dias* "in two days".

(3)   *EDU: era bom a minha mãe ir / comprar qualquer coisa //\$ porque <achei que era uma pena que *daí a dois dias*> +\$ *LUR: [<] <ela acabou por comprar um casaco> (c-oral-rom)
      "*EDU: it would be good if my mother / bought something //\$ because <I thought it was a pity that *in two days*> +\$ *LUR: [<] <she ended out buying a coat>

(4)   os ingleses gostam pouco do alho, mas já se vão habituando porque já têm vindo aqui e começam a querer, claro, *daí a pouco* começam a gostar (PF)
      "English people don't like garlic very much, but they are getting used to it now because they come here and they start wanting it, of course, in a while they will start liking it"

Daí a bocado literally means in an undetermined period of time after a past situation that is mentioned, like in (3), which can be translated as "in two days from then", or after a past but recurrent situation which is told in the present tense, like in (4). Temporal expressions starting with *daí* (e.g., *daí a bocado*) are complementary to the same expressions starting with *daqui* (e.g., *daqui a bocado*). The former are prototypically anchored in the past of the communicative situation, while the later are anchored in the present moment. Such temporal expressions show, at least to a certain degree, the same deictic function as locative adverbs like *aí, aqui, ali*.

However, the temporal reference of *daí* is not solely established in relation to the extra-linguistic context, but also anaphorically, in relation to the event, present or portrayed, expressed previously in the text (the antecedent can be the whole proposition preceding the temporal adverb). In the example, *Ele comprou a casa e daí a dois dias decidiu vendê-la* "He bought the house and in two days from then he decided to sell it", *daí a dois dias* is temporally anchored i) in the past of the communicative occurrence (in opposition to *daqui*), ii) by the previous proposition in the text.

We can summarize the semantic values and reference patterns of *daí* through a semantic and pragmatic cline[3] (Table 1) that starts with a locative meaning (SPACE) followed by a temporal meaning (TIME), where the locative adverb is prototypically deictic, functioning however as a frequent anaphoric element, while the temporal adverb exhibits deictic but mainly anaphoric reference, since it requires a preceding proposition as its temporal antecedent:

SPACE	>	TIME
+ DEICTIC / ANAPHOR		DEICTIC / +ANAPHOR

Table 1. Semantic and pragmatic cline of *daí*: space and time.

Temporal expressions with *daí* are strongly lexicalized with the preposition *a* (*daí a* "in"). *Daí a* occurs in some multiword units that show extremely high frequencies and lexical semi-fixed properties pointing to a lexicalization process. For example, *daí a bocado* does not allow free element insertion (* *daí a esse bocado* "in that while"), although diminutives are possible and corpus attested (*daí a um bocadinho* "in a little while", literally "in a while_little"), while the already mentioned expression *daí a dois dias* "in two days" shows high lexical variation but always in the same two lexical paradigms: numeral *daí a **dois/três/quarto...dez** dias* "in two/three/four...ten days" and time measurement unit (*daí a dois **minutos/dias*** "in two minutes/days"), pointing to a strong colligation "daí a + Numeral + time measurement unit" (cf. Renouf and Sinclair 1991).

Another highly frequent and strongly lexicalized expression involving *daí* is *a partir daí* "since then / that moment", which marks a specific moment in time where a change occurs and the period of time that follows, and is usually preceded, in this corpus, by a conclu-

---

3   Clines capture the fact that "forms do not shift abruptly from one category to another, but go through a series of gradual transitions, transitions that tend to be similar in type across languages" (Hopper and Traugott 1993: 6).

sive prosodic break (//), i.e. with terminal value, and followed by non-conclusive prosodic break (/):[4]

(5)   e para mim aquilo foi uma vitória //$ porque / gostei muito de ir para lá //$ e *a partir daí* / foi lá que eu fiz os meus amigos (c-oral-rom)
        "and for me that was a victory //$ because / I liked very much to go there //$ and *since then* / that's where I made all my friends"

The antecedent of *daí* is the preceding proposition (in (5), the event of moving to another place), usually referring to an event located in the past. However, just like in example (4), the verb of the proposition can be in the present tense when it refers to a recurring event, as in (6):

(6)   com tanto tempo de exposição, queima e depois *a partir daí* é que vai para a máquina de impressão (PF)
        "with so much exposition time, (it) burns and after *from then* (it) goes to the printing machine"

Contrary to the complementary pair *daí a TIME / daqui a TIME*, *a partir daqui* does not establish as referent the present moment of enunciation, in opposition to a past antecedent expressed by *a partir daí*. In fact, *a partir daqui* (a much less frequent expression: 5 occurrences in the corpus, while *a partir daí* occurs 36 times) presents the same interpretation as the expression with *daí*, namely the expression of a transition starting from a moment in the past, or the expression of a recurring sequence of events. The deictic value of *daí* and *daqui* is even less salient in the expression with *a partir daí/daqui* than in the expression *daí/ daqui a*, taking a step further in the cline from deixis to anaphor.

The expression *a partir daí* frequently occurs together with another time delimiter *até aí* "till then", which marks the period of time before the change: *até aí...a partir daí* "till then...since then". Note that both time delimiters use prototypical locative expressions *aí*[5] "there" and *daí* "from there".

---

4   Conventions for prosodic tagging used in the C-ORAL-ROM corpus (cf. Moneglia 2005).
5   For the semantic and pragmatic analysis of the adverb *aí* 'there', see Braga (2003a) and (2003b).

(7)   *até aí* / imagine / nem se sabia / tipicamente o que era o queijo da serra //$ e *a partir daí* / com um trabalho / digamos assim / de extensão rural / com / os pastores e com as queijeiras / é que se definiu / o / o padrão / enfim / típico do queijo da serra //$ (c-oral-rom)
        "*till then* / imagine / no one knew / typically what was the cheese "*queijo da serra*" //$ and *since then* / with a work / let's say / of rural extension / with / the sheperds and the cheese makers / we defined / the / the pattern / well / typical of the cheese "*queijo da serra*" //$"

Corpus occurrences of expressions with *daí* with temporal meaning show a high frequency of other temporal expressions in the near context (underlined in the examples), which reinforce the temporal moment of change (*depois* "after" and *então* "then" in (8), *nunca mais* "never more" in (9)):

(8)   [Conversation on the way students talk] "*ELI: [<] <espontâneos> / espontâneos //$ e *depois* nós *a partir daí* *então* / íamos corrigindo //$ <mas eram>$ *HEL: [<] <exacto> //$ *ELI: / / interessantíssimos //$ &m / pronto //$ e faladores //$" (c-oral-rom)
        "*ELI: [<] <spontaneous> / spontaneous //$ and *after* we *since that moment then* / we corrected //$ <but they were>$ *HEL: [<] <exactly> //$ *ELI: / very interesting //$ &m / well //$ and talkative //$" (c-oral-rom)

(9)   levantaram-se ao meio-dia / creio eu //$ perderam o / a vez //$ *nunca mais* //$ *a partir daí* / eu disse ao Jorge / olha / quero lá saber //$ procurem um emprego (c-oral-rom)
        "$ they got out of bed at noon / I think //$ they lost the / their turn //$ *never more* //$ *since then* / I told Jorge / look / I don't care //$ look for a job"

In (10), a temporal adverb (*depois* "after") occurs even inside the lexicalized expression *daí em diante* "since then", literally "from then in forward", and another one (*então* "then") follows, both adverbs reinforcing the delimitation of a time period that shows discontinuity regarding the previous one:

(10)   teve um certo interesse perante as pessoas, não é, e *daí depois em diante* comecei *então* a expandir-me mais (PF)
        "it had a certain interest for people, you see, and *since* after *then* I started *then* to expand myself more"

Contexts are not always straightforward regarding the delimitation of a spatial or temporal meaning of the form *daí*. For example, in (11), *daí* recovers the locative nominal phrase (underlined) but also identifies a specific temporal point in a succession of events:

(11)   lá em cima, *uma espécie de panela onde se coze a madeira* e *daí* segue então
         para as outras secções (PF)
         "up there, *a sort of pot where the wood is boiled* and *from there/then* it goes
         then to other sections"

3. Anaphor

In the previous examples, *daí* had a deictic / anaphoric function expressing space and/or time. In the following examples, *daí* is an anaphoric element whose textual antecedent (anaphoric (12) or cataphoric (13)) is a nominal phrase expressing an event. In those contexts, the word form *daí* is still recognized as the contraction of (preposition + adverb) and both elements keep their autonomy.

(12)   eu acho que estão a tentar reorganizar, eh, *as competições de clubes* de forma a
         dar... a que... a que os clubes possam *daí* colher mais benefícios. eu acho bem.
         (Redip)
         "I think they are trying to reorganize, eh, *the clubs competition* in sort that ...
         that ... that the clubs can take more benefits *from that*. I think it's fine."

(13)   as meninas são todas desinibidas e tal mas, quer dizer, acho que essa
         desinibição não passa *daí*, exactamente *das farras e essas coisas todas* (PF)
         "the girls are totally uninhibited but, I mean, I think this non inhibition is no
         more *than that*, exactly *the parties and all those things*"

In these contexts, *daí* progresses from an anaphoric temporal function to a function of text organizer, taking as referent another expression in the text, usually expressing an event, and in this use it clearly relates to the temporal anaphor interpretation where it refers to a time period where an event is being realized, showing obvious relations between the different phases of the cline in Table 2.

SPACE >	TIME >	TEXT
+ DEICTIC ANAPHOR	DEICTIC +ANAPHOR	ANAPHOR

Table 2. Semantic and pragmatic cline of *daí*: space, time and text.

4. Connector

The form *daí* also occurs in constructions like the following, where *daí* is followed by a non finite clause (14) or by a nominal phrase (15):

(14)   doenças / &cu / que / que resultam / ou cuja causa / são alterações / num único gene //$ *daí* a gente chamar-lhes doenças monogénicas //$ (c-oral-rom)
"diseases / &th / that / that are the result / or whose cause / are changes / in one gene only //$ *thus* the fact that we call it monogenic diseases//$"

(15)   o futuro passará por aí //$ e passará / por / &ah / a agricultura ligada à água //$ e *daí* / esta grande nosso esforço no sentido de ver se conseguimos / puxar a barragem aqui para esta região (c-oral-rom)
"the future will consist of that //$ and will consist / of / &ah / agriculture related to water //$ and *thus* / our great effort in order to see if we can / bring the dam to this region here"

In (14) and (15) *daí* relates two different propositions in such a way that the second one is a consequence or the natural result of the first one, in other words, *daí* functions as a connector with consecutive value. In these contexts, the word form is no longer understood as a contraction of two elements and is instead recognized as a single, non composite word. In fact, although in the other examples presented *daí* can be replaced by a sequence composed by the same preposition *de* followed by another adverbial or pronominal element (e.g., "sai *daqui*" in (1), "*dali* a dois dias" in (4), "não passa *disso*" in (13)), in (14) and (15) no other element could replace the adverb.

When the connector introduces a finite clause, it is lexicalized as *daí que* "thus that" (16):

(16)   não estão habituados / a engolir / &eh / várias / dezenas de cápsulas / por dia
        //$ *daí que* / o processo de concentração / tenha que ser muito elevado //$ e o
        processo é caro (c-oral-rom)
        "they are not used / to swallow / &eh / several / dozen pills / per day //$ *thus*
        [literally: thus that]/ the concentration process / has to be very high //$ and the
        process is expensive"

We summarize in Table 3 the syntactic and prosodic patterns of *daí*
(*que*) as a conclusive connector, preceded by a proposition that can be
the entire speech turn and by a conclusive break and followed by a
non-conclusive break and by a (non) finite clause:

proposition	[conc. break] *(e) daí* [non-conc. break]	non finite clause (subjunctive) NP
proposition	[conc. break] *daí que* [non-conc. break]	finite clause

Table 3. Syntactic and prosodic patterns of *daí/daí que*.

As a connector, *daí* is lexicalized and has undergone a grammaticalization process, with recategorization from preposition and adverb to
single connector, although it is still anaphoric, like other connectors,
since it recovers the first proposition and could be paraphrased as
"and, from this, the following results".

    The semantic and pragmatic values of *daí* are expressed in the
cline in Table 4, where the domains of space and time become
conceptualizations of logical relations in the text.

SPACE >	TIME >	TEXT >	TEXT
+ DEICTIC ANAPHOR	DEICTIC +ANAPHOR	ANAPHOR	CONNECTOR

Table 4. Semantic and pragmatic cline of *daí*: space, time and text (connector).

In fact, the consecutive reading is difficult to clearly separate from the
interpretation of *daí* as a temporal marker mentioned above, as in the
example (17), where *daí* marks a time period delimitation by anaphorically recovering events expressed by the first proposition (underlined)

and can thus be paraphrased by *a partir daí* "since then", but also expresses a consecutive reading:[6]

(17) "[o patrão] que me levava sempre a ver o Sporting, depois da passei *daí* a gostar do Sporting" (PF)
"[the boss] that always took me to see Sporting (football club), after I started *then* to like Sporting"

Tables 1, 2 and 4 show a progression cline to a function of textual organization without clear-cut categories, since the properties of each phase of the element *daí* are potential motivations for its multifunctionality, which becomes evident when looking at the corpus data where many occurrences of *daí* are ambiguous regarding contiguous steps of the path proposed in Table 4. However, as pointed out by Braga (2003b: 5) in relation to the adverb *aí* (there):

---

6   While the spoken corpus shows full lexicalization of *daí que*, the written corpus shows one occurrence where *daí que* has an inserted parenthetical element:
(i) deixou de haver razão para manter as taxas de juro altas. *Daí, em parte, que* o chanceler tenha abrandado a sua atitude e insistido na redução das mesmas. (CRPC)
'there was no more reason to keep the taxes high. *Hence, in part, [the fact] that* the canceller reconsidered his attitude and insisted on reducing them.
More interesting are the (few) contexts in the written corpus of the construction (*daí* + verb + *que* "that"), like (ii):
(ii) Como também já sabes, as forças de pressão no interior dos líquidos aumentam com a profundidade. Daí se deduz que há uma desigualdade entre as intensidades das forças de pressão (...) (CRPC)
'As you also know, the pressure forces inside liquids augment with depth. From there it is deduced that there is non-equality between the intensities of the pressure forces.'
In these cases, *daí* functions as a prepositional complement of the verb *deduzir* "to deduce" in a pronominal impersonal construction *deduz-se* "it is deduced" literally "deduce-clitic", while the "that-clause" is the direct object: deduz-se [que...]$_{that-clause}$ [daí]$_{PP}$, occurring in the order [daí] deduz-se [que...], and equivalent to the expression *daí que*. Contexts like (ii), occurring in formal written registers in the corpus CRPC, show the path followed by *daí* from a prepositional complement with anaphoric function to a lexicalized consecutive connector.

> The ambiguous occurrences, however problematic for a classic approach of categories, constitute the material that allows the reconstruction of the grammaticalization path of *aí* from anaphoric or cataphoric to junctive. [our translation]

It is the locative deictic nature of *daí* which, by analogy, is associated to a temporal anaphor recovering a preceding or following expression. The consecutive reading is associated to context and is available due to the linearity of events in time, in such a way that precedence is associated to cause. This reading becomes part of the meaning of *daí* as a connector, a process that is similar to the one undergone by the equivalent Spanish form *de ahí*, as mentioned by Bosque and Demonte (1999: 3798):

> From the point of view of the content, the consecutive value that is brought to the group is, however, a contextualized general value, a result of the anaphoric deixis represented by the adverb ahí and its capacity to insert the meaning of the previous discourse as the origin of what is expressed in the clause. [our translation]

The behaviour of *daí* is in no way singular, since other lexical items expressing space and/or time conceptualize textual relations, like the adverbs *logo* "later" (etymologically related to the spatial domain, lat. *locu*), *então* "then" (Macário Lopes and Amaral 1999, Martelotta and Silva 1996) and *pois* (Pinto de Lima 2002), which also express a consecutive/causal reading. In fact, these adverbs point to the language "ability to conceptualize abstract domains of cognition in terms of concrete domains – for example, the domain of space in terms of that of physical objects, the domain of time in terms of spatial concepts, the domain of logical relations in terms of temporal concepts, etc." (Heine et al. 1991: 31).

A comparison with the analysis of the Portuguese adverb *então* "then" shows several points of contact with the properties of *daí*. Martelotta and Silva (1996: 221) refer to the anaphoric and conclusive values of *então* and its grammaticalization process along the path space > (time) > text:

From this process [space > (time) > text] onward, the element display pragmatic-discursive functions, assuming a new and more fixed position inside the clause.

Recent studies, like Martelotta (1994) show that the uses of this argumentative operator can only be satisfactorily understood based on a pragmatic-discursive theory, since its function is not only to syntactically connect clauses, but, mainly, to give an argumentative orientation to the text. [our translation]

5. Discourse

Daí also enters a lexicalized discourse marker, *vai daí*, composed of the verb *ir* "to go" in the 3rd person present and the form *daí*, and used in informal contexts like (18).

(18)   [conversation about a ethnographic group] fazendo uma certa / um certo realce / &eh / à uma área / de actividade / que é as podas e as vindimas //$ *RUI: *vai daí* / dir-se-á que vocês por aqui / neste corpo de baile / arranjaram gente nova (c-oral-rom)

     "giving a certain importance // &eh / to an area / of activity / which consist of pruning and grape-gathering //$ *RUI: *let's see* / so / it seems that you over here / in this dancing goup / you got young people"

This expression is totally fixed (admitting no variation in the verb form, preposition or adverb) and it functions as a colloquial discourse marker ·which refers anaphorically to a previous expression, while expressing a consecutive value, like *daí* (*que*). However, those two expressions show different properties. *Vai daí* is followed by finite clauses, accepting no infinitives or nominal phrases, contrary to *daí* (*que*). While *daí* (*que*) is the introducer of a new clause and can only occur at the beginning, showing a salient connective function, *vai daí* can occur in a parenthetical position inside the new clause (a rapariga não lhe respondeu e o João, *vai daí*, começou a namorar outra "the girl didn't answer him and João, *then*, started dating another one"). While *daí que* is a syntactic connector deriving from an anaphor, *vai daí* is used in less formal registers and has a salient pragmatic value. The data show that the loss in referential meaning of *daí* is concomitant to the gain in new pragmatic values, thus questioning the semantic weakening usually associated to grammaticalization and confirming that "bleaching and grammaticalization must be uncoupled if we are to understand the semantic-pragmatic processes of early stages of diachronic grammaticalization" (Traugott and König 1991: 190).

6. Final remarks

The semantic and pragmatic values of the form *daí* ranging from spatial/temporal deictic and anaphoric to connective and to discourse markers were uncovered in a spoken corpus compiled since the 1970s showing that those different functions are actually in use in contemporary Portuguese and co-exist. This confirms the principle of divergence, i.e., the fact that "existing forms take on new meaning in certain contexts, while retaining old meanings in other contexts" (Hopper and Traugott 1993: 121).

The grammaticalization path of *daí*, from space to discourse, and the connective function with consecutive value that arises point to interesting factors that would gain from a comparative study with other adverbial elements showing such cline, as well as from a contrastive study between spoken and written registers.

7. References

Bosque, Ignacio / Demonte, Violeta 1999. *Gramática Descriptiva de la Lengua Española*. Madrid: Espasa / Real Academia Española.

Braga, Maria Luiza 2003a. *Aí* e *então* em expressões cristalizadas. *Cadernos de Estudos Lingüísticos*, 44, 169-177.

Braga, Maria Luiza 2003b. E Aí se Passaram 19 Anos. In Lamoglia, Maria Eugênia (ed.) *Mudança Linguística em Tempo Real*. Rio de Janeiro: Contra Capa Livraria Ltda. 1, 159-174.

Heine, Bernd / Claudi, Ulrike / Hünnemeyer, Friederike 1991. *Grammaticalization: A Conceptual Framework*. Chicago: Chicago University Press.

Hopper, Paul J. / Traugott, Elizabeth Clauss 1993. *Grammaticalization*. Cambridge: Cambridge University Press.

Macário Lopes, Ana Cristina / Amaral, Patrícia Matos 1999. Pour une approche cognitive intégrée des valeurs de *agora* et *então*. *34th SLE Meeting*, Leuven, August 28-31, 2001.

Martelotta, Mário Eduardo 1994. *Os circunstanciadores temporais e sua ordenação: uma visão funcional*. Pd.D. Thesis: Universidade Federal do Rio de Janeiro (UFRJ).

Martelotta, Mário Eduardo / Silva, Lucilene Rodrigues da 1996. Gramaticalização de *então*. In Martelotta, Mário Eduardo / Votre, Sebastião Josué / Cezario, Maria Maura (eds) *Gramaticalização no Português do Brasil: uma Abordagem Funcional*. Rio de Janeiro: Departamento de Linguística e Filologia, UFRJ, 221-235.

Moneglia. Massimo 2005. *The C-ORAL-ROM resource*. In Cresti, Emanuela / Moneglia, Massimo (eds) *C-ORAL-ROM: Integrated Reference Corpora for Spoken Romance Languages*. Amsterdam: John Benjamins, 1-70.

Pinto de Lima, José 2002. Gramaticalization, subjectification and the origin of phatic markers. In Wischer, Ilse / Diewald, Gabriele (eds) *New Reflections on Grammaticalization*. Amsterdam: Benjamins, 363-378.

Renouf, Antoinette / Sinclair, John 1991. Collocational Frameworks in English. In Ajimer / Altenberg (eds) *English Corpus Linguistics*, London: Longman, 128-143.

Traugott, Elizabeth / König, Ekkehard 1991. The Semantics-Pragmatics of Grammaticalization Revisited. In Traugott, Elizabeth / Heine, Bernd (eds) *Approaches to Grammaticalization*, vol. I. Amsterdam: Benjamins, 189-218.

III. Teaching and Learning Languages
through Oral Corpora

Yukio Tono

The Roles of Oral L2 Learner Corpora in Language Teaching: the Case of the NICT JLE Corpus

1. Introduction

Corpora can provide a wide variety of linguistic information which could be useful in many different fields of language studies. Until two decades ago, most corpora were based on written texts, and with a few exceptions (e.g. the *London-Lund Corpus*, the *Spoken English Corpus*) very few spoken corpora were made available. Although more and more spoken corpora were constructed in the past twenty years, it is not until recently that digitized audio files and their transcripts in an orthographical format are integrated into a corpus in a sophisticated manner.

Today, there is a growing awareness that oral or spoken corpora could serve as useful resources for studying characteristics of human speech, thus being also beneficial for teaching oral skills of a language. Especially corpora of learner language (also known as *learner corpora*) have attracted much attention from researchers working in the field of second/foreign language learning and now there is a growing demand for spoken learner corpora to study oral proficiency skills of second language learners.

This study will first situate spoken learner corpora in learner corpus research and then introduce the *NICT JLE Corpus*, the biggest oral learner corpus in the world as of the beginning of 2007. Next, I will briefly summarize a series of studies using the *NICT JLE Corpus* focusing on the description of various aspects of Interlanguage performance. Finally, the future prospect of research and teaching based on oral learner corpora will be discussed.

2. A brief historical overview on learner language studies

The study of learner language is not new. In the late 19th century, child language acquisition researchers examined the interaction protocol data between a mother and a child. In second language acquisition research, it was not until the middle of the 20th century when Pit Corder wrote the seminal paper called "Significance of learner's errors", in which he stressed the importance of shifting our research focus from mere comparisons of source and target languages, which was then called Contrastive Analysis (CA), to the study of the independent system of learner language by investigating the systematic nature of learner errors (Corder 1967).

This lead to the growing body of research called Error Analysis (EA) in the 1970s. Despite the large number of studies, most research was lacking in the notion of treating the production data in its entirety. In other words, most researchers in those days analyzed the production data in such a way that they looked at only those points that they wanted to examine, thus discarding the data after the data analysis[1].

It was not until the beginning of the 1990s when people started to collect the language production data with a view to sharing it with others in the same research community. In the U.S., child language acquisition data started to be gathered for the project CHILDES. In Europe, the influence of corpus linguistics was seen in several different ways. One was the initiative taken by publishers such as Longman, which started to gather second language learners' writings as a corpus in the early 1980s, which later led to the *Longman Learners' Corpus* (LLC). Second, the *International Corpus of English* (ICE) project was launched in 1990, where they decided to collect not only regional varieties of English, but also a corpus of learner English as one of the varieties of English (Greenbaum 1996), which eventually became one of the first initiatives of collecting learner corpora worldwide, i.e., the *International Corpus of Learner English* (ICLE). Third, a series of conferences such as *Teaching and Language*

---

1   For further detail, see Tono (2002).

Corpora (TALC) provided the opportunities for corpus linguists and researchers in the field of language teaching and learning to discuss the potential of corpus-based approach in various aspects of language education. The present author was one of those who benefited greatly from those meetings. By the beginning of the Millennium, learner corpus projects became the mainstream of corpus applications for language teaching and learning.

3. Major learner corpus projects

Nowadays, we can see a growing number of researchers working on learner production data using a corpus-based approach. The number of major learner corpus projects is somewhat limited, however, because the corpus compilation takes a long time, tremendous effort and a large sum of money. Here I will introduce some of those major learner corpus projects.

There are two commercial learner corpora: the *Longman Learners' Corpus* (LLC) and the *Cambridge Learner Corpus* (CLC). LLC was launched around the mid-1980s, being thus one of the first learner corpora in the world. Now it has about 10 million words in size, and is composed of written compositions, exam scripts, and various other writings by more than 50 different nationalities.[2] CLC was a latecomer, but is growing very rapidly. It contains over 25 million words, and is composed of anonymous exam scripts written by students who took Cambridge ESOL exams all over the world. It currently contains scripts from over 85,000 students with more than 100 first languages and more than 150 nationalities. The unique feature of CLC is its learner error-coded scripts. According to their website,[3] approximately 13 million words (45,000 scripts) were tagged for errors.

---

2   For the use of LLC, see Gillard and Gadsby (1998).
3   <http://www.cambridge.org/elt/corpus/learner_corpus2.htm>

Another important learner corpus project in Europe is the *International Corpus of Learner English* (ICLE) (Granger 1998). ICLE started in 1990, aiming to describe the Interlanguages of homogeneous groups of English learners (the third- or fourth-year students majoring in English as a foreign language at a university level) with approximately 15 different mother tongue backgrounds. Their primary goal is to identify similarities and differences in overuse, underuse or misuse phenomena across different first language (L1) background groups, which, they hope, will clarify universal vs. L1-related developmental patterns in second language.

Granger also launched a project of compiling an oral corpus of learner English in 1995, called LINDSEI (*Louvain International Database of Spoken English Interlanguage*). There are currently 11 different groups of learners from different L1 backgrounds, each of which contains 50 transcripts of 15-minute oral interviews.

In Asia, various projects for compiling learner corpora arose and disappeared in the last decade, and now a few of them survived. The *HKUST Learner Corpus* is one of the first learner corpora built in Asian regions. It contains more than 25 million words of exam scripts and term papers written by Chinese-speaking learners of English. John Milton has developed the web learning materials as well as a concordancer (Word Pilot) based on this corpus (Milton and Chowdhury 1994, Pravec 2002). In Japan, the present author has been involved in developing two major learner corpora: the *NICT JLE Corpus* and the *JEFLL Corpus*. The *NICT JLE Corpus* is an oral learner corpus of more than 1200 Japanese-speaking learners of English, based on the oral proficiency interview test transcripts. The *JEFLL Corpus* contains more than 10,000 Japanese secondary school students' writings (approximately 0.7 million). These two corpora are the biggest second language developmental corpora in the world, in the sense that the subcorpora are controlled by the proficiency level guidelines (either the test grades or the school years).

4. The NICT JLE Corpus: its design criteria

This section describes in more detail the *NICT-JLE Corpus*, the first oral corpus of EFL (English as a Foreign Language) learners in Japan.[4] The project started in 2001, funded by the Japanese government and led by the National Institute of Information and Communications Technology (NICT). It contains close to 1300 examinees' interview transcripts, which is approximately 2 million words in size. What makes this corpus quite unique is the fact that each subject is tagged for his or her oral proficiency test score based on the *Standard Speaking Test*[5] (SST), thus making it possible to compare across groups of different proficiency levels. SST is modeled after ACTFL (The American Council on the Teaching of Foreign Languages) OPI. There are nine levels, ranging from Level 1 for Novice Low to Level 9 for Advanced. Each interview test lasts 15 minutes, in which there are five stages: (1) warm-up, (2) the task for eliciting simple present tense narration, (3) the task for eliciting questions or testing the ability to negotiate in English, (4) the task for eliciting simple past tense narration, and (5) wrap-up. The three stages in the middle involve tasks such as picture descriptions, role plays or story-telling. The interviewer will decide the tasks spontaneously as they interact with the subjects. Since SST is a test disguised as a natural conversation, it is by nature interactive and adaptive to the examinee's profile. The recorded interviews are then evaluated by at least two certified SST raters, following the SST evaluation scheme.

The project also provided added value to the corpus by supplying a partially error-tagged version and a comparable corpus, in which the same interview tests were administered to native speakers of English. It also provides the version of a back-translation corpus, the one whose original English interview transcripts were translated into Japanese in order to investigate the first language influence. They also developed some useful tools for the project: (a) *TagEdit*, an editor for

---

4   For general introduction, see Tono (2001).
5   The Standard Speaking Test was developed by ALC Press based on ACTFL OPI.

supporting oral data transcription (Fig.1) and error annotation, which manages transcriptions and tag insertions, and (b) *Analyzer*, a tool for basic concordancing and frequency and statistical analyses (Fig. 2).

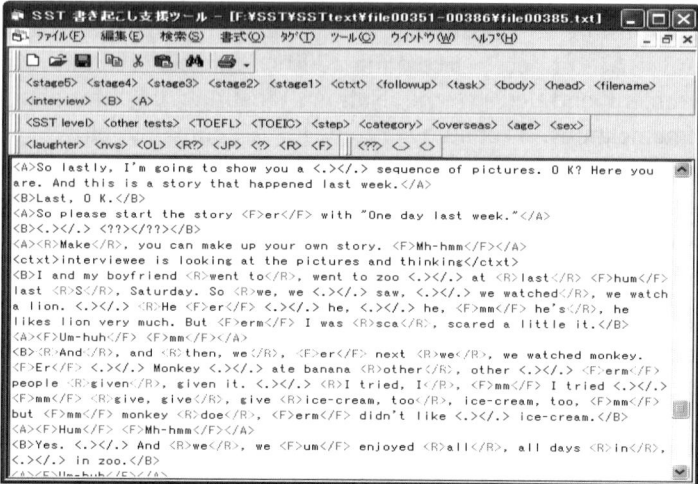

Figure 1. Screenshot of *TagEdit*.

Figure 2. Screenshot of *Analyzer*.
(Window showing the analysis of article errors.)

5. Some findings using the NICT JLE Corpus

This section will describe on-going research into a spoken learner language, using the NICT JLE Corpus. Since the corpus was developed in collaboration between humanities researchers and Natural Language Processing (NLP) researchers, it has involved an interesting mixture of psycholinguistic, computational and pedagogical research. I will report mainly on the following two aspects: first, various research projects to identify the characteristics of spoken Interlanguages at different proficiency levels. Secondly, I will briefly summarize NLP people's research into (a) automatic error detection and identification, and (b) automatic identification of speakers' proficiency levels.

5.1. What basic text characteristics tell us

Tono (2004) examined basic text characteristics of the different proficiency level groups of the NICT JLE Corpus.[6] The measures include (a) average corpus size (the total size of the subcorpora (Level 1-9) divided by the number of subjects in each level), (b) Standardized Type/Token Ratio (STTR), and (c) Mean Length of Utterances (MLU). See Table 1 for the results. The mean sample corpus size for Level 1 was 338 words, and it increased to 790 words at Level 3, 1412 words at Level 6, and 1715 words at Level 8 respectively. This indicates that the total amount of speech made in the given time (15 min) is a strong indicator of the proficiency levels. In STTR, there was a sharp increase between Level 1 and 2, then followed by a gradual increase from Level 2 up to Level 7, which shows that STTR, an index of lexical density, distinguishes the low-mid groups effectively while it is not useful for discriminating the upper levels. MLU also shows a similar tendency as STTR. It increases constantly from Level 1 to Level 6, and then seems to reach the ceiling. It seems that in order

---

6   The version used for Tono (2004) was a pre-release version of the corpus, and it contained 1,313,293 words (1,201 examinees' utterances only).

to discriminate the upper levels (Level 7-9), we need to identify different types of Interlanguage features.

	1	2	3	4	5	6	7	8	9
Mean sample corpus size	338	457	790	1060	1298	1412	1505	1715	1632
Standardized TTR	36.67	42.03	42.48	44.20	46.22	47.58	49.02	49.00	49.35
MLU	3.09	4.04	5.90	7.44	8.44	9.00	9.14	9.25	9.24

Table 1. Basic text characteristics of the NICT JLE subcorpora.

5.2. Patterns in word/POS n-grams

One way to examine overall text characteristics is to obtain n-gram statistics for words and parts-of-speech. Figure 3 below shows the bird's-eye view of the top 100 trigrams of each level of the NICT JLE Corpus.[7]

Let me summarize some interesting findings from this diagram:
➤ The use of fillers is very frequent in the lower-proficiency groups, which gradually decreases to the minimum at the upper levels. The types of the fillers were also different; at the lower levels, fillers sound very Japanese (e.g. EETTO) but later sound more like English (e.g. erm, Uh-huh), and lexically more target-like and sophisticated (e.g. well, how can I say).
➤ The trigram patterns of "AT (article) + X" and "ADJ (adjective) + X" increased in number and types, which shows that learners tend to use more complex noun phrases.
➤ The trigram patterns of "PP*(personal pronoun) + X" and "V (verb) + X" also increased in number and types, which shows that learners have a tendency to use more complex predicate patterns, especially the use of modal auxiliaries and verb patterns.

---

7 This diagram was made by extracting the top 100 trigrams from each level, then sorted alphabetically. The patterns containing punctuations in the middle were deleted for the sake of simplicity.

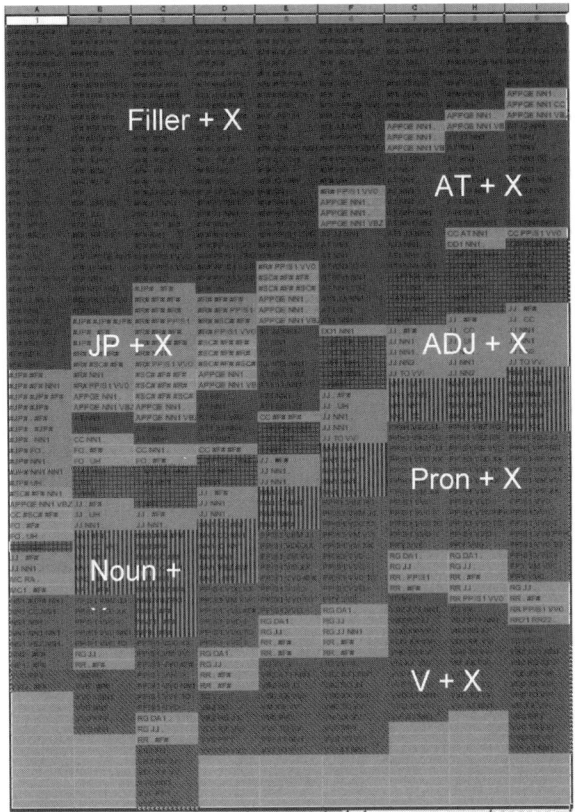

Figure 3. Trigram transition patterns across the NICT JLE Corpus.

These changes of trigram patterns are found to be much more frequent in oral learner corpora than written ones (Tono 2007).[8] This may be partly due to the fact that in the case of written essays, learners can spend more time monitoring their use of language as compared to speech, which helps them produce relatively more complex sentences from the beginning. It is worth noting, therefore, that attention has to be paid to different linguistic characteristics in evaluating oral and written performance.

---

8   Fillers are, of course, not usually observable in writings.

Patterns in word or POS n-grams are quite revealing, for it provides an overall picture of transition patterns of lexical as well as syntactic combinations across different stages of learning. By carrying out a thorough investigation on the similarities and differences in n-gram patterns between oral and written learner corpora, we will be able to describe the transitional structures of Interlanguage in a more systematic way.

5.3. Acquisition of verb subcategorization patterns

N-gram analysis is useful, but the technique is somewhat limited when it comes to examining a syntactic development. The analysis of verb complementation or subcategorization patterns, in particular, is a difficult job, for it involves grammatical categories such as noun phrases or prepositional phrases as a constituent, which cannot be captured by a simple n-gram analysis.

We conducted a preliminary investigation about the use of the verb "*get*" to compare the oral and written corpora, NICT JLE and JEFLL[9]. All the instances of the verb "*get*" were retrieved and classified according to the following verb categories:[10]

a.   Basic structures (get + N; get + Adj; get + Part/Prep; get + Past Participle; get + Ving; get + to do)
b.   Get + object + verb form (get + N + Ving; get + N + to do; get + N + Past Participle)

The classification was partly done automatically by searching for the POS patterns following the verb. The identification of noun phrases in learner production data was too difficult to automate, thus we categorized complex patterns by hand.

Tables 2 and 3 show the normalized frequencies (per 100,000) of subcategorization patterns for the verb "*get*".

---

9   I would like to thank Rie Suzuki, my postgraduate student, for her initial analysis of this work. Correspondence analysis was performed by the author.
10   The classification was based on Swan (2005).

JEFLL Level	Verb patterns of "get"							Active Margin
	get + N	get + Adj	get + Part/Prep	get + p.p.	get + to do	get+ N to do	get + N p.p.	
JH1	27.992	2.896	21.236	.000	.965	.000	.000	53.089
JH2	95.505	5.847	56.524	.650	.650	.000	.000	159.176
JH3	41.788	18.619	98.885	1.241	.000	.000	.414	160.947
SH1	34.886	18.660	36.509	2.434	.000	.000	.000	92.489
SH2	57.606	18.055	42.989	2.293	.573	.000	.000	121.516
SH3	108.982	26.439	46.430	2.579	2.579	.645	.000	187.655
Active Margin	366.759	90.516	302.573	9.197	4.768	.645	.414	774.872

Table 2. Correspondence Table. Patterns for the verb "*get*" (JEFLL).

SST Level	Verb patterns of "get"							Active Margin
	get + N	get + Adj	get + Part/Prep	get + p.p.	get + to do	get + N to do	get + N p.p.	
Level 3	17.694	1.083	13.000	1.083	.000	.000	.000	32.861
Level 4	27.559	4.039	17.106	2.970	.119	.000	.119	51.911
Level 5	35.876	10.250	24.297	4.176	.190	.000	.190	74.979
Level 6	48.062	22.491	24.955	6.162	2.773	.616	.000	105.059
Level 7	46.991	21.834	33.226	10.917	1.424	.000	.475	114.866
Level 8	61.078	32.888	42.285	12.920	8.809	.000	1.175	159.155
Level 9	53.215	38.225	61.460	11.243	5.996	2.249	3.748	176.134
Active Margin	290.476	130.810	216.328	49.471	19.311	2.865	5.705	714.966

Table 3. Correspondence table. Patterns for the verb "*get*" (NICT JLE)[11].

The first four patterns (get + N, get + Adj, get + Part/Prep, get + p.p.) show a steady increase in frequencies as the stages go up in both written and spoken corpora. In the case of the pattern "get to do", JEFLL shows an increase only in the last year (Year 12) while NICT JLE shows a gradual increase across the levels. Correspondence analysis was performed for the data from the NICT JLE Corpus in order to capture the relationship between proficiency levels and the use of different subcategorization patterns (see Figure 4 below).

In Figure 4, Dimension 1 explains 61.1% of the relationship between the two variables (SST level x Verb patterns of "get") and Dimension 2 explains 25.1%. As the diagram shows, Dimension 1 seems to indicate the proficiency levels, for the dots showing Level 3

---

11   Level 1 and 2 were omitted because there was only one occurrence of the verb *get* in these levels.

to Level 9 are plotted along the horizontal dimension. Dimension 2 can be interpreted as "the complexity of the verb subcategorization patterns". The two dots "get + N+ p.p." and "get + N + to do" are far away from all the groups, further down in the bottom right of the space, which indicates that these two verb patterns are seldom used by any of the groups. Level 9 is the only group slightly closer to these two categories. Thus, we can say that the presence of these two patterns in spoken data indicate that the speakers are very competent in using the verb "*get*".

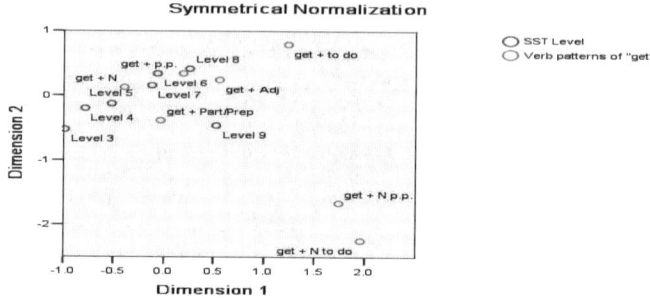

Figure 4. Correspondence analysis (NICT JLE).

In Figure 4, the use of the subcategorization pattern "get + N" is more closely associated with lower levels while such patterns as "get + Adj" and "get + Part/Prep" are plotted closer to upper levels. While all three patterns steadily increase along the proficiency levels, the frequent use of "get + Part/Prep" (i.e. phrasal verbs) or "get + Adj" patterns demonstrates that the speakers acquire the colloquial use of the verb "*get*", which resulted in closer plots between these patterns and upper levels. This is not the case with JEFLL; in the case of written data, the use of "get + N" is more prominent than other patterns. We can see that secondary school students have a rather limited repertoire of subcategorization patterns, as compared to the adult learners taking the SST. However, the JEFLL data shows that the pattern "get + N" is used with increasing frequency, which indicates that the learners become able to use different nouns within this pattern. In other words, the patterns of use in spoken and written learner corpora are different; in speech, a wider range of subcategorization patterns become available as the level goes up. In writing, on the other hand, the repertoire of lexical choices within the simple pattern "get + N" becomes wider, whilst the subcategorization patterns are rather limited throughout the different developmental stages.

5.4. Automatic detection of learner errors

The NICT JLE Corpus has been used also by NLP researchers in order to apply natural language processing techniques to solve practical problems regarding learner language analysis. One of the areas is automatic detection of learner errors. Izumi, Uchimoto, and Isahara (2004), for example, investigated the possibility of identifying three types of learner errors (omission, replacement, insertion) based on the error-tagged data of the NICT JLE Corpus. They considered error detection as similar to text categorization and applied the machine learning model to solve this task. For this, they selected the Maximum Entropy (ME) model. By using the original error-tagged corpus as the training data, they obtained the recall of article errors to be approximately 35 percent and the precision to be around 48 percent, which was not very encouraging. In order to improve the results, they added corrected sentences and artificially-made errors, which led to better recall and precision (43 percent and 68 percent respectively).

5.5. Automatic identification of learners' proficiency levels

Another area of application in NLP using the NICT JLE Corpus is to automatically identify the proficiency levels of learners using linguistic features in the speech data. Since every individual file in the NICT JLE Corpus has proficiency level information as meta-data, it would be interesting to explore the possibility of how well computers can identify proficiency levels by looking at features of each speech data. Sakata et al. (2007) used the measurement called BLEU, which is proposed as a method of automatic evaluation of machine translation. It basically compares n-grams of machine translated texts against human translation and yield the rating (0.0 to 1.0 scaling) based on the overlapping ratio of n-grams between the two.

In the same vein, Sakata et al. used word n-grams of the speech data labeled with different proficiency levels in the NICT JLE Corpus in place of human translation, and proposed two ways of automatic evaluation using BLEU: one is to use word n-grams only, and the other is to use word and POS n-grams, whose weight was optimized by Support Vector Regression. The results show that the method using word and POS n-grams as feature vectors outperformed the word only method. Using this method, the accuracy rate of identifying the proficiency levels is approximately 65%.

If this type of research is carried out further, it would be possible to see the computer system for the future, which can determine the learner's proficiency level based on the input text features. This will be potentially very useful in developing the CALL system, where learners are guided to different levels of tasks based on their language proficiency levels. The same thing can be possible with human speech in the future, if speech recognition system is fully implemented. The NICT JLE Corpus can serve as an invaluable resource for such a direction of research.

6. Pedagogical implications

So far I have presented some findings based on the NICT JLE Corpus. It is exciting to see a growing number of studies conducted on various aspects of oral learner corpora; description of various linguistic features at different stages of L2 development, comparison between oral and written performance of the learners, computational analysis of learner corpora for automatic identification of errors and proficiency levels. Each of these findings will surely lead to a new paradigm of foreign language teaching and learning. To conclude this paper, let me discuss pedagogical implications of the studies mentioned above.

First, as we know more about the learning process, we will be able to adjust the learning environment to an appropriate learning level. Most foreign language teaching materials thus far do not take into account a scientific analysis of Interlanguage process. They largely rely on teachers' own experience and their forerunners' wisdom. I used the frequency data from the British National Corpus for developing my TV English conversation program for NHK (Nihon Hosou Kyokai: Japan Broadcasting Corporation), which ran from April, 2003 to March, 2006 and more than one million people watched the show. The book based on the program, called *Corpus Renshu-cho* (Corpus Drill Book) became a best-seller. I realized that people knew the value of such resources, if they were properly packaged and presented. Since I did not use learner corpora for my program, I will definitely produce something in the future, using spoken learner data. The analysis of oral learner corpora against written ones, together with the comparison with native speakers' corpora, will shed light on the learning path and the related problems on the way. This will benefit various areas such as syllabus construction, textbook writing, task design and creation, among others.

Second, teachers' attitude toward learner performance will change as more findings will be provided regarding the Interlanguage process. Examples of some features of the spoken learner corpus shown above (e.g., the transition of patterns in fillers or verb subcategorization) will provide teachers with a different viewpoint. The way a teacher evaluates students will be different with such insights into their language use.

Third, learners themselves can benefit from accessing the oral corpus directly. After my corpus-based TV programs, many teachers started to use corpora in the classroom. They make exactly the same comments: "We need corpora which are more accessible and easy to read." Corpora tuned to novice-intermediate learners are still hard to find. Oral corpora are also beneficial for learners because they are usually simpler than written corpora and students can learn useful colloquial expressions from them. Most spoken corpora, however, are often too difficult or too natural to understand the contexts fully. Therefore, I would like to propose an alternative: oral learner corpora with their corrected counterparts. Learners can access the oral learner corpora and if they wanted to know the proper way to say it, they can access the corrected version of the corpus. This will be an excellent way to provide resources for writing classes or for preparing the speech or debate classes. I hope that research into oral learner corpora and their applications in the classroom should go hand in hand so that teachers and learners of foreign languages will get maximum benefit from this wonderful resource.

7. References

Corder, Pit 1967. The significance of learners' errors. *International Review of Applied Linguistics*, 5, 161-170.

Gillard, Patrick / Gadsby, Adam 1998. Using a learners' corpus in compiling ELT dictionaries. In Granger, Sylviane (eds) *Learner English on Computer*. Addison-Wesley: Longman, 159-171.

Greenbaum, Sydney 1996. *Comparing English Worldwide*. Oxford: Clarendon Press.

Izumi, Emi / Uchimoto, Kiyotaka / Isahara, Hitoshi 2004. Jido Eigo Ayamari Kensaku System No Kaihatu. (Developing an automatic error detection system for English learner corpora). In Izumi, Emi/ Uchimoto, Kiyotaka / Isahara, Hitoshi (eds). Nihonjin 1200 Nin no Eigo Speaking Corpus (A spoken corpus of 1200 Japanese-speaking learners of English), Tokyo: ALC Press. 141-153.

Milton, John and Chowdhury, Nandini 1994. Tagging the Interlanguage of Chinese learners of English. In Flowerdew, Lynne / Tong, Anthony K.K. (eds) *Proceedings of Joint Seminar on Corpus Linguistics and Lexicology*, Guangzhou and Hong Kong, 19-22 June, 1993. Hong Kong: Language Centre, HKUST, 127-143.

Pravec, Norma A. 2002. Survey of learner corpora. *ICAME Journal*, 26, 81-114.

Sakata, Kosuke / Shimbo, Hitoshi / Matsumoto, Yuji 2007. Automatic estimation of language proficiency levels based on corpora.

(original in Japanese). ANLP. *Proceedings of the annual meeting of the Association for Natural Language Processing*, March 2007, 793-796.

Swan, Michael 2005. *Practical English Usage*. Oxford: Oxford University Press.

Tono, Yukio / Kaneko, T./ Isahara, Hitoshi / Saiga, Toyomi. / Izumi, Emi 2001. The Standard Speaking Test Corpus: a 1 million-word spoken corpus of Japanese learners of English and its implications for L2 lexicography. In Lee, S. (ed.) *ASIALEX 2001 Proceedings: Asian Bilingualism and the Dictionary. The Second Asialex International Congress*, August 8-10, 2001, Yonsei University, Korea. 7-17.

Tono, Yukio 2002. *The Roles of Learner Corpora in SLA Research: The Multiple Comparison Approach.* Unpublished Ph.D. thesis. Lancaster University.

Tono, Yukio 2004. On the use of productive vocabulary in the NICT JLE Corpus. In Izumi, Emi / Uchimoto, Kiyotaka / Isahara, Hitoshi (eds) *Nihonjin 1200 Nin no Eigo Speaking Corpus* (*A spoken corpus of 1200 Japanese-speaking learners of English*), Tokyo: ALC Press, 97-112.

Tono, Yukio 2007. Comparing the NICT JLE Corpus with the JEFLL Corpus: Analyzing the word/POS-tag sequences. Paper given at the 29th JAECS (Japan Association for English Corpus Studies) conference. Dokkyo University, Kyoto, Japan, 28 April, 2007.

JOHN OSBORNE

Investigating L2 Fluency through Oral Learner Corpora

In the early 1960s the British intelligence services set up a unit called the "Fluency Committee". The purpose of this unit was not, as the name might suggest, to improve the language skills of their agents, but to identify a suspected "mole" at the heart of the organisation. The mole was never formally identified, and it is not clear whether he ever really existed. In many respects, the quest for language fluency has a similarly elusive target. It is widely believed that such a thing as fluency exists, and indeed that it is a major goal of language learning; most people recognise fluency (or lack of fluency) when they encounter it, but it is difficult to identify exactly what fluency consists of and what causes it.

In this chapter, I should like to look at the ways in which the analysis of oral learner corpora can contribute to identifying the factors which affect fluency in spoken L2 production. Recent work with learner corpora has mostly been concerned with written corpora, and has focussed principally on non native-like patterns of lexico-grammatical or phraseological usage, or on aspects of morpho-syntactic development in L2 acquisition. The compilation of oral L2 corpora opens the possibility for studying other characteristics of oral production – hesitations, pauses, fillers, repetitions and retracing – which are not necessarily errors in themselves, but which are marks of disfluency, and which may in fact be more detrimental to effective language use than formal errors. The analysis of these features raises many interesting questions. What is oral fluency, and how can it be measured? How are particular types of disfluency related to morpho-syntactic or lexical difficulties? To what extent do pauses and fillers occur within units rather than at syntactic and phraseological boundaries? In what ways does the relatively non-fluent production of less proficient learners differ from fluent production by advanced learners, or indeed by native speakers? What kinds of disfluencies disappear as overall proficiency increases, and which kinds persist? To what extent do disfluencies vary according to task, according to L1-L2 pairings, or to individual differences between learners?

Following earlier studies of the role played by temporal factors in speech production (notably those collected in Dechert and Raupach, 1980), there has been a renewed interest in defining, measuring and understanding fluency in second language production (see for example Riggenbach 2000). Various measures of fluency have been proposed – words per minute, length of runs, number of pauses, proportion of pause time, etc. (Lennon 1990, Towell, Hawkins and Bazergui 1996, Freed, Segalowitz and Dewey 2004) – and in some cases have been correlated with subjective ratings from native and non-native listeners to try to determine which features are a good prediction of whether an L2 speaker will be perceived as fluent or non-fluent (Lennon 1990, Kormos and Dénes 2004, Mizera 2006).

1. The *PAROLE* corpus

In what follows, I should like to compare some examples from an oral corpus, to illustrate the kinds of features that may distinguish fluent from non-fluent production. The examples are taken from the *PAROLE* corpus (*PARallèle, Oral, en Langue Etrangère*), presently being compiled at the Université de Savoie. This corpus consists of oral productions from learners of French, Italian and English. The samples are collected at various levels of proficiency, from lower intermediate to advanced, and are obtained from guided and semi-guided oral pro- duction tasks based on picture and video prompts, and from free narration of personal experiences. It is thus possible to compare pro- ductions on identical tasks across languages and across proficiency levels. These data are complemented by a battery of tests chosen to measure other aspects of the learners' language aptitude (vocabulary size, grammatical aptitude, oral comprehension skills, etc.) and by recordings of native speakers accomplishing the same tasks.

The digital recordings are transcribed and annotated using the *CHILDES* system (MacWhinney 2000). This system, although extensively used in child language acquisition studies, has been less widely used in compiling L2 corpora; for some examples, see Housen 2002, Myles 2005, Myles and Mitchell 2004. For the transcription of non-native oral corpora, however, the system offers a number of useful features. Application of *CHAT* transcription conventions reduces individual transcribing decisions and ensures maximum consistency across transcribers and across languages. The transcription format used provides a detailed and well-tried system for coding filled and unfilled pauses, repetitions, retracings, incomplete words or utterances, indistinct or indeterminate forms, overlap, code-switching and use of non-target forms. Accurate measurement of pauses is also possible, using the *Sonic Mode* facility. The corpus can then be searched for occurrences of the features that have been coded in this way, and for the contexts in which they occur.

In the following microanalysis, I will look at examples of three types of potential disfluency markers: speech rate and pauses, retracing, and length of runs. The aim is to illustrate how these temporal factors might be related to more qualitative aspects of speech fluency. To ensure comparability, all the examples are taken from the same production task, the "fridge" video, where the subjects watch and then describe a short (35s) video clip showing a group of men trying to hoist a large fridge up to the window of a third floor apartment. At the moment when the men try to catch the fridge to bring it through the window, it tips over and crashes down on to the roof of a small car parked below. Six productions will be considered, three in English and three in French. For each language, the three speakers are respectively a low intermediate learner (A2-B1), an upper intermediate or advanced learner (B2-C1) and a native speaker. All the speakers are students in higher education, aged between 18 and 25. The full transcripts of the examples are given in the appendix.

2. Speech rate and pauses

Table 1 summarises the temporal measures for each of the six speakers. Proficiency level is measured by results on three parts of the *DIALANG* test[1] (vocabulary, oral comprehension and structures); this is not intended as a rigorous test of language competence, but provides a rough indication of the relative level of the non-native speakers. In the last two lines of the table, "segment length" is the duration of continuous speech between two pauses.

	003A	*025A*	*N01A*	*407A*	*417A*	*N47A*
Language of production / L1	English/ French	English/ French	English/ English	French/ Chinese	French/ English	French/ French
Level of proficiency	A2	C1	Native	B1	B2	Native
Speaking time (seconds)	88.798	35.873	25.931	72.056	44.173	22.330
N° of words	77	105	52	92	82	84
Speech rate (wpm)	52.03	175.62	120.32	76.61	111.38	225.71
N° of pauses	62	20	14	29	21	9
Total pause time	51.939 58.5%	6.427 17.9%	8.086 31.2%	24.561 34.1%	10.649 24.1%	2.142 9.6%
Mean pause time	1.574	0.428	1.011	1.445	0.887	0.536
Mean segment length	2.54	5.8	5,5	3.69	4.14	8.3
Max. segment length	7	17	15	13	12	23

Table 1. Fluency measures for the 6 recordings.

The most obvious difference between these speakers is in the rate of speech, ranging from 225 to 52 words per minute. Rate of speech, whether measured in words per minute or in syllables per minute, has

---

1   <http://www.dialang.org>

been found to correlate well with perceived fluency, as evaluated by untrained native-speaker judges (Lennon 1990, Riggenbach 1991, Freed 2000, Cucchiarini et al 2002, Kormos and Dénes 2004, Mizera 2006: 61-79). However, speech rate is subject to considerable variation, both individual and according to task. Although in this small sample the fastest speaker of French is a native, the fastest speaker of English is non-native. At the same time, a relatively high rate of speech will not necessarily give an impression of fluency, if it is accompanied, for example, by frequent errors or retracing. This can be seen in the following fragment:

(1)   417: et <ils ont> [/] ils ont essayé de [/] de saisir la [/] la [*] &fr [//] réfrigérateur mais ils [/] ils ont échoué .

This uninterrupted 17-word fragment lasts just under 7 seconds, corresponding to a speech rate of 146 words per minute, which is comparable to that of many native speakers. However, the fragment contains 5 repetitions and a morphological error (*la réfrigérateur*), which detract from the impression of fluency that it produces. Methodologically, it is possible to counteract this effect by "pruning" productions to exclude all repeated elements, or by introducing a separate criterion to measure the effect of repetitions. By themselves, though, repetitions do not seem to be a good measure of perceived fluency, as will be discussed below.

Another possible indicator of fluency is the number of pauses, filled and unfilled, their average length, and the total duration of pauses. Measures such as these will nevertheless smooth out the differences between a speaker who produces a lot of relatively short pauses and one who produces fewer but more protracted pauses. In the *PAROLE* corpus, a silence of more than 200ms is transcribed as a pause, since this is the minimum duration that can be distinguished from regular articulatory activity. However, it is pauses of 500ms or more that are likely to be perceived as disfluent, and up to 3 seconds before listeners sense a breakdown in communication (Griffiths 1991, Rieger 2003). Isolated unfilled pauses rarely exceed 1.5 seconds even in learner speech; beyond this, longer hesitation is usually marked by pause complexes – pausal groups made up of one or more unfilled

pause plus one or more filled pause, for example: *<e:r # &=bouche>*
[#3_221] who were <u:m # &=bouche> [#1_607] er at the window ↑
, which contains two such pausal groups, occupying a total of nearly 5
seconds. Although these pausal groups are less frequent in NS
production, they are used even by the most rapid speaker, N47: *le*
frigo tombe sur la voiture et <euh #> [#0_883] il est cassé. In native
speaker production, however, and in fluent non-native speech, such
pausal groups tend to serve as planning pauses and to occur at
propositional boundaries, as in the above example, where the pause
group is realised as a prolongation of the conjunction *et*, by
centralising and lengthening the vowel (on vowel lengthening as a
pause marker in French, see Candea 2000). For English, there is some
evidence that when native speakers' pausal groups include a filler, the
filler will tend to be *um* rather than *uh/er*, suggesting that these fillers
are not chosen at random, but are functionally differentiated (Clark
and Fox Tree 2002). Since the filler and accompanying pause are thus
meaningful, their use will appear motivated, rather than being just
disfluent.

Less fluent non-native speakers, by contrast, also produce
pausal groups within syntactic units, where they appear not as
discourse planning pauses but as holders for lexical or morpho-
syntactic searches. This can be seen in the examples below, where in
addition, fillers such as *er*, *um* or *euh* are used more randomly:

(2)   *Morpho-syntactic search:* bu:t [/] <e:r #> [#4_123] but the [/] the fridge <e:r
       #> [#3_553] fallen [*] [//] #0_812 non@s

(3)   *Lexical search:* et [/] et il veut <euh # um #> [#2_766] apporter le frigo au [//]
       le [*] premier étage &s par la fenêtre.

Objectively, the number and duration of pauses are factors that affect
fluency, and overall, more proficient speakers produce fewer and
shorter pauses. But perceived fluency is influenced also by other
factors such as the placement of pauses and the transfer of L1-specific
characteristics of filled pauses to the target language, or more subtly,
by non-use of "authentic" L2 fillers, such as *ben*, *(en)fin* or vowel
lengthening, all used by N47 but not by the two non-native speakers
of French.

3. Retracing

Disfluency may also be marked by repetition of morphemes, words or syntactic groups. In some cases, repetition is clearly a mark of lexical or syntactic difficulty, as in the following example:

(4)   *407: <euh #> [#1_122] <mais [/] mais [/] mais> [#3_798] <il ne veut pas> [/] #0_777 <il ne veut pas> [//] #1_596 il ne peut pas <# &=bouche> [#1_596] tirer le frigo

In other cases, the status of repetition is more ambiguous. Table 2 gives the number of repetitions, both without and with modification, for each of the speakers.

	003A	*025A*	*N01A*	*407A*	*417A*	*N47A*
repetitions	7	0	1	9	12	3
modifications	4	0	2	5	2	1
total	11	0	3	14	14	4
/ 100 words	14.3	0	5.8	15.2	17.1	4.8

Table 2. Retracing, without and with modification.

Although there is a general tendency for more fluent speakers to produce fewer repetitions, these variations are considerably blurred by individual differences. Speaker 417, for example, who is more proficient in L2 French than speaker 407, nevertheless produces a greater number of repetitions. Similarly, both of the native speakers produce more repetitions than the non-native speaker 025.

Given these individual variations, it is perhaps not surprising that repetition and self-correction do not appear to be good predictors of perceived fluency (see, for example, Lennon 1990, Mizera 2006: 53-54). In addition, retracing can have a variety of causes, not all of which are related to disfluency: emphasis, lexical fine-tuning, stylistic improvement, reformulation, backtracking to introduce an afterthought, etc.

There are also practical difficulties in measuring the extent of retracing in oral production. Detecting plain repetition is easy enough, but it is not always so straightforward to identify occurrences of retracing with modification. If a speaker immediately reuses lexical items in a different context, or uses a new lexical item in an apparently similar context, should this be interpreted and transcribed as a continuation or as a modification of an ongoing utterance? As the following example will illustrate, the boundary is not always clear.

(5)   N01: there's a #0_327 crane manoeuvring a fridge up to a window #0_630 trying to er get it in through the window <of the> [//] #0_418 to the apartment <um #> [#1_031] trying to manoeuvre it .

In this extract, there is one clear case of retracing (*the window <of the> [//] #0_418 to the apartment*). Immediate repetition or substitution of closed-class items such as prepositions is usually unambiguous and operates within a syntactic unit. However, the extract also contains repetition of two open-class items: *manoeuvre* and *try*, in the three fragments *manoeuvring a fridge / trying to get it through the window / trying to manoeuvre it*. Should these be considered as "new" non-finite clauses, or as successive attempts to formulate the same thing?

These are not trivial questions, since the decision whether or not code these fragments as retracings will not only affect the overall count of repetitions for a given speaker but also, if repeated items are "pruned" from the word count, will modify the rate of speech. In non-native speech, one might be tempted to see fragments such as *manoeuvring a fridge / trying to get it through the window* as rehearsals for *trying to manoeuvre it*. Mature native speakers do not normally need to rehearse their syntax, although they do often break down complex syntactic structures into simpler units. They also monitor their speech and retrace if they detect inappropriate usage. The example below is a clear case of self-correction, replacing the informal *le gars d'en dessous* ("the guy down below") by the more formal *le monsieur du dessous*.

(6)   N47 : il est cassé et euh <le gars d'en dessous> [//] (en)fin #0_476 le [/] le monsieur du dessous est en train de crier

Similarly, for non-native speakers, the ability to monitor speech and make substitutions smoothly does not necessarily constitute a disfluency. Retracing, like pausing, is clearly a factor in fluency, but quantitative measures of the number of repetitions need to be combined with analysis of the onset of retracing and of whether it concerns lower-level phenomena (*407: c'est le &propri #0_311 &prié [///] #0_491 propriétaire de la voiture; 417: jusqu'à le [///] la fenêtre*) or higher stylistic or discourse-level phenomena (see Kormos 1999; 2000).

4. Automaticity and islands of reliability

A third measure of fluency is to look at what lies between pauses, i.e., the nature of uninterrupted segments or fluent chunks. For the most proficient speakers (the two native speakers and 025), the longest fluent segments contain complete clauses or even combinations of clauses:

(7)   N47: le monsieur du dessous est en train de crier parce qu'il est pas content par rapport à ça

(8)   N01: which is obviously unfortunate for the car owner

(9)   025: and they were trying to catch something heavy I think it was a fridge

For the less proficient speakers, the longest runs constitute progressively more complex but incomplete syntactic fragments, respectively a simple existential clause plus a hedge (*003 : there is a fridge I think*), the end of a clause plus a coordinate clause (*407: propriétaire de la voiture et il a crié*) and the end of a principal clause plus a subordinate clause (*417: voiture qui &=rire était directement en dessous*). One component of fluency is the ability to handle increasing syntactic complexity without obvious processing effort, and to generate continuous chunks that cross clause boundaries. Two main factors seem to contribute to this ability. One is the increasingly skilful application of syntactic rules; the other is the use of multi-word segments which are formulaic in nature (N47: *il est pas content par rapport à ça; N01: which is obviously unfortunate*). Less fluent speakers lack these "islands of reliability" (Dechert 1983), or their islands are so small and far apart that they are not a sufficient basis for alternating smoothly between formulaic and creative speech. This can be seen in recording 003A, where the only apparently formulaic sequence is *I think*. Consequently, even though 003's final utterance is syntactically well-formed, it is produced as a succession of one or two word segments punctuated by pauses:

(10)   *003: and # there is &a another # man # who is # I think # very angry # because # I think # it was # her car .

Another factor which is partially reflected in syntactic complexity is the propositional richness or semantic density of speech production, the second of Fillmore's (2000: 51) four kinds of fluency. Fillmore had in mind a native speaker's ability to articulate complex ideas, but even everyday events have their complexity. This can be seen most clearly in the initial stage of the "fridge" incident, describing the movement of the fridge up towards the window. The event in question has the following six components:

- a moving object (the fridge)
- the process of movement (go, lift, move…)
- the path of movement (up / to),
- a target (the window)
- an instrument (the crane)
- the instigators of the movement (two or three men)

To these can be added two peripheral components: a purpose (take the fridge into the apartment through the window) and a justification (because it is too big to go up the stairs).

The least fluent speakers present each component separately or in minimal associations, sometimes omitting the path and the instrument altogether (003: *I have seen mans who were at the window / and I think it is a remover / and there is a fridge I think / and they try to take the fridge),* while more proficient speakers combine several components into a single structure (N01: *there's a crane manoeuvring a fridge up to a window / trying to er get it in through the window <of the> [///] to the apartment*). From one language to another, the components may be combined in different ways. For example, a verb-framed language such as French (see Talmy 2000, Slobin 2004) will tend to combine movement and path into a single verb (*soulever, amener*) while a satellite-framed language such as English will tend to code the path separately through a preposition (*bring/lift up to*). Thus we have N47: *une grue qui* amène *un: [/] un espèce de (en)fin je crois que c'est un frigo,* compared with N01: *a crane manoeuvring a fridge* up to *a window.* Non-native speakers may not be able to make these choices spontaneously. In L2 French, both 407 and 417 have difficulty making an appropriate lexical choice for the verb and rely more heavily on prepositions:

(11)   407 : et [/] et il veut <euh # um #> [#2_766] apporter le frigo au [//] le [*] premier étage &s par la fenêtre

(12)   417 : #0_621 et on enlève un [/] un &réfr réfrigérateur <# euh #> [#1_783] jusqu'à le [//] la fenêtre .

Conversely, in L2 English, subject 003 chooses not to code the path at all, and even 025, an advanced learner of English, expresses movement and path through a single verb:

(13)   025: so &th the fridge was lifted by #0_308 a crane or whatever it was .

Like phraseological knowledge, the ability to opt for language-specific preferences in coding events helps to reduce processing effort and to improve temporal fluency by avoiding lexical searching. It no doubt also contributes to a greater impression of naturalness, by conforming to the choices made spontaneously by native speakers, and thus enhances perceived fluency.

5. Applications

Corpus-based analysis of fluency has practical applications in the assessment of L2 learners' oral competence. Descriptors such as those used in the Common European Framework often qualify "Can Do" statements with hedges of the type "...even though pauses, false starts and reformulations are very evident" (A2) or "...although he/she can be hesitant as he/she searches for patterns and expressions" (B2). In order to evaluate fluency differences consistently between levels, oral examiners need to know how to interpret these statements, and be able to relate such descriptors to objective criteria, illustrated with concrete examples. This is one of the objectives of the *WebCEF* project,[2] started in late 2006, and which will provide language teachers and learners with online samples of video-recorded oral productions from L2 learners, along with annotations indicating how these samples – initially in L2 English, and subsequently in Dutch, Finnish, French, German and Polish – can be related to the levels of the Common European Framework.

Fluency is only one dimension of overall proficiency in the spoken language, but it is important to be able to distinguish between the hesitations and repetitions that are a normal part of speech production, either in native or accomplished non-native production, and those which are signs of imperfect mastery. Kormos and Dénes (2004: 158) distinguish between low-order fluency (temporal variables) and high-order fluency (accuracy, lexical diversity). This is a useful distinction, and analysis of the samples presented here suggests that syntactic complexity, formulaic knowledge and semantic density are also factors in high-order fluency. A lot of interesting work remains to be done to study the precise nature of the interaction between higher-order fluency and purely temporal factors, and spoken corpora are invaluable in investigating these relations.

6. References

Candea, Maria 2000. *Contribution à l'étude des pauses silencieuses et des phénomènes dits "d'hésitation" en français oral spontané.* Unpublished doctoral dissertation. Université de Paris 3.

---

2   <http://www.webcef.eu/>

Clark, Herbert / Fox Tree, Jean 2002. Using *uh* and *um* in spontaneous speaking. *Cognition,* 84, 73-111.

Council of Europe 2001. *Common European Framework of Reference for Languages: Learning, Teaching, Assessment.* Cambridge: Cambridge University Press.

Cucchiarini, Catia / Strik, Helmer / Boves, Lou 2002. Quantitative assessment of second language learners' fluency: Comparisons between read and spontaneous speech. *Journal of the Acoustical Society of America,* 111/6, 2862-2873.

Dechert, Hans 1983. How a story is done in a second language. In Faerch, Claus / Kasper, Gabriele (eds) *Strategies in Interlanguage Communication.* London: Longman, 175-195.

Dechert, Hans / Raupach, Manfred (eds) 1980. *Temporal Variables in Speech.* The Hague: Mouton.

Fillmore, Charles 2000. On fluency. In Riggenbach, Heidi. *Perspectives on Fluency*, Ann Arbor: University of Michigan Press, 43-60. First published in Fillmore, Charles *et al.* (eds) 1979. *Individual Differences in Language Ability and Language Behavior.* New York: Academic Press 85-101.

Freed, Barbara / Segalowitz, Norman / Dewey, Dan 2004. Context of learning and second language fluency in French: Comparing regular classroom, study abroad, and intensive domestic immersion programs. *Studies in Second Language Acquisition,* 26/2, 275-301.

Freed, Barbara 2000. Is fluency, like beauty, in the eyes (and ears) of the beholder? In Riggenbach, Heidi (ed.) *Perspectives on Fluency.* Ann Arbor: University of Michigan Press, 243-265.

Griffiths, Roger 1991. Pausological research in an L2 context: A rationale, and review of selected studies. *Applied Linguistics,* 12, 345-364.

Housen, Alex 2002. A corpus-based study of the L2-acquisition of the English verb system. In Granger, Sylviane / Hung, Joseph / Petch-Tyson, Stephanie (eds) *Computer Learner Corpora, Second Language Acquisition and Foreign Language Teaching.* Amsterdam: Benjamins, 77-116.

Kormos, Judit 1999. Monitoring and self-repair in L2. *Language Learning,* 49/2, 303-342.

Kormos, Judit 2000. The timing of self-repairs in second language speech production. *Studies in Second Language Acquisition,* 22, 145-167.

Kormos, Judit / Dénes, Mariann 2004. Exploring measures and perceptions of fluency in the speech of second language learners. *System,* 32, 145-164.

Lennon, Paul 1990. Investigating fluency in EFL: A quantitative approach. *Language Learning,* 40/3, 387-417.

MacWhinney Brian. 2000. *The CHILDES Project: Tools for Analyzing Talk.* Mahwaw NJ: Lawrence Erlbaum.

Mizera, Gregory 2006. *Working Memory and L2 Oral Fluency.* Unpublished PhD dissertation, University of Pittsburgh.

Myles, Florence / Mitchell, Rosamund 2004. Using information technology to support empirical SLA research. *Journal of Applied Linguistics,* 2, 169-196.

Myles, Florence 2005. Interlanguage corpora and SLA research. *Second Language Research,* 21/4, 373-391.

Rieger, Caroline 2003. Disfluencies and hesitation strategies in oral L2 tests. *Proceedings of DiSS'03. Gothenburg Papers in Theoretical Linguistics,* 90, 41-44.

Riggenbach, Heidi 1991. Towards an understanding of fluency: A microanalysis of non-native speaker conversations. *Discourse Processes,* 14, 424-41.

Riggenbach, Heidi (ed.) 2000. *Perspectives on Fluency.* Ann Arbor: University of Michigan Press.

Slobin, Dan 2004. The many ways to search for a frog: Linguistic typology and the expression of motion events. In Strömqvist, Sven / Verhoeven, Ludo (eds) *Relating Events in Narrative: Vol 2. Typological and Contextual Perspectives.* Mahwah, NJ: Lawrence Erlbaum, 219-257.

Talmy, Leonard 2000. *Toward a Cognitive Semantics. Vol II: Typology and Process in Concept Structuring.* Cambridge MA: MIT Press.

Towell, Richard / Hawkins, Roger / Bazergui, Nives 1996. The development of fluency in advanced learners of French. *Applied Linguistics,* 17, 84-19.

Appendix: transcriptions of the samples

For the recording and transcription of data, thanks are due to other members of the *PAROLE* project, in particular Heather Hilton and Marie-Jo Derive.

The following conventions are used in the transcription : # pause (followed by duration of the pause in ms); [*] non-target form; [/] retracing ; [//] retracing with modification; < > is a scoping symbol, indicating that the following symbol applies to everything within the angle brackets; @s marks use of a language other than the target language (usually the learner's L1); &=rire and &=bouche respectively indicate laughter and sounds made with the mouth, most frequently lip noises.

For a full description of *CHAT* conventions, see MacWhinney (2000) or the regularly updated pdf manual, available on the *CHILDES* website.[3]

Recording 003A

*003:   yes <e:r #> [#1_754] I [/] <I have seen <u:m # &=bouche> [#1_501] a: few> [//] #2_127 I have seen <um &=bouche #> [#1_575] mans [*] <e:r # &=bouche> [#3_221] who were <u:m # &=bouche> [#1_607] er at the window ↑ .

*003:   #0_657 and <er #> [#0_828] I think <er #> [#1_242] it is a: [/] #0_779 a mover [*] [//] #0_536 a remover [*] #0_926 +...

*003:   u:h <je@s sais@s pas@s> ["] .

*003:   #1_250 and <e:r #> [#1_510] there is a fridge I think .

*003:   #0_568 and <e:r #> [#1_778] they: [/] they try <u:h #> [#1_761] to [/] <u:m #> [#2_110] to take [*] er the fridge ↑ .

*003:   &=bouche but <e:r #> [#1_964] he [*] <e:r # &=bouche> [#2_354] &=laugh [/] #1_2 bu:t [/] <e:r #> [#4_123] but the [/] the fridge <e:r #> [#3_553] fallen [*] [//] #0_812 non@s [//] +/.

*INV: mm .

*003:   +, falls <er # &=bouche> [#1_267] e:r on e:r a car ↑ .

*003:   &=bouche and <u:m #> [#1_875] there is &a another [*] #0_935 man <uh #> [#2_257] u:h who is uh I think uh very angry [*] #0_910 because <uh #> [#0_893] I think <uh #> [#0_917] it was <e:r #> [#1_022] her [*] car ↑ .

*INV: #1_436 okay .

Recording 025A

*025:   okay #0_278 0det first [*] thing I saw #0_163 in the video was a big white building .

*025:   #0_145 and um inside that building #0_163 there was a window with two or three people inside .

*025:   #0_604 0subj can't [*] remember I think it was two

*025:   #0_540 and they were trying to catch [*] something heavy I think it was a fridge

*025:   <&=bouche # um> [#1_167] so &th the fridge was lifted by #0_308 a crane or whatever it was .

*025:   &=bouche but they didn't manage to catch it .

*025:   #0_621 and in the end uh the: fridge f:ell #1_132 on a car &=rire .

*INV: oh dear !

*025:   and I think # the car's owner was screaming .

*025:   +^ he was um raising his hands and he was um screaming +"/.

*025:   +" what happened to my car ?

*INV: +< oh god !

*025:   he was mad .

*INV: +< yeah ?

*025:   and that's it &=rire !

*INV: www .

Recording N01A

*N01:   yes #0_458 er right <there's a:> [/] <oh &=rire &=bouche> [#1_613] there's a #0_327 crane manoeuvring a fridge up to a window .

*N01:   #0_630 trying to er get it in through the window <of the> [//] #0_418 to the apartment <um #> [#1_031] trying to manoeuvre it .

*N01:   but <um #> [#1_080] it [//] the: er link broke and it fell on a car.

*N01:   <# um # > [#2_529] which is obviously unfortunate for the car owner but &=rire +...

*INV: +< &=rire

*INV: ok

Recording 407A

*407:   oui um #0_844 il 0*y a [*] #0_532 une [*] #0_475 ascenseur [*] &=rires ascenseur [*] qu'il [*] apporte <une [*] frigo> [//] <un &f> [//] un frigo .

*407:   #0_450 et [/] et il veut <euh # um #> [#2_766] apporter le frigo au [//] le [*] premier étage &s par la fenêtre.

*407:   <# euh> [#0_818] mais aussi il y a deux personnes qui <euh #> [#3_345] [/-]
        <je sais pas comment> ["] euh il y a deux personnes pour [/] <euh #>
        [#1_604] pour [/] <euh # &=rire> [#2_857] pour euh ressoir +/.
*INV: oui.
*407:   +, ressoir [*] le frigo .
*INV: um um .
*407:   <euh #> [#1_122] <mais [/] mais [/] mais> [#3_798] <il ne veut pas> [/]
        #0_777 <il ne veut pas> [//] #1_596 il ne peut pas <# &=bouche> [#1_596]
        tirer le frigo et [/] et après le [/] le frigo tomber [*] euh sur une voiture .
*407:   et [/] et <euh #> [#1_179] peut+être c'est le &propri #0_311 &prié [//]
        #0_491 propriétaire de la voiture et il a crié .
*INV: <très bien> [/] très bien .

Recording 417A

*417:   j'ai [/] j'ai entendu euh cet événement c'est un [/] c'est un déménagement .
*417:   <# euh> [#1_207] au <euh # > [#1_121] j'ai oublié le: [/] #0_308 le premier
        ou [/] ou deuxième étage .
*417:   #0_621 et on enlève un [/] un &réfr réfrigérateur <# euh #> [#1_783] jusqu'à
        le [//] la fenêtre .
*417:   et <euh #> [#1_521] il y a deux hommes euh dedans .
*417:   <# um # &= bouche> [#2_682] et <ils ont> [/] ils ont essayé de [/] de saisir la
        [/] la [*] &fr [//] réfrigérateur mais ils [/] ils ont échoué .
*417:   et euh #0_406 le réfrigéreur [*] est tombé #0_303 et il a frappé un [/] un [*]
        voiture qui &=rire était directement en dessous .
*417:   <euh #> [#0_697] et a écrasé le [/] le toit de [/] de la voiture .

Recording N47A

*N47:   euh donc on voit en fait une [/] une grue qui euh amène un: [/] un espèce de
        (en)fin je crois que c' est un frigo .
*N47:   et euh il y a des gens qui sont à la fenêtre et qui essaient de l' attraper .
*N47:   #0_446 malheureusement #0_337 ça 0ne marche pas et le frigo tombe sur la
        voiture et <euh #> [#0_883] il est cassé &=rire .
*INV: il est cassé ?
*N47:   il est cassé et euh <le gars d' en dessous> [//] (en)fin #0_476 le [/] le
        monsieur du dessous est en train de crier parce qu' il 0n' est pas content par
        rapport à ça

Winnie Cheng

"Sorry to interrupt, but …": Pedagogical Implications of a Spoken Corpus

1. Introduction

Corpora, corpus-analytic tools and corpus evidence have been increasingly used in English language teaching and learning for the last two or three decades (see, for example, Sinclair 1987, 1991, 2004). In English language teaching and English Studies, the potential of corpus-driven research (Tognini Bonelli 1996) to make a significant contribution is vast. "Corpus-driven" research emphasizes that theoretical statements are a product of the evidence from the corpus (Tognini Bonelli 2002: 75). An important application of corpora in language teaching is to focus on the pedagogical application of corpus research findings. Examining the role of corpora in English Studies, Kettermann and Marko (2004) argue that the use of corpora and corpus-analytic techniques helps to strengthen learners' language awareness, in particular their discourse awareness. In other words, students will be able to distinguish more clearly between different types of texts or discourses within the discipline. In addition, corpus data have helped researchers to identify patterning that differs from traditional models of the English language, and have demonstrated the shortcomings of relying solely on intuitive models of language in use. Recent studies comparing English presented in ELT textbooks and English used in natural communicative situations outside of the classroom have, however, found that textbook accounts of language use are often decontextualised and lack an empirical basis (Cheng and Warren 2005, Römer 2005). For example, in their studies of the speech acts of disagreement, and giving an opinion, Cheng and Warren (2005, 2006) conclude that English textbook writers need to incorporate a wider range of and more accurate forms into their materials in order to better reflect the realities of actual language use.

In Hong Kong, starting with the 1998 school year, English is the medium of instruction in 25% of secondary schools, with the remaining adopting mother-tongue (i.e., Cantonese) teaching (Pan 1999). Altogether 114 schools were allowed to continue with English-medium instruction because of their previous high achievement (Hong Kong Department of Education 1997). English is also the main language of legal statutes, ordinances and the courts, government documentation and, of course, widely used by the Hong Kong business community. In upper secondary schools in Hong Kong, the focus in English language learning is the preparation of students for their future workplaces and tertiary education. Oral English, particularly group discussion, is considered an important skill for the students to master. Nevertheless, a consistent comment made by oral examiners of the Use of English of the Advanced Supplementary Level Examination (2002, 2003 and 2004), a public examination taken by 17/18 year olds in Hong Kong, is that in general candidates are weak in interaction in group discussion. Examiners of the English Language examination of the Hong Kong Certificate of Education Examination also point out that the lack of communication skills and discussion techniques were the reasons for the poor performance of the candidates (HKEAA 2004). As highlighted in examination reports from HKEAA 2000-2004, some ELT textbooks offer misleading and inaccurate descriptions of language use and do not always mirror actual language use, creating problems for foreign language teachers and learners.

2. The teaching of interruption in Hong Kong

Motivated by the comments found in these examiners' reports, the present study sets out to examine the important interactional strategy of "interrupting" someone in group discussion, which is explicitly taught in class in preparation for the examination. According to Sacks,

Schegloff and Jefferson (1974: 706-707), an "interruption" can be of variable size and of various construction unit types, and may occur "by competing self-selectors for a next turn". Schegloff (1987) defines "interruption" as simultaneous talk that does not occur at or near a Transition Relevance Place (TRP), and that occurs when a participant begins to talk when the current speaker is still taking his or her turn-at-talk, but not yet approaching a TRP. In contrast to simultaneous talk that involves the apparent violation of the rules of the turn-taking system (i.e., interruption), another type of simultaneous speech, "overlap", is resultant from participants' orientation to those rules. "Overlap" can arise in several ways: premature self-selection related to the upcoming TRP, occurring in conjunction with the current TRP, self-selection at the same time as the current speaker elects to continue (Sacks, Schegloff and Jefferson 1974). This type of simultaneous talk occurs within a syllable or two of the TRP where interactional participants are entitled to take turns.

The present study argues that "interrupting", as used in Hong Kong English language textbooks, is a less than satisfactory term to be used, and instead, suggests that "simultaneous talk" should be used (Cheng 2003). "Simultaneous talk" encompasses "interruptions" and "overlaps" as used in the literature, which have very often been used for various meanings, and have been subjected to a range of interpretations, as well as laden with value judgement (West and Zimmerman 1983, Houtkoop and Mazeland 1985, Murray 1985, Thomas 1985, Schiffrin 1986, Goldberg 1990, Nofsinger 1991, Makri-Tsilipakou 1994, Tannen 1994).

3. Aim of study

When examining what is taught in some English language textbooks used in secondary schools in Hong Kong, the author felt that many of the examples of spoken language forms were not an accurate reflection of real-world language use. Mindful of Trudgill's (1996: xii) insightful comment that "in the final analysis if linguistics is not about language as it is actually being spoken and written by human beings, then it is about nothing at all", the author decided to put her opinion regarding textbook contents to the test. The present study reviews what school textbooks in Hong Kong say about "interrupting" others and compares the findings with how intercultural speakers in a variety of communicative contexts and discourses in Hong Kong "interrupt" their interlocutors, namely which group of speakers initiate simultaneous talk (ST) more often, and how ST behaviour compares across the four different domains of use of English, and lastly, what speakers say to initiate ST.

4. Methodology of study

The present study examines 40% of the two-million-word Hong Kong Corpus of Spoken English (HKCSE) (Cheng and Warren 2000, Cheng, Greaves and Warren 2005), primarily between Hong Kong Chinese (HKC) and native English speakers (NES) of English, to determine the ways in which the "simultaneous talk" strategies are linguistically realised in real-life communication, and compares the findings with the forms that are taught to students in school textbooks. All of the participants in the HKCSE were monitored in terms of place of birth, age, gender, occupation, educational background, time spent living or studying overseas (for the HKC) and mother tongue (Cantonese in the case of the HKC participants). Importantly, the HKCSE is not a learner corpus, but rather it is comprised of competent speakers of English communicating in the kinds of typical intercultural contexts which account for much, if not most, of the English spoken in today's world. The four sub-corpora represent the main overarching spoken genres found in the Hong Kong context: academic discourse (lectures, seminars, supervisions, student presentations, telephone interviews etc.), business discourse (meetings, service encounters, workplace presentations, job and placement interviews, informal office talk, etc.), conversation (conversations recorded in restaurants, pubs, cafés, homes etc.) and public discourse (public speeches (followed by Q&A), forum discussions, radio and television broadcasts, press briefings (followed by Q&A), etc.).

Table 1 describes the data for this study, which consist of 778,018 words, spoken by 686 HKC, 223 NES, and 33 Other Speakers whose mother-tongue is neither Cantonese nor English. Considering only the HKC and NES groups, HKC speak 75.5% of the words and NES 24.5%. Table 1 also shows the number of words across the four sub-corpora, with more or less equal proportion of words in the academic, conversational and public sub-corpora, and a much smaller business sub-corpus.

Sub-corpora	No. of Words	No. of HKC	No. of NES	No. of Other Speakers
Academic	204,700 (26.3%)	216	19	3
Business	131,022 (16.8%)	181	84	9
Conversation	229,187 (29.5%)	109	79	11
Public	213,109 (27.4%)	180	41	10
Total	778,018 (100%)	686	223	33

Table 1. Data set for the study.

The HKCSE was interrogated using the software iConc© [1] (see Cheng, Greaves, and Warren 2005 for more details) to determine the frequency of occurrences of instances of ST, both their overall usage, as well as the relative usages by the two groups of speakers and across the four sub-corpora. In the prosodically transcribed component of the HKCSE, ST was marked up with a double asterisk '**'. Figure 1 shows some concordance lines in the conversation sub-corpus generated by iConc©.

---

[1]   iConc© is designed and written by Chris Greaves, Senior Project Fellow at The Hong Kong Polytechnic University, specifically to interrogate the HKCSE.

1   ** { = a̲ [^ PART] time < JOB > } { \ [^ BOTH] <
2   a3:   ** { / < Mhm > }   ** { = a̲ < LONG > } a3:   { / < UH > huh } a3:
3   ME] poSItions < FInish > } a3: ** { = a̲ very < POpular > } { \ < Area > } a3:   { = [
4   ** a̲: { \ < MM > mm } a: { \ < MM > mm } a: { \ <

5   ** { \ < YEAH > }   ** { = [ACtually] < I > }   ** { = < I > like
6   oing < THAT > } ((laugh)) a3: ** { = actually < I M > } { = i m not [QUITE] famil
7   to } a2:   ** { \ < ^ ACtually > } { \ lok fu is [NOT] that FA
8   ** { = < ^ ACtually > } { = < ER > } { \ there s [ON
9   ** { \ < _ YEAH > } a3:   ** { \ [AH] oKAY > } a2:   ** { \ < MM > } {
10 > } { = < THAT > } a3:   ** { ? ah } (.) { / [MORE] than < TEN > } ((laugh))

Figure 1. A sample of concordance lines showing simultaneous talk (ST).

5. Textbook findings

A survey of fifteen English language textbooks used in the upper forms in Hong Kong schools has shown that eleven of them (Appendix 1) teach interruptions in group discussions explicitly, with varying focuses and space devoted to the topic. Generally, the textbooks contain materials about when and how to interrupt others, how to deal with interruptions, as well as what to say to interrupt others and to return to the original point after being interrupted. One textbook writer, however, seems to give contradictory advice: Potter (2003a: 40) remarks that "In a real discussion, interrupting is natural – people don't always wait for others to finish talking", but in Potter (2003b: 39), the writer cautions students, and teachers: "Remember you should wait until the speaker has paused before interrupting – never interrupt while someone is actually saying something". Duncan and Sutton (1999) equate "not interrupting unnecessarily" to saying "something relevant when another candidate has finished speaking". They present interrupting others as someone's effectiveness in turn-taking, although they have mistakenly placed interrupting, which involves the apparent violation of the rules of the turn-taking system (Sacks, Schegloff and Jefferson 1974), on a par with Sacks's (1971,

1992) observation in American English conversation that "at least and not more than one party talks at a time".

Some textbooks point out the "rude" nature of interruptions and suggest that interrupting someone "can be done politely" (Potter 2003a: 49, Potter 2003b: 5). Interrupting others will "lose marks and may get a warning from the examiner" but still candidates should stand up for their own rights (Free Press 2002: 58). Other books suggest that interrupting others is appropriate verbal behaviour if someone is "an aggressive candidate" (Esser 2003: 10), "dominating the discussion" (Potter 2003b: 5), and "speaking unreasonably long or for a long time" (Li and Leetch 2003: 28), or after "someone interrupts inappropriately" (Lee and Holzer 1999: 96). Regarding knowing when to interrupt, Potter's (2003a: 49) suggestions are at the end of a complete thought, at the end of a sentence, and during a silent hesitation. These suggestions are, nevertheless, either unclear or wrong, as discussed above, confusing legitimate turn-taking, turn-holding and turn-yielding with "interruption" (Sacks, Schegloff and Jefferson 1974).

The functions of interruptions described in the eleven textbooks can be summarised as follows: to interrupt someone who has been dominating the discussion and preventing others from speaking; to check that you understand what someone is saying; to clarify a point that seems unclear; to ask for an explanation as you do not understand what the others are saying; to clarify yourself as you think others have misunderstood you or are ignoring you; to stop repetitive or irrelevant discussion, and move on to a new point; to keep your turn after someone interrupts inappropriately; and when you think two of the other candidates have misunderstood each other (Duncan 1994, 2001, Duncan and Sutton 1999, Esser 1999, 2003, Lee and Holzer 1999, Free Press 2002, Li and Leetch 2003, Potter 2003a, 2003b,).

A range of language forms are introduced in the textbooks. There are the conventional politeness markers, "Excuse me", "Sorry" and "I am sorry", to apologise for interrupting someone, as follows:

> *Excuse me.*
> *Excuse me, but ...*
> *Excuse me, I'd just like to finish this point ...*
> *Excuse me, I'd like to make a point ...*

Excuse me, perhaps we can hear Miss X's opinion. Miss X, do you have any other suggestions?
Excuse me, if I could jump in her, I think ...
Excuse me, may I say something here?
Excuse me, Mr X, can I say something here?

Sorry, (name), but ...
Sorry to interrupt.
Sorry to interrupt, but ...
Sorry to interrupt, I think ...
Sorry, can i come in here?
Sorry, may I interrupt here?
Sorry, but I don't quite understand.
Sorry, but I'm not with you.
Sorry could you say that again, please?
Sorry, would you mind explaining that again, please?
Sorry Miss Y, we haven't heard from Miss M yet, shall we ask for her opinion? Miss M, what do you think?
I'm sorry, but can I get a word in /say something?
I'm sorry, but the rest of us would like to speak.

Just a moment, ...
By the way ... (to change the subject)

There are then interrogative requests, the negative politeness strategy "conventionalised indirectness" (Brown and Levinson 1987: 132) to effectively ask to be allowed to interrupt someone, as follows:

Can I just break in there?
Can I have a turn?
Could I just finish my point first?

Interrupting others can also be linguistically realised by using conditionals, another realisation of negative politeness (Brown and Levinson 1987: 135-6), as follows:

If I could just say something ...
If I could just come in here ...
If I could just say something ...

Another way of interrupting someone is by the speaker verbalising his or her mental process of 'wanting' to 'say something', with the politeness marker "please", as in the following:

> *I want to say something, please.*

The speaker can also verbalise the mental process of 'thinking', giving his or her opinion that interrupting the dominant current speaker is called for, namely:

> *I think we are losing balance here. Everyone is supposed to be joining in.*

Another way of interrupting someone is to begin the turn with discourse particles such as "well", "O.K.", or "actually", as follows:

> *Well, O.K. – let's see what everyone else has to say about it.*
> *Well, I know it doesn't say that, but don't you think …*
> *O.K. Look, I don't think we're going to agree on this.*
> *OK. Shall we talk about how we are going to organize our arguments now?*
> *Actually, I'm not with you. Could you please repeat what you said?*
> *Actually, that reminds me …*

According to Stenström (1994: 67), "well" can function as an <uptake>, accepting what was said and leading on, or a <staller> that plays on time; and "OK" can be a <frame> to mark a boundary in the discourse, an <answer> to a question or request, or an <appealer> to invite feedback. Cheng and Warren (2001) identify five functions of "actually" when used as a discourse particle, namely to mitigate correction, rephrasing or contradiction, to introduce a new topic or sub-topic, to act as a filler, to introduce or mitigate a point of view, and to imply a sense of solidarity, friendliness and intimacy.

Some textbooks also teach what to say when being interrupted, as follows:

> *As I was saying …*
> *To return to my point.*
> *To get back to what I was just saying*
> *Going back to what I was saying …*

6. HKCSE simultaneous talk findings

Analysis of the 778,018 words in the HKCSE has produced 12,016 instances of ST (Table 2). When the number of occurrences of ST is compared with the relative sizes of the four sub-corpora, it is found that ST occurs most frequently in conversation (58.32%), followed by business (22.44%) and public discourse (12.81%). In academic discourse, ST rarely occurs (only 6.43%). In the HKCSE, group discussions occur in the form of academic tutorials, broadcast forum discussions, and organisational meetings. The findings have therefore shown that ST is a highly common phenomenon in everyday social interaction, i.e., conversation, and much more so than in other text-types with different contexts of situation.

HKCSE Sub-corpora	HKC as initiator of ST	NES as initiator of ST	Other Speakers as initiator of ST	Total number of occurrences of ST
Academic (26.3%)	600	101	72	773 (6.43%)
Business (16.8%)	2,046	641	9	2,696 (22.44%)
Conversation (29.5%)	3,768	2,865	374	7,007 (58.32%)
Public (27.4%)	1,454	66	20	1,540 (12.81%)
Total (100%)	7,868	3,673	475	12,016 (100%)

Table 2. Number of occurrences of ST initiated by HKC and NES.

Then the HKCSE data set was searched in terms of the language forms that the Hong Kong school textbooks teach. Table 3 shows that the total number of occurrences of ST is 557 (4.64%), out of 12,016 recorded in the data set. In other words, 11,459 (95.36%) of the ST instances are not initiated by any of the language forms taught in the textbooks.

Language form	Academic	Business	Conver-sation	Public	Total
Excuse me.	0	1	2	0	3
Sorry.	2	3	0	0	5
I'm sorry.	0	1	0	0	1
Just a moment,...	0	0	0	0	0
Well ...	3	11	81	37	132
O.K. / Okay	36	188	131	39	394
Well, O.K.	0	0	1	0	1
Actually	2	8	10	1	21
As I was saying ...	0	0	0	0	0
By the way ...	0	0	0	0	0
Can I just break in there?	0	0	0	0	0
Can I have a turn?	0	0	0	0	0
Could I just finish my point first?	0	0	0	0	0
If I could just say something ...	0	0	0	0	0
If I could just come in here ...	0	0	0	0	0
I want to say something, please.	0	0	0	0	0
I think we are losing balance here.	0	0	0	0	0
To return to my point.	0	0	0	0	0
To get back to what I was just saying.	0	0	0	0	0
Going back to what I was saying.	0	0	0	0	0
Total	43	212	225	77	557

Table 3. Number of occurrences of simultaneous talk in the HKCSE.

The most interesting finding is that the most frequently-occurring forms are discourse particles which serve as "complementary acts" (Stenström 1994: 37): "OK/Okay" (394 times), "Well" (132 times), and the infrequent "Actually" (20 times). Another finding is that contrary to what textbooks say, the numbers of occurrences of politeness markers of apology "Excuse me", "Sorry" and "I am sorry" are negligible, with only five instances of "Sorry", 3 instances of "Excuse me", and one instance of "I'm sorry". All of the other suggested language forms do not occur at all in the data set examined.

The two most frequently occurring language forms, "Well" and "Okay", are then examined, across the four sub-corpora spoken by the HKC, NES, and Other Speakers, in relation to the relative sizes of the four sub-corpora. Table 4 shows that the ST introduced by "Well" and "OK/Okay" occur most frequently in conversation (40.31%) and business discourse (37.83%), even though the latter constitutes only 16.8% of the data set. The percentage of occurrence is comparatively low for public discourse (14.44%), and 7.42% in academic discourse.

Language Form	Academic (26.3%)	Business (16.8%)	Conversation (29.5%)	Public (27.4%)	Total (100%)
Well ...	3 (2.27%)	11 (8.3%)	81 (61.4%)	37 (28.03%)	132 (100%)
O.K./Okay	36 (9.14%)	188 (47.72%)	131 (33.24%)	39 (9.9%)	394 (100%)
Total	39 (7.42%)	199 (37.83%)	212 (40.31%)	76 (14.44%)	526 (100%)

Table 4. Number of occurrences of 'Well' and 'OK/Okay' across four sub-corpora.

7. Conclusions and recommendations

A few tentative conclusions can be drawn. First of all, the value of a corpus-driven study has been demonstrated and confirmed. Second, some Hong Kong school textbooks do not seem to provide a proper view about the function of the interactional strategy of "interruptions", and in particular many adopt a negative view about interrupting others and being interrupted. Third, many of the language forms taught in the textbooks are not an accurate reflection of real-world language use. The textbooks contain language forms that are rarely, if ever, used in the real world and are overly influenced by academic genres. The study shows that the most common forms found in the HKCSE are syntactically simpler than those in the textbooks. Fourth, all the textbooks focus too narrowly on the use of "interruptions" in the context of simulated group discussion, and have hence ignored other, and more, prevalent contexts of interaction.

In order to provide effective English language education and promote effective communicative competence among learners, it is important that textbook writers and teachers alike use teaching materials which better reflect the realities of actual language use, and so enhance learners' language awareness. Greater attention needs to be given to real-world language use when exemplifying "interruptions" and, if space is limited, the most frequently occurring interruption markers should feature prominently in the textbooks. Corpora, such as the HKCSE, will be very useful resources for contextualized examples and teaching materials. It is not enough for the textbooks just to list out the language forms. Rather, any language forms should be contextualized for the purposes of validity and authenticity, and more importantly, meaningful interaction and exchange between speakers that take place in naturally occurring situations that learners can relate to, both currently and in future. It is also important to help learners to increase their awareness of the great variety of communicative functions served by "interrupting" others in different contexts of interaction, for instance, in social conversation, classroom interaction, during someone's speech presentation, in a meeting, a service encounter, and so on. This study also argues for the use of the neutral term "simultaneous talk", which is free from any value judgement (Cheng 2003). Finally, assessing learners' compe-tence in using interactional strategies such as "interrupting" others should imply assessing student performance against language as it is actually spoken, rather than against the intuitive notions of examiners and textbook writers.

Future research studies need to look at both the wider and the immediate context of interaction, including the intent, the cultural meaning of the genre, distance, status and power relations of the participants. In addition, examining a much larger corpus and a wide range of text types would increase the extent to which the conclusions drawn from the research can be generalised. All of the 12,016 instances of ST in the HKCSE can be examined to address the research purpose of the study comprehensively to investigate the sub-genres in the academic, business and public sub-corpora, and to describe what speakers in the sub-genres say to initiate ST, apart from "OK" and "Well".

Acknowledgements

The work described in this paper was substantially supported by a grant from the Research Grants Council of the Hong Kong Special Administrative Region (Project No. PolyU 5374/03H).

8. References

Brown, Penelope / Levinson, Stephen C. 1987. *Politeness. Some Universals in Language Usage.* Cambridge: Cambridge University Press.
Cheng, Winnie 2003. *Intercultural Conversation.* Amsterdam: John Benjamins.
Cheng, Winnie / Warren, Martin 2000. The Hong Kong Corpus of Spoken English: Language Learning through Language Description. In Burnard, Lou / McEnery, Tony (eds) *Rethinking Language Pedagogy from a Corpus Perspective.* Frankfurt am Main: Peter Lang, 133-144.
Cheng, Winnie / Warren, Martin 2001. The Functions of *Actually* in a Corpus of Intercultural Conversations. *International Journal of Corpus Linguistics*, 6/2, 257-280.
Cheng, Winnie / Warren, Martin 2005. // → well I have a DIFferent // ↘ THINking you know //: A Corpus-driven Study of Disagreement in Hong Kong Business Discourse. In Bargiela-

Chiappini, Francesca / Gotti, Maurizio (eds) *Asian Business Discourse(s)*. Frankfurt am main: Peter Lang, 241-270.

Cheng, Winnie / Warren, Martin 2006. I Would Say be Very Careful of …: Opine Markers in an Intercultural Business Corpus of Spoken English. Bamford, Julia / Bondi, Marina (eds) *Managing Interaction in Professional Discourse. Intercultural and Interdiscoursal Perspectives*. Rome: Officina Edizioni, 46-58.

Cheng, Winnie / Greaves, Chris / Warren, Martin 2005. The Creation of a Prosodically Transcribed Intercultural Corpus: The Hong Kong Corpus of Spoken English (Prosodic). *International Computer Archive of Modern English (ICAME) Journal*, 29, 47-68.

Goldberg, Julia A. 1990. Interrupting the Discourse in Interruptions: An Analysis in Terms of Relationally Neutral, Power- and Rapport-oriented Acts. *Journal of Pragmatics*, 15, 883-903.

Hong Kong Department of Education. (September, 1997). *Medium of Instruction Guidance for Secondary Schools*. Hong Kong SAR.

Hong Kong Examinations and Assessment Authority. (2002, 2003, 2004). *Examination Reports, Advanced Supplementary Level Use of English Oral Examination*. Hong Kong SAR: HKEAA.

Hong Kong Examinations and Assessment Authority (2000, 2001, 2002, 2003, 2004). *English Language (Syllabus A)*. Hong Kong SAR: HKEAA.

Houtkoop, Hanneke / Mazeland, Harrie 1985. Turns and Discourse Units in Everyday Conversation. *Journal of Pragmatics*, 9, 595-619.

Kettemann, Bernhard / Georg, Marko 2004. Can the L in TALC Stand for Literature?. In Aston, Guy / Bernardini, Silvia / Stewart, Dominic (eds) *Corpora and Language Learners*. Amsterdam: Benjamins, 169-93.

Makri-Tsilipakou, Marianthi 1994. Interruption Revisited: Affiliative vs. Disaffiliative Intervention. *Journal of Pragmatics*, 21, 401-426.

Murray, Stephen O. 1985. Toward a Model of Members' Methods for Recognizing Interruptions. *Language in Society*, 14/, 31-40.

Nofsinger, Robert E. 1991. *Everyday Conservation*. Newbury Park, California: Sage.

Pan, S. 1999. Bilingual policy change in Hong Kong and its impact on bilingual education. Paper presented at Symposium on

Bilingualism and Biliteracy through Schooling, Long Island University, Brooklyn, N.Y.

Römer, Ute 2005. *Progressives, Patterns, Pedagogy. A Corpus-driven Approach to Progressive Forms, Functions, Contexts and Didactics.* Amsterdam: Benjamins.

Sacks, Harvey 1971. Unpublished lecture notes. 1992. *Lectures on Conversation. Vols. I-II.* Jefferson, Gail (ed.) Cambridge: Blackwell.

Sacks, Harve / Schegloff, Emanuel A. / Jefferson, Gail 1974. A Simplest Systematics for the Organization of Turn-taking for Conversation. *Language.* 50/4, 696-735.

Schegloff, Emanuel A. 1987. Recycled Turn Beginnings: A Precise Repair Mechanism in Conversation's Turn-taking Organization. In Button, Graham / Lee, John R. E. (eds) *Talk and Social Organization.* Clevedon, England: Multilingual Matters, 70-85.

Schiffrin, Deborah 1986. Turn-initial Variation: Structure and Function in Conversation. In Sankoff, David (ed.) *Diversity and Diachrony*, Amsterdam: John Benjamins, 367-380.

Sinclair, John McH. 1987. The nature of the evidence. In Sinclair, J. McH. (ed.) *Looking Up: An Account of the COBUILD Project in Lexical Computing.* London: Collins, 150-159.

Sinclair, John McH. 1991. *Corpus Concordance Collocation.* Oxford: Oxford University Press.

Sinclair, John McH. 2004. (eds) *How to Use Corpora in Language Teaching.* Amsterdam: Benjamins.

Stenström, Anna-Britta 1994. *An Introduction to Spoken Interaction.* London and New York: Longman.

Tannen, Deborah 1994. *Gender and Discourse.* New York: Oxford University Press.

Thomas, Jenny 1985. The Language of Power: Towards a Dynamic Pragmatics. *Journal of Pragmatics*, 9, 765-783.

Tognini-Bonelli, Elena 1996. *Corpus Theory and Practice.* Birmingham: TWC Monographs.

Tognini-Bonelli, Elena 2002. Functionally Complete Units of Meaning across English and Italian: Towards a Corpus-driven Approach. In Altenberg, Bengt / Granger, Sylviane (eds) *Lexis in Contrast: Corpus-based Approaches.* Amsterdam: John Benjamins, 73-96.

Trudgill, Peter 1996. Series Editor's Preface. In Stubbs, Michael. *Text and Corpus Analysis: Computer-assisted Studies of Language and Culture*. Oxford; Cambridge, Mass: Blackwell, xi-xii.

West, Candace / Zimmerman, Don 1983. Small Insults: A Study of Interruptions in Cross-sex Conversations between Unacquainted Persons. In Thorne, Barrie (ed.) *Language, Gender and Society.* Cambridge, Mass.: Newbury House, 102-117.

Appendix

Duncan, J. 1994. *Expression: Oral Practice for AS-level*. Hong Kong: Precise Publications.

Duncan, J. 2001. *Expression: Oral Practice for AS-level*. Hong Kong: Precise Publications.

Duncan, J. and Sutton, M. E. 1999. *Speaking Precisely 2*. Hong Kong: Precise Publications.

Esser, D. 1999. *Teach & Practice: AS-level Oral English for Form 7*. Hong Kong: Pilot Publications.

Esser, D. 2003. *Teach & Practice: AS-level Oral English for Form 6.* Hong Kong: Pilot Publications.

Free Press. 2002. *The Use of English Oral Handbook*. Hong Kong: Free Press.

Lee, I. and Holzer, V. 1999. *Skills Building for AS Use of English*. Hong Kong: Longman.

Li, A. and Leetch, P. 2003b. *Use English! Volume 2*. Hong Kong: Macmillan New Asia.

Potter, J. 2003a. *Steps & Skills - Oral* 6. Hong Kong: Witman.

Potter, J. 2003b *Steps & Skills - Oral 7*. Hong Kong: Witman.

Sutton, M. E. 1999. *Speaking Precisely 1*. Hong Kong: Precise Publications.

SYLVIE DE COCK

Routinized Building Blocks in Native Speaker and Learner Speech: Clausal Sequences in the Spotlight

1. Introduction

Most aspects of human existence are marked by habit and recurrence. The way we use language is no exception to this: we have a tendency to recurrently say again what we have said before. As was noted by Kjellmer (1994: ix), "[t]here is no doubt that natural language has a certain block-like character. Words tend to occur in the same clusters again and again". Over the past two decades, the prevalence of these routinized building blocks has been brought to light in an un-precedented manner by a number of corpus linguistic studies of combinations of words (e.g., Sinclair 1991, Kjellmer 1994, Altenberg 1998, Biber *et al.* 1999, Biber and Conrad 1999, Biber *et al.* 2004, Cortés 2004). These studies have been particularly instrumental in widening the scope of phraseology in that they have demonstrated that beside the psychologically salient but comparatively rare classical idioms with figurative meanings such as *kick the bucket*, which used to lie at the heart of traditional phraseology, there is a large number of recurrent sequences of words, which, even though they have not traditionally been labelled as phraseological and tend to go virtually unnoticed in everyday language because they are not very salient psychologically, can however not be dismissed as uninteresting from a broader phraseological perspective. Although linguists such as Cowie (1999) have convincingly shown that frequency of recurrence is not a criterion for strict phraseological status, it can nevertheless be seen to give us some guarantee that the strings are current in the language variety under study (Fernando 1996). In other words, recurrent sequences of words give us access to what is typical (Stubbs 2002), to the "tendencies in the encoding of text by native speakers" (Béjoint 2000: 216), or in Schmitt and Carter's words (2004: 10) to "the pre-ferred choice". Recurrent sequences of words as typical or preferred ways of saying things or routinized building blocks can directly be related to one of the four components making up Hymes's (1972) communicative competence, "Whether (and to what degree) some-thing is done" or, to put it differently, what is actually performed. As Hymes (1972: 286) points out "[s]omething may be possible, feasible, and appropriate and not occur". He also believes that "[t]he capabili-ties of language users do include some (perhaps unconscious) knowl-edge of probabilities". Recurrent sequences of words can thus also be seen to reflect and to play a major role in idiomaticity taken in the wide sense of Pawley and Syder's (1983: 191) "native-like selection", i.e., "the ability of the native speaker routinely to convey his meaning by an expression that is not only grammatical but also nativelike [...] he selects a sentence that is natural and idiomatic from among a range of grammatically correct paraphrases".

The aim of this paper is to paint a picture of the clausal sequences of words that native speakers and advanced learners of English as a foreign language use as their routinized building blocks in spoken English. The first section provides a description of the data and the method used in the investigation. The paper then sets out to characterise and contrast the preferred clausal sequences in the two corpora used before focusing on some of the major differences between the native speakers' and the learners' repertoire of recurrent sequences conveying attitudinal stance. The paper is rounded off by a concluding section that suggests possible practical implications for English language teaching (ELT).

2. Data and method

The spoken data used in the study consists of a corpus of informal interviews with EFL learners (henceforth NNS corpus) and a comparable control native speaker corpus (henceforth NS corpus). Each corpus totals approximately 100,000 words of interviewee speech: the NS corpus is made up of 117,417 words and the NNS corpus of 90,300 words. The learner spoken corpus is the French-speaking component of the Louvain International Database of Spoken English Interlanguage (LINDSEI). The LINDSEI project was launched in 1995 at the Centre for English Corpus Linguistics, Université catholique de Louvain, as the spoken counterpart of the International Corpus of Learner English (ICLE, Granger 1998). A number of other LINDSEI components have been or are currently being complied: Bulgarian, Chinese, Dutch, German, Greek, Italian, Japanese, Polish, Spanish and Swedish to date. The native speaker corpus is the Louvain Corpus of Native English Conversation (LOCNEC), which was compiled within the framework of De Cock 2003. LOCNEC is actually something of a misnomer as it is made up of informal interviews and not (spontaneous) conversations.

The informal interviews in LINDSEI and LOCNEC are of similar length (approximately 2,000 words of interviewee speech each) and follow the same set pattern: the main body of the interviews takes the form of an informal and open discussion mainly centred around topics such as university life, hobbies, foreign travel or plans for the future, although many different subjects were touched upon when the interviewees introduced them into the conversation. Each interview starts with one of three topics (topic 1: an experience that taught them a lesson, topic 2: a country that impressed them, topic 3: a film or play they liked / disliked), which the students were given a few minutes to choose and think about. This was designed to make the interviewees, and especially the learners, feel at ease. The students were, however, specifically asked not to make any notes as it was intended for the spoken productions to be as spontaneous as possible. Each interview concludes with a short picture-based story-telling activity.

The method used is essentially corpus-driven: native speakers' and learners' routinized building blocks are investigated on the basis of automatically extracted continuous sequences of two-, three-, four-, five- and six-word sequences that recur in identical form at least 12, 6, 4, 3 and 3 times respectively in the NS or NNS corpus. A different frequency threshold was set for each sequence size bearing in mind that the length of recurrent word combinations is inversely related to their frequency (Altenberg 1990). The thresholds were also scaled so that approximately 10%-12% of recurrent sequence types are taken into consideration for each length. Frequency thresholds were adopted mainly because the focus is on routinized building blocks. Following Altenberg (1998), the thresholds are regarded as giving us at least some guarantee that the sequences have some currency in NS and NNS speech and are part of a group's shared repertoire of preferred ways of saying things. They also go some way towards ensuring that the sequences extracted are not the result of local textual repetition. This corpus-driven method can be regarded as particularly well-suited to the study of routinized building blocks, not least because of their familiar, common and psychologically non-salient character, and because there are as yet no comprehensive widely agreed upon lists of preferred ways of saying things.

It is important to point out that studies of learners' routinized building blocks that make use of this recurrent word combination method are rather few and far between (Milton and Freeman 1996, Sugiura 2002, Adolphs and Durow 2004). Unlike most investigations of recurrent sequences in NS and learner speech and writing, our study is not restricted to one specific sequence length (e.g., Biber 2004 focuses on four-word sequences; Adolphs and Durow 2004 concentrate on three-word sequences) and also includes two-word sequences, which have usually been left out because of their sheer number.

Recurrent sequences occurring	Symbol
less than 10 times per 100,000 words (NB: 3-word sequences recur at least 6 times, 4-word sequences at least 4 times, 5- and 6-word sequences at least 3 times)	△
10 to 19 times per 100,000 words	▲
20 to 49 times per 100,000 words	▲ ▲
50 to 74 times per 100,000 words	▲ ▲ ▲
over 74 times per 100,000 words	▲ ▲ ▲ ▲

Table 1. Frequency of recurrence of routinized sequences.

Table 1 above outlines the system that will be used to give an indication of the frequencies with which the sequences can be seen to recur in the corpora.

3. Clausal sequences in NS and NNS speech

A structural analysis of the recurrent sequences yielded after the extraction phase outlined above reveals that the lion's share of the recurrent sequences in the NS and NNS corpora used are clausal. There are just under three times as many sequence types such as *it's very interesting, it was very, it's just a, when you're,* or *and I thought that was* as phrasal sequence types like *quite difficult, off campus, my friends, for about, one of the, a sort of, at the moment, all the time, at the end of the, a lot of people,* and *things like that,* or *quite a lot of.* While some clausal sequences are structurally complete (e.g., *no I don't think so, I went to the States, while I was there, if you know what I mean, I'd like to teach*), the majority are structurally incomplete (approximately 90 % in each corpus) and tend to recur at the beginning of clauses. These findings echo the results of other studies of recurrent sequences (e. g., Altenberg 1998, Biber *et al.* 1999).

3.1. Preferred ways of getting started

Recurrence appears to be essentially a clause initial phenomenon in our corpora of spontaneous speech. High frequency function words such as coordinators tend to cluster recurrently with high frequency 'given', and therefore easily accessible, subject pronouns, high frequency discourse items and verbs (e.g., *be, have, want*) to form recurrent "thematic springboards" (Altenberg 1998: 111) or "light starting points" (Chafe 1987) at the beginning of clauses, a point of considerable planning pressure for the speaker (Biber *et al.* 1999). Speakers appear to use recurrent 'light' thematic springboards as their preferred ways of getting started at points where they have to plan, encode and articulate what they want to say in real time. The high number of thematic springboards that start with the linkwords *and*, *but*, *so*, *because*, or *cos* is in line with the 'clause chaining style' or clause 'add-on strategy' that have been presented as particularly well-suited to the demands of on-line production (Pawley and Syder 1983, Chafe 1987, Altenberg 1984, Biber *et al.* 1999). Loosely chaining single clauses beginning with coordinating conjunctions in a linear fashion enables speakers to plan their clauses more or less independently of each other, thereby reducing the risk of syntactic and communication breakdown. As was pointed out by Biber *et al.* (1999), Altenberg (1984) and Chafe (1982, 1987), although *because*, *cos* and *so* are not technically coordinators, they can be seen to behave as such in spontaneous speech, where they are used to introduce clauses that follow rather than precede and that are loosely connected with main clauses.

A closer inspection of native speakers' and learners' routinized ways of getting started reveals that the learners tend to use a significantly higher number of sequences containing repeats and / or hesitation items (e.g. *I think er* ▲▲, *and er it's* ▲▲, *I I didn't* ▲, *you have to to* ▲, *and it was er* ▲, *if you if you* ▲) than the native speakers. This seems to suggest that, rather unsurprisingly, having to plan a clause in a language other than one's mother tongue increases the planning pressure speakers face at the beginning of a clause, which leads them to use more 'wobbly thematic springboards' than native speakers.

3.2. Interaction and involvement

From a functional point of view (Chafe 1982, 1987, Chafe and Danielewicz 1987, Biber 1988) the majority of the clausal sequences of words favoured by the native and non-native speakers in the corpus are essentially interactional in nature and contribute to the involved character that is typical of informal speech. Many recurrent sequences contain response items, discourse items, first and second person pronouns, private verbs (*think, know, remember*) and / or are used to convey attitudinal stance, i.e., speakers' likes and dislikes, speakers' evaluations of events and personal experiences as well as speakers' wishes and intentions (*I really enjoyed, it was very, I'd like to, I'm hoping to, I don't want to, I wouldn't mind, I'm gonna*) or epistemic stance, i.e., speakers' commitment to the truth of the proposition expressed (*but I think, I don't know if, I can't remember*).

Table 2 lists the non-verbal ingredients that characteristically make up the clausal sequences in the corpora under study. The items that are particularly prevalent in either the NS corpus or the NNS corpus (both in terms of the number of sequence types and in terms of the frequency of these sequences) have been highlighted in bold.

	NS speech	NNS speech
Response items	**yeah,** *oh, well, yes*	**yes,** *well*
Connectors	**cos,** *and, but, so, because*	*and, but, so, because,* **in fact**
Discourse items and adverbs	**you know, I mean, like, sort of, just, really**	*you know, I mean, just, really*
Subjects	*I (we, you)* *it / that / this / there*	*I (we, you)* *it / that / this / there*
Examples of sequences	*oh I; yeah it's, yeah that's right, but I mean; I just thought, we sort of, and I was like, it was like, it's sort of, cos it's, cos I was, you know it's, I mean I've, I just*	*yes that's, well it's, in fact I and in fact, yes but I, in fact it was, because it was, so it was, and there are, yes it's not, well I think*

Table 2. Typical ingredients of clausal sequences in the NS and NNS corpus.

Typical NS sequence types containing the discourse items *you know, I mean, just, sort of* and *like*, which have been shown to be characteristic of informal interactions (Aijmer 2002) are either relatively rare (*I mean, you know*) or non-existent in the NNS spoken data (e.g. there are no types containing *sort of* or *like*). Learners can also be seen to underuse other sequences that contain elements that are typical of informal interactions, namely sequences containing *cos* or *yeah* and sequences containing contracted forms. Note that learners' marked preference for the use of sequences containing *in fact*, sequences which are notably absent from NS sequence types, and the functions the sequences are used to fulfil can be related to transfer from their mother tongue (De Cock 2003).

In short, learners' preferred ways of getting started tend to be less interactional and involved, less informal and more hesitant than native speakers'. This tendency is confirmed by the analysis of the whole set of clausal and phrasal routinized sequences in the two corpora (De Cock 2003 and 2004). Learners' overall greater use of sequences containing hesitation items and repeats, combined with their underuse of informal and interactional sequences such as markers of vagueness (e.g. *and things like that, a bit of a*) or informal quantifying expressions (*loads of, a couple of*) and their tendency to favour some more formal and forceful sequences such as *yes of course, in fact, and so on*, or *for instance / example* (De Cock 2003 and 2004) may well cause them to sound rather formal and detached in informal interactions.

Other studies of recurrent sequences of words in spoken English such as Altenberg (1998) and especially in Biber *et al.* (1999) have highlighted the considerable number of typically interactional recurrent sequence types that are (parts of) questions, typically yes-no question fragments and wh-question fragments (e.g. *how would you, have you got, can I have a, are you going to*). These sequences are very few and far between in our data. Table 3 includes an exhaustive list of these comparatively rare sequences in our corpora.

	NS corpus	NNS corpus
▲	do you know; what else; can I	do you
△	where else did we go; do you know what I mean; have you seen; do you want	how do you say that

Table 3. Recurrent sequence types that are (parts of) questions in the NS and NNS corpus.

Only the sequences *have you seen, do you know, how do you say that* and some instances of *do you want* and *do you* can be regarded as (parts of) genuine questions to speakers' interlocutors. (see examples 1 and 3) The remaining sequences in Table 3 and the remaining instances of *do you want, do you* either occur as part of direct reported questions as in (1) or act as rhetorical questions which enable speakers to carry on talking while thinking about what to say next (example 2) and / or to establish 'rapport' with the interlocutor (*do you know what I mean*). The sequence *how do you say that* explicitly bears witness to learners' encoding problems. It is used as a communication strategy and more specifically as a direct appeal for assistance (Tarone *et al.* 1983).

(1)   <B> [<laughs> because sometimes when I go to when I went last year to Cirencester they told me why <u>do you</u> have this American accent (NNS corpus)

(2)   spaghetti black beans manioc flour . and .. <u>what else</u> did we have .. I can't remember now .. some sort of like potato (NS corpus)

(3)   <B> yes in in Europe or . even in the United States but sometimes you . you realise that eh like for instance human rights are also em .. <u>how do you say that</u> eh <\B>
       <A> violated <\A>
       <B> violated in in in Europe as well <\B> (NNS corpus)

The very limited number of (parts of) questions can directly be related to the type of spoken data used here, i.e., informal interviews. More specifically, it can be related to the fact that interviews, however informal they may be, do not share two of Clark's (1996) typical features of face-to-face conversation, namely self-determination and self-expression. While the free exchange of turns is a fundamental organizing factor of conversations, in interviews the participants do not determine for themselves what actions to take when. Instead of being "locally managed" as in conversations (Lazaraton 1992: 383), the turn-taking system is pre-specified: interviews are organised according to a question-answer format. Besides taking actions as themselves (Clarke's self-expression), the participants in an interview also take actions as 'interviewer' or 'interviewee'. As Fiksdal (1990) points out, the participants have rights and obligations as interviewer or interviewee: the interviewer has the right and obligation to ask questions and the interviewee has the obligation to answer these questions. What these results clearly indicate is that, as was also pointed out by Stubbs and Barth (2003) and Nesi and Basturkmen (2006), recurrent sequences and phraseology (taken in a wide sense) tend be largely genre-sensitive.

4. Attitudinal stance

As was mentioned above, a significant set of routinized clausal sequences convey attitudinal stance in the NS and NNS corpora. A comparison of the frequencies (relative frequencies per 100,000 words) of recurrence of the sequences that are used to express likes, dislikes and evaluations in our corpora and in the spoken component of the British National Corpus that contains spontaneous conversations reveals that most of these sequences tend to be far more frequent in our corpora than in the BNC (e.g. *it was good*: NS corpus 13.626 vs. BNC 1.569; *I really enjoyed*: NS corpus 5 vs. BNC 0.309). The high degree of recurrence of these sequences can arguably to a large extent be seen to stem from the type of data used and in particular to the content of the questions the interviewees were asked (cf. Section 2. above). This seems to suggest that the informal interviews in LINDSEI and LOCNEC appear to lend themselves particularly well to the study of a group of speakers' shared repertoire of preferred ways of expressing likes / dislikes and evaluations.

This section focuses on some of the major differences between interactional clausal sequences used to express likes, dislikes and evaluations in the NS corpus and the NNS corpus.

One of the striking differences that emerges when contrasting native speakers' and learners' preferred ways of conveying attitudinal stance is that while native speakers make use of recurrent sequences with the verbs *LIKE*, *ENJOY* and *LOVE* (NS sequences only: e.g. *I really like* △, *I do like* △, *I love* ▲▲ , *I really enjoy(ed)* ▲, *I enjoy(ed)* it ▲), the learners in the corpus tend to cling to sequences with the verb *LIKE* such as *(yes) I like it* (NNS corpus: ▲▲ vs. NS corpus △). This can be seen to tie in with the more general observation that learners tend to make a repeated use of a smaller stock of preferred ways of saying things that do not contain repeats and / or hesitation items than native speakers (De Cock 2003 and 2004).

A group of recurrent clausal sequences native speakers appear to favour when conveying attitudinal stance are sequences in which the adjective *good* is used predicatively after forms of the verb *BE*.

These sequences are typically used to evaluate a situation or a personal experience considered as 'enjoyable' as in examples (4) to (6). While there are ten different recurrent sequence types of this nature in NS speech (e.g. *it's good* ▲, *it was good* ▲, *it was really good* △, *and / yeah it was really good* △, *it was quite good* △, *that was good* △, *it's really good* △), not a single recurrent combination of this type can be found in NNS speech. The same incidentally also applies to the (admittedly less common) NS evaluative clausal sequences containing the adjective *bad* such as *it's not too bad* (△).

(4)   <A> but did you enjoy working in <\A>
        <B> yeah <u>it was good</u> I love working <\B>

(5)   <B> erm .. but it's fun living here I like living in a house <u>it's good</u> <\B>

(6)   <B> and it's absolutely amazing fun and everyone's just . soaking wet and
        they don't care and <u>it's really good </u><\B>

A significant way speakers can introduce and express their attitudes towards and evaluations of experiences and situations which emerges from the list of recurrent sequences in the NS corpus and which would probably not have been identified in a manual investigation of routinized combinations is the use of sentential relative clauses. A very large proportion of the relative clauses (over 60%) introduced by the recurrent sequences *which is* (▲▲▲▲), *which was* (▲▲), *which is quite* (▲), *which was a* (△), *which is a bit* (△), and *which is very* (△) are sentential relative clauses with evaluative function (examples 7 to 10). One evaluative sentential relative clause, i.e., *which is good* (△), can even be seen to recur as a complete clausal sequence in the NS corpus (example 11). Sentential relative clauses have been regarded by Chafe (1982) and Biber (1988) as a feature typically associated with the involved, interactive and non-informational style of spontaneous speech.

(7)   they didn't sort of give me any frog's legs or snails or anything .. <u>which was</u>
        quite a relief <laughs> <\B>

(8)   <B> and er .. and then some caribou there was one person who saw some
        caribou but nobody else saw them <u>which is a</u> shame <\B>

(9)   <B> they all come and visit me cos they think it's great having a student life so close to <X> so a lot of them travel up at weekends and that [which is quite nice <B>

(10)   we did a quiz the[i:] other night er and the[i:] executive the committee got completely thrashed like everybody else which is a bit embarrassing <\B>

(11)   I've got other people to hitch with which is good

(12)   and we've seen: Havana . which is an amazing town

(13)   Oldham actually which is near Manchester

(14)   I'm at Charlotte Mason which is the[i:] other campus

Many of the remaining instances of non-sentence relative clauses introduced by *which is / was* are also evaluative in nature as in (12). There are only few non-sentence relative clauses introduced by *which is / was* that offer 'neutral' additional information on the referent (example 13). It should be noted that all the relative clauses introduced by *which is the* (△) are of this type (example 14). The high number of evaluative relative clauses introduced by *which is / was* in the NS spoken corpus is in line with the findings of Tao and McCarthy's (2001) study of non-restrictive *which*-relative clauses in British and American spoken English. Tao and McCarthy found that the bulk of relative clauses under study, many of which are sentential relative clauses, have evaluative function displaying speakers' affective involvement with and attitudes to the events and experiences they are relating.

There are only two recurrent sequence types that can potentially introduce evaluative sentential relative clauses among the clausal sequences in NNS speech, i.e. *which are* ▲ and *which is* ▲▲. On closer inspection, only a handful of the instances of *which is* do actually introduce this type of relative clause (examples 15 and 16)

(15)   they don't ask me to pay so . this is sometimes for just one article for thirty pages of something er I don't have to pay which is really eh interesting <\B>

(16)   <A> so you were studying your German vocabulary <\A>

> <B> <begin_laughter> in place of speaking English <u>which is</u> a very stupid thing to do <end_laughter> I just [you know <\B>

Some of the remaining instances of non-sentential relative clauses introduced by *which is / are* are evaluative in nature as in (17) but the vast majority are non-evaluative as in (18).

(17)   <B> and so we went in Italy we went to: Assise . <u>which is</u> a wonderful city <\B>

(18)   <B> and <X> we were a group of fi= five girls and we wanted to go to er . to a beach <u>which is</u> er .. fifteen kilometres away eh of er . from Salou eh

5. Concluding remarks: implications for ELT

As pointed out by Granger (forthcoming), "features of learner language uncovered by LC [learner corpus] research need not necessarily lead to targeted action in the classroom", textbooks or grammar books. A number of factors such as learner needs, teaching objectives and teachability should guide linguists and ELT practitioners when attempting to determine which features should or should not be focused on in ELT. Bearing this in mind, let us briefly outline two possible practical implications of some of our findings for ELT.

As was highlighted above, clause beginnings appear to be a real challenge for learners even at an advanced level of proficiency. Learners would therefore definitely benefit from speaking courses that would equip them with a series of alternatives to wobbly thematic springboards. A second possible implication concerns our findings about attitudinal stance. It is not difficult to see how some of them could be used to inform the section on relative clauses in a con-textualised discourse-oriented grammar of speech, a section where more prominence would be given to the description and use of evaluative (sentential) relative clauses. The integration of suggestions of this type into ELT material might go some way towards helping

learners improve their fluency and increase their degree of involvement in informal interactions, which would be good!

6. References

Adolphs, Svenja / Durow, Valerie 2004. Social-cultural integration
    and the development of formulaic sequences. In Schmitt,
    Norbert (ed.) *Formulaic Sequences*. Amsterdam / Philadelphia:
    Benjamins, 107-126.
Aijmer, Karin 2002. *English Discourse Particles. Evidence from a
    Corpus*. Amsterdam: Benjamins.
Altenberg, Bengt 1984. Clausual Linking in Spoken and Written
    English. *Studia Linguistica,* 38, 20-69.
Altenberg, Bengt 1990 Speech as linear composition. In Caie, Graham
    / Haastrup, Karin *et al.* (eds) *Proceedings from the Fourth
    Nordic Conference for English Studies, Helsingor, May 11-13
    1989*. Copenhagen University, Department of English, 133-143.
Altenberg, Bengt 1998. On the Phraseology of Spoken English: The
    Evidence of Recurrent Word-Combinations. In Cowie, Antho-
    ny. P. (ed.) *Phraseology: Theory, Analysis, and Applications*.
    Oxford: Oxford University Press, 101-122.
Béjoint, Henri 2000. *Modern Lexicography. An Introduction*. Oxford:
    Oxford University Press.
Biber, Douglas 1988. *Variation across Speech and Writing*. Cam-
    bridge: Cambridge University Press.
Biber, Douglas 2004 Lexical Bundles in Academic Speech and
    Writing. In Lewandowska-Tomaszczyk, Barbara (ed.) *Practical
    Applications in Language and Computers (PALC 2003)*.
    Frankfurt am Main: Peter Lang, 165-178.
Biber, Douglas / Conrad, Susan 1999. Lexical Bundles in Conversa-
    tion and Academic Prose. In Hasselgård, Hilde / Oksefjell,
    Signe (eds) *Out of Corpora. Studies in Honour of Stig Johans-
    son*. Amsterdam and Atlanta: Rodopi, 181-190.

Biber Douglas / Conrad, Susan / Cortes, Viviana 2004. *If you look at ….:* Lexical bundles in university teaching and textbooks. *Applied Linguistics.* 25/3, 371- 405.

Biber, Douglas / Johansson, Stig / Leech, Geoffrey / Conrad, Susan / Finegan, Edward 1999. *Longman Grammar of Spoken and Written English.* London: Longman.

Chafe, Wallace. L. 1982. Integration and involvement in speaking, writing, and oral literature. In Tannen, Deborah (ed.) *Spoken and Written Language: Exploring Orality and Literacy.* Norwood: Ablex, 35-54.

Chafe, Wallace L. 1987. Cognitive Constraints on Information flow. In Tomlin, Russell S. (ed.) *Coherence and Grounding in Discourse. Outcome of a Symposium, June 1984, Eugene, Oregon.* Amsterdam / Philadelphia: John Benjamins, 21-51.

Chafe, Wallace L. / Danielewicz, Jane 1987. Properties of Spoken and Written language. In Horowitz, Rosalind / Samuels, Jay S. (eds) *Comprehending Oral and Written language.* New York: Academic Press, 82-113.

Clark, Herbert H. 1996. *Using Language.* Cambridge: Cambridge University Press.

Cortes Viviana 2004. Lexical Bundles in Published and Student Disciplinary Writing: Examples from History and Biology. *English for Specific Purposes,* 23/4, 397-423.

Cowie, Anthony P. 1999. Phraseology and corpora: some implications for dictionary-making. *International Journal of Lexicography.* 12/4, 307-323.

De Cock, Sylvie 2003. *Recurrent Sequences of Words in Native speaker and Advanced Learner Spoken and Written English.* Unpublished PhD thesis, Université catholique de Louvain.

De Cock, Sylvie 2004. Preferred Sequences of Words in NS and NNS Speech. *Belgian Journal of English Language and Literatures New Series,* 2, 225-246.

Fernando, Chitra 1996. *Idioms and Idiomaticity.* Oxford: Oxford University Press.

Fiksdal, Susan 1990. *The Right Time and Pace: A Microanalysis of Cross-cultural Gatekeeping Interviews.* New Jersey: Ablex Norwood.

Granger, Sylviane 1998. The Computerized Learner Corpus: A Versatile New Source of Data for SLA Research. In Granger, Sylviane (ed.) *Learner English on Computer*. London: Longman, 3-18.

Granger, Sylviane. Forthcoming. The Contribution of Learner Corpora to Second Language Acquisition and Foreign Language Teaching: A Critical Evaluation. In Aijmer, Karin (ed.) *Corpora and Language Teaching*. Amsterdam and Philadephia: Benjamins.

Hymes, Dell 1972. On Communicative Competence. In Pride, John / Holmes, Janet (eds) *Sociolinguistics: Selected Readings*. Harmondsworth: Penguin, 269-293.

Kjellmer, Göran 1994. *A Dictionary of English Collocations*. 3 Vols. Oxford: Clarendon Press.

Milton, John / Freeman, Robert 1996. Lexical Variation in the Writing of Chinese Learners of English. In Percy, Carol E. / Meyer, Charles F. / Lancashire, Ian (eds) *Synchronic Corpus Linguistics. Papers from the Sixteenth International Conference on English Language Research on Computerized Corpora (ICAME 16)*. Amsterdam: Rodopi, 121-131.

Lazaraton, Anne 1992. The Structural Organization of a language Interview: A Conversation Analytic Perspective. *System,* 20/3, 373-386.

Nesi, Hilary / Basturkmen, Helen 2006. Lexical Bundles and Discourse Signalling in Academic Lectures. *International Journal of Corpus Linguistics*, 11/3, 147-168.

Pawley, Andrew / Syder, Frances H. 1983. Two Puzzles for Linguistic Theory: Nativelike Selection and Nativelike Fluency. In Richards, Jack C. / Schmidt, Richard W. (eds) *Language and Communication*. London: Longman, 191-226.

Schmitt, Norbert / Carter, Ronald 2004. Formulaic sequences in action. An introduction. In Schmitt, Norbert (ed.) *Formulaic Sequences*. Amsterdam / Philadelphia: Benjamins, 1-22.

Sinclair, John M. 1991. *Corpus, Concordance, Collocation*. Oxford: Oxford University Press.

Stubbs, Michael 2002. *Words and Phrases: Corpus Studies of Lexical Semantics*. Oxford: Blackwell.

Stubbs, Michael / Barth, Isabel 2003. Using Recurrent Phrases as Text-type Discriminators: A Quantitative Method and some Findings. *Functions of Language,* 10/1, 61-104.

Sugiura, Masatoshi (2002) Collocational Knowledge of L2 Learners of English: A Case Study of Japanese Learners. In Saito, Toshio, Nakamura, Junsaku / Yamazaki, Shunji (eds) *English Corpus Linguistics in Japan.* Amsterdam / Atlanta: Rodopi, 303-323.

Tao, Hongyin / McCarthy, Michael J. 2001. Understanding Non-restrictive W*hich*-clauses in Spoken English, which is not an Easy Thing. *Language Sciences,* 23/6, 651-677.

Tarone, Elaine / Cohen, Andrew / Dumas, Graham 1983. A Closer Look at Some Interlanguage Terminology: A Framework for Communication Strategies. In Faerch, Claus / Kasper, Gabriele (eds) *Strategies in Interlanguage Communication.* London: Longman, 4-14.

Fiona Farr

Spoken Language Analysis as an Aid to Reflective Practice in Language Teacher Education: Using a Specialised Corpus to Establish a Generic Fingerprint

1. Background and context

In recent years, corpus exploitation has been finding its way into the language classroom in many different applications and formats (for examples, see contributions in Sinclair 2004, O'Keeffe, McCarthy, and Carter 2007, Chambers and Thompson Forthcoming). For practical reasons associated with availability and cost, much corpus-based instruction has engaged the use of written language corpora, which are now relatively easy to acquire. Somewhat more slowly, the use of spoken corpora is becoming more feasible (see McEnery, Xiao, and Tono 2006: 62) with increased access to appropriate collections such as MICASE, CSPAE, the Scottish Corpus of Texts and Speech, collections available through ICAME and the Oxford Text archives, and the spoken components of the BNC, to name a few. At the same time it has been fully acknowledged that if the language teaching profession is to see increased integration of corpus use, this integration must firstly and most importantly happen also at the level of language teacher education (LTE) (Conrad 2000, Chapelle 2001). In the context of LTE, thus far, we have seen the exploitation of corpora primarily for the development of grammatical/discourse awareness (for example, Hunston 1995, Coniam 1997) and pedagogic awareness (O'Keeffe and Farr 2003, Amador-Moreno, O'Riordan, and Chambers 2006), and indications are that this is an effective and well-liked mode of instruction among student teacher cohorts (Farr Forthcoming). The present chapter will explore how the established tradition of spoken corpus manipulation can be used in an innovative way through the examination of a specialised corpus of spoken interactions to enhance and offer an alternative route to reflective practice and continued professional development in language teacher education, and while the focus here will be primarily on the professional development of tutors, it can and could equally apply to student teachers, and indeed qualified and practising teachers wishing to develop further.

Many professions have found the road of continued and reflective learning to be highly effective (Schön 1991), and this, along with co-operative growth (Edge 2002), has taken root. In LTE, many now hold strong convictions that, "[...] one of the most effective ways of solving professional problems, and of continuing to improve and develop as a teacher, teacher educator, or manager in ELT is through reflection on our professional practice" (Wallace 1998: 1). This has often been done within the framework of action research, which involves the identification of a problem or issue in existing practices, the investigation of this problem using formal research procedures, and the subsequent documentation of findings so that the problem can be eliminated or reduced through changing the original practices appropriately. It is a more official way in which actions and experiences are recorded and shared so that we can better understand the processes in which we are involved, and ultimately make a difference to the quality of these actions and experiences. The intention, according to Edge (2001: 6), must be to learn and not justify. Freeman (2001: 7), in his discussions on the current state of teacher education, emphasises the need to draw on the past to forecast the present. This, he argues, can be most effectively done through reflection on practices which have been appropriately documented. Wallace (1998: 4) identifies four additional reasons:

1. It is a way of accelerating and enhancing our expertise, and it turns problems into positive versus negative experiences
2. It allows us to identify areas for self-development and at the same time raises awareness of professional strengths
3. It results in increased effectiveness
4. It promotes a healthy spirit of inquiry and research.

There is also the added dimension of the obligation to engage in such activity based on what we now know about the ways in which student teachers learn from their tutors. In the relevant setting of practice teaching Koerner, O'Connell-Rust, and Baumgartner (2002) highlight the relatively high priority teachers in training give to the personal qualities of co-operating teachers and educators, and Woodward (1997: 5) suggests that "when you ask teachers what they like and remember about their trainers, many will mention personal qualities such as sensitivity, flexibility, and a sense of humour rather than strategies and techniques used and often rather even than the content or knowledge passed on". If this is the case, it increases the formal obligation on educators to develop the necessary skills and traits which will help them to achieve their goal more effectively and affectively. Edge (2002), adapting earlier work by Egan (1986), details nine essential skills which those in a position to facilitate the teaching performance of others should ideally possess. These include the abilities to attend, reflect, focus, thematise, challenge, disclose, set goals, trail, and plan. He also explores the strategies of questioning, commenting, and silence, which can help to realise these in inter-actional contexts (Edge 1992: 69). The examination of the specialised spoken corpus (POTTI) reported in this chapter investigates the presence of these and other skills in action, which, it is suggested, might advance our understanding of the issues involved and help this particular community to better understand, and if necessary, modify its own practices.

Myers and Clark (2002: 50) conclude that continued profe-ssional development is crucial for individuals and their organisations, should be continuous and lifelong (Randall and Thornton 2001: 55), and should happen at the meta level so that any resultant modifica-tions in practice are more than superficial. Additionally, reflection based on action research allows for the localisation of solutions based on local problems, an approach which has been advocated in teacher training (Gill 1997), and was a core rationale for the present author to engage in the collection of POTTI from the local and most relevant context. Until now, in language teacher education circles, such reflection and development has been implemented largely by means of reflective diaries, peer discussion groups, on-going monitoring, video recordings, seminar attendance etc (for example, Bax 1995, Reicheld 2000), in an era of prospective versus retrospective educational practices. Here I aim to investigate the complementary role which a spoken corpus can have.

2. The POTTI Corpus: data and methodology

The data for the reported study exists in the form of a small spoken language corpus of post-observation teaching practice (TP) feedback sessions between tutors and student teachers (the POTTI Corpus) working together on an MA in English Language Teaching education programme in an Irish University. It contains the talk which occurs between tutor/observer and student teacher/observee in the feedback sessions which take place after observed TP has occurred. Teaching practice takes place in the university where the LTE programme runs. It consists of approximately 80,000 words and is a sub-corpus of the larger one-million-word Limerick Corpus of Irish English (L-CIE, see Farr, Murphy, and O'Keeffe 2004).

2.1. The feedback location

Feedback takes place in the physical context of the university-based office of the relevant tutor. The physical context therefore belongs to the tutor. Only the relevant tutor and student teacher are present in each session. This location in which recording takes place is that used in all feedback sessions in normal situations and is not therefore artificial in that sense. "In this way, though natural behaviour is not guaranteed, the likelihood of untypical behaviour is reduced" (Phillips 1999: 40).

2.2. The feedback timing

Feedback usually takes place at any time up to three days after the TP lesson, although there is a general tendency to do feedback the following day. Each session lasts between twenty-five and forty-five minutes, with an average of thirty minutes per session. The feedback sessions recorded in POTTI take place in Weeks 6, 7 and 8 of the first semester of the two semester MA course. TP started in Week 4, so each student teacher had participated in a minimum of two feedback sessions before the POTTI recordings commenced.

2.3. The participants

Two tutors, one of whom is the participant researcher (and present author), and seven student teachers are recorded. Both tutors are female. Fionnuala (all names are pseudonyms) is older with considerable teaching experience and had been employed on a part-time basis by the university for seven years at the time of the recordings. She holds a BA, a Higher Diploma in Education, and a Graduate Diploma in TEFL. Edwina, was a newly employed tutor / academic, with just three years' training experience at the time. She holds a BA, an MA in TEFL, and a PhD. Four of the student teacher participants are female and three are male. All but one of the males is Irish. Participants are aged between twenty and thirty-five years of age, and only one of the males had any considerable teaching experience before starting the programme. All student teachers hold primary degrees from a range of academic disciplines.

2.4. The atmosphere

As is the case for many institutional meetings there is an asymmetry of power between the participants. The tutor is considered to be more expert than the student teacher. These roles and power relations have consequences for the discourse of POTTI. Additionally, the situation is one where the normal conventions of politeness have been temporarily suspended and in the name of professional development and improvement, which allow typically face-threatening acts, such as direction and criticism, to be included. Using a framework presented in Brown and Levinson (1987), we can say that the power distance (P) is high, the social distance (D) is average, and the rating of impositions (R) is high. Therefore, feedback has the potential to cause considerable anxiety (Mann 2003). Nonetheless, the ethos of collaboration and constructive criticism is strongly promoted and advocated by the tutors concerned in this and other aspects of their contributions on the programme.

2.5. The recordings

The audio recordings were made using a Marantz Professional System and a table-top microphone. The full consent of all participants was secured on each occasion prior to recording, and anonymity in the transcription was guaranteed. An option to delete the recording was given immediately after each recording and all participants were finally afforded the opportunity to read, edit or remove the transcribed data before the initial analysis began. What remains as the corpus are those sessions which were not removed or edited in any way and for which full supporting questionnaires were completed and submitted to the researcher (full details of questionnaires can be found in Farr 2005c). In total fourteen sessions are included amounting to 81,944 words. One session for each student teacher with each tutor is incorporated, providing two sessions for each of the seven student teachers, and seven sessions for each of the two tutors. The following table details the data included in the POTTI corpus, including a number assigned to each feedback session for the purposes of identification in this study, the week and time of recording, the pseudonym of the tutor and student teacher and the total number of transcribed words per recording.

Feedback Session Number	Week and Time of Recording	Tutor	Student Teacher	Number of Words
1	Week 6, 16.00	Edwina	Lorna	2833
2	Week 6, 13.00	Fionnuala	Roseanna	5245
3	Week 6, 12.00	Fionnuala	Jim	9300
4	Week 6, 16.45	Edwina	Petra	4534
5	Week 6, 14.15	Fionnuala	Peter	7223
6	Week 6, 15.15	Edwina	Michael	8346
7	Week 6, 14.00	Fionnuala	Joanne	5443
8	Week 7, 17.30	Edwina	Jim	8646
9	Week 7, 16.15	Edwina	Roseanna	6251
10	Week 7, 16.45	Edwina	Joanne	4701
11	Week 7, 14.00	Fionnuala	Lorna	4073
12	Week 7, 14.30	Fionnuala	Michael	3740
13	Week 7, 13.30	Fionnuala	Petra	6387
14	Week 8, 16.00	Edwina	Peter	5222
Total				**81,944**

Table 1. The POTTI Corpus.

2.6. Corpus linguistics as an investigative approach

Two different but related aspects of the talk are of interest when investigating POTTI. Firstly, who is participating and to what extent, and secondly, what is the nature of the dyadic communication? Both of these questions are complex and require a variety of analytical techniques to begin to uncover some answers, and indeed it is fair to assume that general academic wisdom in applied linguistics and educational investigation now accepts that no research framework, methodology, nor procedure, can be all things to all researchers for all purposes. Different and combined approaches are necessary to even begin to understand the complexity of human interactions in social space (Hammersley 2004). For this reason, the corpus analysis presented here was complemented with data from diary entries and also three sets of questionnaires (for full details see Farr 2005c). However, a corpus-based analysis can help the investigator, and practitioner in this case, to go a long way in uncovering relevant information to build answers to both of the questions. This is especially true if one considers the two broad approaches that have developed within the field of corpus linguistics. McCarthy *et al.* (2002: 70), exemplify as follows,

> Broadly, corpus linguistics may be performed in two ways: quantitative and qualitative. The quantitative approach usually looks for the largest corpus possible [...] from as wide a range of sources as possible. These data are then analysed computationally and the output comprises sets of figures that tell the discourse analyst about the frequency of occurrence of words, phrases, collocations or structures. These statistics are then used to produce dictionaries, grammars, and so on. But for the discourse analyst, statistical facts raise the question "*Why?*", and the answers can only be found by looking at the contexts of the texts in the corpus. Discourse analysts, therefore, work with corpora in a qualitative way.

This does not mean to suggest that one approach excludes the other, simply that one takes precedence over the other resulting from differences in research interest and objectives. This befits the premise that "neither the quantitative data of a corpus alone nor the one-off analysis of conversational fragments is sufficient, [...] much extra insight can be gained by [...] keeping both in constant dialectal relationship" (McCarthy and Handford 2004: 190).

3. Results and analysis

3.1. Participation

Using Wordsmith Tools 3 (Scott 1999), statistical corpus generated information gives insights into levels of participation and interactivity in the POTTI interactions, shedding light on potential power differentials and influences which may be at play. Taking all of the sessions, and based on word counts, we find that the tutors occupy 63.57% of the talk, while the student teachers account for just 36.43% (for full details see Farr 2005a, 204-206). Although slightly disappointing from the perspective of the tutors, whose stated objective is to get the student teachers to engage in critical self-reflection, these results are not surprising given the asymmetry of the professional relationship and the high imposition associated with context. Both of these factors, taken from pragmatic models of politeness may provide and explanation for the relative reluctance for the student teachers to become overly involved. There may be a fear of losing face by being 'wrong' in their interpretation of events vis a vis the 'expert', and also of exposing themselves further to potentially harmful imposition. Double threat to both positive and negative face (Brown and Levinson 1987). Nonetheless, it is gratifying to see that these student teachers are playing some part in the encounter, albeit less than that of the tutor. Such findings are in line with previous results from research examining the feedback context (Phillips 1999). Moving towards exploring the nature of the talk, a quantitative analysis using frequency and keyword lists begins to take us towards understanding in a more contextualised way what is happening in the feedback sessions.

3.2. Frequency analysis

Comparative frequency lists are a useful indicator of the relative characteristics of genres such as POTTI. The following table compares the top 50 most frequent words in four spoken corpora: POTTI, the one-million word L-CIE corpus, an academic English corpus of 340,000 words (ACAD), and a spoken business English corpus of 250,000 words (CANBEC). The frequency lists for CANBEC and ACAD come from McCarthy and Handford (2004). Table 2 presents the results. The words which are exclusive to POTTI are shaded on the table.

	POTTI	L-CIE	ACAD	CANBEC
1	I	THE	THE	THE
2	YOU	I	AND	AND
3	THE	AND	OF	TO
4	TO	YOU	YOU	I
5	THAT	TO	A	YOU

	(POTTI)	(L-CIE)	(ACAD)	(CANBEC)
6	AND	IT	TO	A
7	IT	A	THAT	IT
8	YEAH	THAT	IN	YEAH
9	OF	OF	IS	THAT
10	A	IN	IT	OF
11	WAS	YEAH	I	WE
12	IN	WAS	ER	ER
13	THEY	IS	SO	IS
14	IS	LIKE	IT'S	IN
15	KNOW	KNOW	THIS	SO
16	THEM	HE	WHAT	IT'S
17	EM	THEY	YEAH	ERM
18	BUT	ON	ERM	BUT
19	WHAT	HAVE	ARE	ON
20	HAVE	THERE	BUT	FOR
21	SO	NO	ON	KNOW
22	JUST	BUT	HAVE	THEY
23	DO	FOR	BE	BE
24	WERE	BE	WE	WELL
25	THINK	WHAT	RIGHT	HAVE
26	ON	SO	KNOW	MM
27	AT	DO	AS	IF
28	DID	WE	THEY	DO
29	NOT	IT'S	IF	THAT'S
30	WOULD	AH	OR	WHAT
31	WELL	NOW	DO	JUST
32	THIS	OH	NOT	WITH
33	BECAUSE	SHE	WITH	ALL
34	OR	ARE	ALL	RIGHT
35	AS	ALL	FOR	THIS
36	ARE	ONE	WHICH	GOT
37	ONE	THAT'S	AT	NO
38	IF	THIS	ONE	AT
39	THERE	WITH	THERE	WAS
40	WITH	JUST	CAN	ONE
41	BE	OR	ABOUT	NOT
42	HAD	AT	THAT'S	THERE
43	OKAY	NOT	LIKE	THINK
44	FOR	WELL	WAS	CAN
45	IT'S	DON'T	MM	AS

	(POTTI)	(L-CIE)	(ACAD)	(CANBEC)
46	MMHM	IF	JUST	ARE
47	ABOUT	THEM	VERY	DON'T
48	VERY	WOULD	HE	THEM
49	MEAN	GOING	OKAY	GET
50	YOUR	OUT	BECAUSE	THEN

Table 2. Frequency comparisons POTTI, L-CIE, ACAD, and CANBEC.

In line with findings by McCarthy and Handford (2004) these lists show a common core high frequency vocabulary, with none of the top ten words in POTTI not appearing in the top ten of at least one of the other lists. Only seven of the words on the POTTI list do not appear on any of the other lists (illustrated by shading on Table 2). Two of these, *em* and *mmhm*, can be discounted as they are most probably attributable to differences in transcription systems. Three of the different words, *were*, *did* and *had*, past tense verb forms, indicate the relatively factual and descriptive narrative nature of POTTI. *Mean* may be indicative of much exemplification and clarification in POTTI, or more likely its dual function as a hedge accounts for its above average frequency. The only other word unique to POTTI's list is *your*. The use of this possessive determiner might be explained by the personalised commentary of student teacher behaviour and teaching performance, a more detailed concordance analysis presented below will provide more subtle insights.

The importance afforded to interpersonal language use in this research provides an imperative to compare tutor and student teacher talk. We have already seen a very uneven distribution in quantity of talk between both parties and comparative frequency lists for tutors and student teachers may provide further insights into differences in the relative quality and content of their talk. Table 3 shows both lists. Shaded items are those which are exclusive to the tutor or student teacher lists, and will be commented on further below.

	TUTOR		STUDENT TEACHER	
1	YOU	2,955	I	2,398
2	THE	2,220	THE	1,023
3	TO	1,525	YEAH	932

	(TUTOR)		(STUDENT TEACHER)	
4	THAT	1,502	TO	771
5	I	1,198	AND	729
6	IT	1,182	WAS	699
7	AND	1,129	THAT	671
8	OF	963	IT	670
9	A	933	OF	543
10	IN	853	YOU	427
11	IS	673	A	423
12	YEAH	631	EM	394
13	THEY	555	KNOW	390
14	WAS	534	THEY	377
15	WHAT	501	IN	364
16	THEM	469	THEM	303
17	BUT	450	JUST	286
18	DO	420	BUT	255
19	HAVE	415	HAVE	250
20	WERE	397	THINK	240
21	KNOW	383	SO	237
22	THIS	378	WELL	223
23	ARE	358	MM	217
24	SO	353	BECAUSE	185
25	EM	347	DID	181
26	ON	343	WHAT	179
27	YOUR	326	MMHM	176
28	WOULD	322	HAD	175
29	NOT	314	DIDN'T	171
30	AT	310	IS	170
31	IF	297	WERE	170
32	JUST	290	AT	169
33	BE	289	OR	165
34	THINK	283	AS	155
35	IT'S	279	THERE	155
36	AS	277	ONE	154
37	DID	277	DO	153
38	FOR	276	MEAN	151
39	OR	269	ON	150
40	WITH	268	RIGHT	149
41	ONE	254	AH	146
42	VERY	253	DON'T	142
43	BECAUSE	252	NO	139

	(TUTOR)		(STUDENT TEACHER)	
44	OKAY	247	KIND	136
45	THERE	240	NOT	135
46	ABOUT	239	SAID	129
47	NOW	239	LIKE	127
48	SAY	225	OKAY	127
49	WELL	219	WOULD	125
50	HAD	202	THEN	120

Table 3. Tutor and student teacher frequency lists (top 50 words).

Again there are many similarities but the two lists diverge in 12 cases on each. The following words appear in the tutors' list only: *this, are, if, be, for, with, one, very, about, now, say, had. This, for, with, about* and *one* suggest the type of informative and rationalising narrative engaged in by the expert speaker. *If* and *had* indicate a tutor strategy to move the discourse into hypothetical and irealis mode. *About* and *say* hint at hedging, while *very* points to the tutor's right to make evaluative judgements, either positive or negative. The use of *be* merits further analysis to investigate its directive function. Some words feature more highly in the student teacher list also. These include: *mm, mmhm, ah, right, no, didn't, mean, kind, like, don't, said,* and *then.* The first five on the list can function as response tokens and the listenership role of the student teacher. *Mean, kind* and *like* suggest a high degree of hedging. *Didn't* and *don't* may be used for negative evaluations or uncertainty, while *said* and *then* are to be expected in the type of personal reporting engaged in by the student teacher.

3.3. Keyword analysis

Although frequency list comparisons like those just presented are a useful starting point when attempting to establish the shared and distinguishing characteristics of a particular type of discourse, they do not tell us which words are statistically significant. A keyword comparison against a larger reference corpus, in this case L-CIE (containing the genre of casual conversation), reveals more specific distinctions. Table 4 presents the top 100 keywords in POTTI. Using even the arbitrary cut-off point of 100 words, this list tells something of what makes POTTI unique as a genre.

	WORD		WORD
1	MMHM	51	VIDEO
2	EM	52	CLASSROOM
3	I	53	HAD
4	YOU	54	YEAH
5	LESSON	55	AWARE
6	CLASS	56	THEY
7	THEM	57	EXERCISES
8	THAT	58	GROUP
9	MM	59	EXAMPLES
10	WORDS	60	LITTLE
11	STUDENTS	61	BOOK
12	EXERCISE	62	WORD
13	VOCABULARY	63	TP
14	ACTIVITY	64	DID
15	QUESTIONS	65	WAS
16	BECAUSE	66	LEVEL
17	OKAY	67	GROUPS
18	WERE	68	INFORMAL
19	TEACHING	69	PLAN
20	VOCAB	70	PICKED
21	SORT	71	INTERMEDIATE
22	FORMAL	72	PROBING
23	INSTRUCTIONS	73	WHOLEMEAL
24	MEAN	74	TIME
25	DICTIONARY	75	APPROACH
26	FELT	76	PAUSE
27	ASKED	77	QUITE
28	DICTIONARIES	78	FOCUS
29	MORE	79	STAGE
30	EXPLAIN	80	SECONDS
31	THINK	81	LANGUAGE
32	NEED	82	HISTORIC
33	THINGS	83	CONSCIOUS
34	DIDN'T	84	YOURSELF
35	PAIRS	85	WANTED
36	TAUGHT	86	PETRA
37	TO	87	PREP

38	TERMS	88	ANSWER
39	CORRECTION	89	OTHERS
40	BIT	90	SOME
41	ASK	91	CARRIE
42	QUESTION	92	MONITORING
43	MAYBE	93	PREPARATION
44	TEACH	94	FEEL
45	DIFFICULT	95	TEACHER
46	DEFINITIONS	96	DEFINITION
47	USE	97	VERY
48	FIONNUALA	98	CHALLENGING
49	JUST	99	DIFFERENT
50	DESCRIBE	100	EXPLAINED

Table 4. Keywords in POTTI (top 100 words).

The keywords listed on Table 4 can be analysed and grouped into the following five broad categories:

3.4. Metadiscourse

Some of the defining characteristics that a 'Community of Practice' has formed are the use of "jargon and shortcuts to communication [...] specific tools, representations, and other artefacts" and "certain styles recognized as displaying membership" (Wenger 1998: 125-126). The use of "metadiscourse" (Hedgcock 2002: 305) in LTE is expected to include metalanguage used to describe language and also conventions to describe the art of teaching. Both are apparent in the lexical choices made by the speakers in POTTI and the top 100 keywords contain a very high proportion of such vocabulary. These include: *lesson, class, words, students, exercise, vocabulary, activity, questions, teaching, instructions, formal, dictionary, pairs, correction, definitions, video, examples, level, groups, plan, intermediate, probing, prep, monitoring,* and so on.

3.5. Cognitive and cathartic words

In line with the cognitive, reflective and affective focus of LTE it is not surprising to find the following among the differentiating lexical repertoire of tutors and student teachers in the feedback session: *mean, felt, think, aware, conscious, wanted, feel* and *challenging.*

3.6. Reference

POTTI data contain relatively more reference items than casual conversation found in L-CIE. Among the keywords are: personal pronouns, *I, you, they,* and *them*, the reflexive pronoun *yourself,* the demonstrative pronoun *that*, the names *Fionnuala, Carrie, Petra* (although these could not really be considered key), and other reference words like *things* and *others* (for a full account see Farr 2005b: 216-223).

3.7. Words indicating interactivity

Tokens signifying mutual and reciprocal engagement are again in the keyword list and include *mmhm, mm, okay,* and *yeah* (see Farr 2003).

3.8. Hedging words

Indicators of hesitation such as *em*, and other lexis associated with the realm of vague, fuzzy, or hedgy language can be found in the examples, *sort, mean, think, terms, bit, maybe, just, little,* and *some.*

3.9. Cluster analysis

The area of formulaic language use has received much attention in recent times with many insightful findings emanating from corpus-based studies (see for example Wray 2002, Adolphs and Durow 2004,

Schmitt 2004, Spöttl and McCarthy 2004). In addition to individual lexical choices in POTTI, it is interesting to examine whether there are significant reoccurrences of phrases in the form of clusters. Table 5 below details the three, four, and five word clusters found in the data. The top 20 clusters were examined in each case and any partially repeated clusters are included in one section only. There are examples of clusters which are directive or critical, contain metadiscourse as illustrated above, and lots of pragmatic hedges and mitigators.

5 WORD CLUSTERS	OCCURRENCES
AT THE END OF THE	13
YOU NEED TO LOOK AT	8
THE END OF THE DAY	7
I WAS GOING TO SAY	6
YOU KNOW WHAT I MEAN	6
ABOUT THAT A LITTLE BIT	5
AM I GOING TO DO	5
AND I WOULD SAY THAT	5
I SHOULD HAVE TOLD THEM	5
TALK TO ME ABOUT THAT	5
THAT PART OF THE LESSON	5
A MINUTE TO LOOK AT	4
AND I DIDN'T WANT TO	4
AND I WAS TRYING TO	4
DID YOU WANT THEM TO	4
DO YOU KNOW WHAT I	4
EM I MEAN I DIDN'T	4
HOW AM I GOING TO	4

4 WORD CLUSTERS	
OR SOMETHING LIKE THAT	17
A LITTLE BIT MORE	14
I DON'T KNOW WHAT	13
I THINK IT WAS	12
I THINK THAT WAS	12
I DON'T KNOW I	11
I DON'T THINK I	11
I MEAN YOU KNOW	11
I WAS A BIT	11
YOU NEED TO BE	11

A BIT OF A	10
GET THEM TO DO	10
TO BE AWARE OF	10

3 WORD CLUSTERS	
I MEAN I	60
YOU KNOW I	56
I WOULD SAY	51
IN TERMS OF	51
I THINK YOU	49
ONE OF THE	49
A LOT OF	44
I THINK THAT	44
AND I WAS	42
I MEAN YOU	41
I THINK I	41
YOU HAVE TO	41
SOME OF THE	38

Table 5. Clusters in POTTI.

Although clustering does not seem to be as formulaic as in other genres such as business discourse (see for example, McCarthy and Handford 2004), POTTI nonetheless contains at least one fixed phrase shared with other registers: *at the end of the day*. This is an encouraging finding in light of the fact that over-routinisation and over-formulaic language use has been considered poor practice (Maingay 1997). Some clusters are directive and used to give advice and exemplification, for example, *you need to look at, talk to me about that, you need to be, get them to do, to be aware of, you have to*. Others contain some of the metadiscourse referred to earlier, for example, *that part of the lesson*, or indicate the critically reflective nature of the discourse, for example, *I should have told them, I didn't want to, I was trying to, I don't know what, I think it was*. Most predominately, however, we can find polite phrases used as mitigators, or hedges, for example, *I was going to say, you know what I mean, I would say, about that a little bit*.

4. Discussion and conclusion

This chapter, based primarily on a qualitative analysis, reveals a number of interesting facts about the nature of the POTTI genre. Measure of speaker participation and utterance length per participant indicates that the majority of talk is conducted by the tutor. Despite the attested aim for student teachers to participate fully and be critically reflective, this might have been anticipated, given that most of the student teachers are inexperienced and relatively young. In the second part of the analysis, the generation of frequency lists and keyword lists identify the shared and distinctive characteristics of POTTI talk relative to other genres. It shares the typical lexicon associated with spoken genres, such as highly frequent use of personal pronouns. On the other hand, it displays a higher frequency of specific metadiscourse relating to the teaching of languages and the TP context, more cognitive and cathartic words, more reference in the form of pronouns and vocatives, and many tokens indicating inter-activity, such as *okay*, *mm*, and *yeah*. And finally, the cluster analysis reinforces some of the findings of the keyword analysis and presents some formulaic sequences relating to exemplification, the critically reflective nature of the talk, and many polite phrases used as mitigators and hedges. We therefore have a generic fingerprint of POTTI, which can be instrumental in a number of ways. It can provide the statistical justification and basis for a more detailed and perhaps more qualitative contextualised account of some of the identified items, by means of concordance searches, patterns and collocations. This would allow for the investigation of hypotheses generated from the initial quantitative findings. Indeed to this end, I have elsewhere examined in much more detail the phenomena of engaged listenership (Farr 2003), reference (Farr 2005b), participation and interactivity (Farr 2005a), and modality (Farr 2006a), and am currently working on a combined analysis of the corpus findings and the questionnaire and diary data (Farr 2006b). However, this is a time expensive endeavour, and though very insightful, is not always one easily available to many teacher educators. Nevertheless there are many who may wish to engage in some sort of reflection and development in the realm of teaching practice feedback, and even a generic analysis like the one above can be useful in a reflective practice loop.

If we are to return to just the second of Wallace's reasons for engaging in reflective practice 'It allows us to identify areas for self-development and at the same time raises awareness of professional strengths' (Wallace 1998: 4), and apply it to what we have seen in the analysis above, we can identify several areas for development, for example, to increase student teacher participation, perhaps to avoid formulaic language clusters that have become devoid of meaning, and to reduce the potential occurrences of negative retrospection without positive outlook. On the other hand, we can also find much evidence of professional strengths, for example, the ability to engage the student teachers using the appropriate metadiscourse, ample use of hedging and modal structures suggestive of a pragmatically sensitive encounter attempting to minimise the imposition, and many inter-active listening devices being used by both parties. Only when this awareness is made explicit through the use of documented evidence, in this case in the form of a spoken corpus, can professional educators begin to modify their practices for improved future engagement with student teachers. Of course, this is but one means among others already mentioned, but a spoken language corpus can be a valuable instrument in the toolbox for professional development, and in turn using a corpus in this way is a new departure for the potential applications of corpus linguistics in teacher education contexts.

5. References

Adolphs, Svenja / Durow, Valerie 2004. Social-cultural Integration and the Development of Formulaic Sequences. In Schmitt, Norbert (ed.) *Formulaic Sequences*. Amsterdam: John Benjamins, 107-126.

Amador-Moreno, Carolina / O'Riordan, Stephanie / Chambers, Angela 2006. Integrating a Corpus of Classroom Discourse in Language Teacher Education: the Case of Discourse Markers. *ReCALL*, 18/1, 83-104.

Bax, Stephen 1995. Principles for Evaluating Teacher Development Activities. *English Language Teaching Journal*. 49/3, 262-271.

Brown, Penelope / Levinson, Stephen 1987. *Politeness: Some Universals in Language Usage*. Cambridge: Cambridge University Press.

Chambers, Angela / Thompson, June (eds) Forthcoming. Incorporating Corpora in Language Learning and Teaching. Special Issue of *ReCALL* 2007.

Chapelle, Carol 2001. CALL in the 21st Century: Looking Back on Research to Look Forward for Practice. In: *CALL in the 21st Century CD-ROM*. Whitstable: IATEFL.

Coniam, David 1997. A Practical Introduction to Corpora in a Teacher Training Language Awareness Programme. *Language Awareness*, 6/4, 199-207.

Conrad, Susan 2000. Will Corpus Linguistics Revolutionize Grammar Teaching in the 21st Century? *TESOL Quarterly*, 34/3, 548-560.

Edge, Julian 1992. Co-operative Development. *English Language Teaching Journal*, 46/1, 62-70.

Edge, Julian 2001. Search and Re-search. *English Teaching Professional*, 20, 5-7.

Edge, Julian 2002. Continuing Cooperative Development. A Discourse Framework for Individuals as Colleagues. Ann Arbor: University of Michigan Press.

Egan, Gerard 1986. *The Skilled Helper: A Systematic Approach to Effective Helping*. Pacif Grove, Calif: Brooks / Cole Pub. Co.

Farr, Fiona 2003. Engaged Listenership in Spoken Academic Discourse: the case of student-tutor meetings. *Journal of English for Academic Purposes*, 2/1, 67-85.

Farr, Fiona 2005a. Reflecting on Reflections: the Spoken Word as a Professional Development Tool in Language Teacher Education. In Hughes, Rebecca (ed.) *Beyond Words. The Challenge of Spoken English for Applied Linguistics and Language Teaching*. Hampshire: Palgrave Macmillan, 182-215.

Farr, Fiona 2005b. Relational Strategies in the Discourse of Professional Performance Review in an Irish Academic Environment: the Case of Language Teacher Education. In Schneider, Klaus / Barron, Ann (eds) *The Pragmatics of Irish English*. Berlin: Mouton de Gruyter, 203-234.

Farr, Fiona 2005c. *Reflecting on Reflections: a Corpus-based Analysis of Spoken Post TP Interactions in an ELT Academic Environment*. Unpublished PhD Thesis, College of Humanities, University of Limerick.

Farr, Fiona 2006a. Modality in Context: Spoken Language, Variety and the Classroom. In Gallgher, Anne / Ó Laoire, Muiris (eds) *Language Education in Ireland: Current Practice and Future Needs*. Dublin: Irish Association for Applied Linguistics, 165-184.

Farr, Fiona 2006b. Strengthening Interpretative Research through the Use of Complementary Data Sources in Corpus-based Spoken Discourse Analysis. Paper presented at the 3rd International IVACS Conference, University of Nottingham. 23-24 June, 2006.

Farr, Fiona Forthcoming. Evaluating the Use of Corpus-based Instruction in a Language Teacher Education Context: Perspectives from the Users. *Language Awareness*.

Farr, Fiona / Murphy, Brona / O'Keeffe, Anne 2004. The Limerick Corpus of Irish English: Design, Description and Application. *Teanga,* 21, 5-29.

Freeman, Donald 2001. Rethinking the Tools of the Trade: Teacher Learning and Trainer Learning. *The IATEFL Teacher Trainers and Educators SIG Newsletter,* 1, 7-8.

Gill, Simon 1997. Local Problems, Local Solutions. In McGrath, Ian (ed.) *Learning to Train: Perspectives on the Development of Language Teacher Trainers*. Hemel Hampstead: Prentice Hall, 215-224.

Hammersley, Martyn 2004. Social science methodology today: diversity or anarchy? Paper presented at the CALL Conference, Antwerp. September, 2004.

Hedgcock, John 2002. Toward a Socioliterate Approach to Second Language Teacher Education. *Modern Language Journal,* 86/3, 299-317.

Hunston, Susan 1995. Grammar in Teacher Education: the Role of a Corpus. *Language Awareness,* 4/1, 15-31.

Koerner, Mari / O'Connell-Rust, Frances / Baumgartner, Frances 2002. Exploring Roles in Student Teaching Placements. *Teacher Education Quarterly,* 29/2, 35-58.

Maingay, Peter 1997. Raising Awareness of Awareness. In McGrath, Ian (ed.) *Learning to Train: Perspectives on the Development of Language Teacher Trainers.* Hemel Hempstead: Prentice Hall, 117-126.

Mann, S. George 2003. An Evaluation of Tutor-led Feedback in the Context of Initial Teacher Training in EFL. In Gollin, Jacqueline / Ferguson, Gibson / Trappes-Lomax, Hugh (eds), Proceedings of Symposium for Language Teacher Educators, Edinburgh, 2000, 2001, 2002. Edinburgh: IALS, CD Publication.

McCarthy, Michael / Handford, Michael 2004. 'Invisible to Us': a Preliminary Corpus-based Study of Spoken Business English. In Connor, Ulla / Upton, Thomas (eds), *Discourse in the Professions: Perspectives from Corpus Linguistics.* Amsterdam: John Benjamins, 167-201.

McCarthy, Michael / Matthiessen, Christian / Slade, Diana 2002. Discourse Analysis. In Schmitt, Norbert (ed.) *An Introduction to Applied Linguistics.* London: Arnold, 55-73.

McEnery, Tony / Xiao, Richard / Tono, Yukio 2006. *Corpus-based Language Studies: an Advanced Resource Book.* London: Routledge.

Myers, Mel / Clark, Sue 2002. CPD, Lifelong Learning and Going Meta. In Edge, Julian (ed.) *Continuing Professional Development. Some of our Perspectives.* Kent: IATEFL, 50-62.

O'Keeffe, Anne / Farr, Fiona 2003. Using Language Corpora in Language Teacher Education: Pedagogic, Linguistic and Cultural Insights'. *TESOL Quarterly,* 37/3, 389-418.

O'Keeffe, Anne / McCarthy, Michael / Carter, Ronald 2007. *From Corpus to Classroom.* Cambridge: Cambridge University Press.

Phillips, Diane 1999. *The Feedback Session within the Context of Teacher Training and Development: An Analysis of Discourse, Role and Function.* Unpublished PhD Thesis, University of London.

Randall, Mick / Thornton, Brabara 2001. *Advising and Supporting Teachers.* Cambridge: Cambridge University Press.

Reichelt, Melinda 2000. Case Studies in L2 Teacher Education. *English Language Teaching Journal,* 54/4, 346-351.

Schmitt, Norbert (ed.) 2004. *Formulaic Sequences.* Amsterdam: John Benjamins.

Schön, Donald 1991. *The Reflective Practitioner: How Professionals Think in Action.* Aldershot: Arena.

Scott, Michael 1999. *Wordsmith Tools 3.* Oxford: Oxford University Press.

Sinclair, John 2004. *How to Use Corpora in Language Teaching.* Amsterdam: John Benjamins.

Spöttl, Carol and M. J. McCarthy, 2004. Comparing knowledge of formulaic sequences across L1, L2, L3, and L4. In Schmitt, Norbert (ed.) *Formulaic Sequences.* Amsterdam: John Benjamins, 191-226.

Wallace, Michael 1998. *Action Research for Language Teachers.* Cambridge: Cambridge University Press.

Wenger, Etienne 1998. *Communities of Practice. Learning, Meaning, and Identity.* Cambridge: Cambridge University Press.

Woodward, Tessa 1997. Trainer Training: a Question Matrix. In McGrath, Ian (ed.) *Learning to Train: Perspectives on the Development of Language Teacher Trainers.* Hemel Hampstead: Prentice Hall, 3-10.

Wray, Alison 2002. *Formulaic Language and the Lexicon.* Cambridge: Cambridge University Press.

Notes on Contributors

MARÍA JOSÉ LUZÓN (University of Zaragoza, Spain) is Senior Lecturer in English for Specific Purposes at the University of Zaragoza, Spain. She has published widely in the area of corpus-based analysis of academic and professional discourse and on language teaching and learning in the field of English for Specific Purposes. Her current research interests are the corpus-based analysis of digital genres, especially those used in professional and academic communication, and the use of Internet resources and tools to design tasks for ESP. She is co-editor of the volume *Corpus Linguistics. Applications for the Study of English* (Peter Lang, 2006).

MARI CARMEN CAMPOY (University Jaume I, Spain) is the Head of the Department of English Studies of Jaume I University, Spain. She has co-edited *Oral Skills: Resources and Proposals for the Classroom* and *Computer-Mediated Lexicography in the Foreign Language Learning Context*. She is a member of the *LAELA* research group (Lingüística Aplicada a l'Ensenyament de la Llengua Anglesa), a research group that is currently involved in projects dealing with interaction in second language acquisition. Her main research interests are in the areas of lexicography and the application of corpus linguistics to the teaching of foreign languages.

MARÍA DEL MAR SÁNCHEZ obtained her degree in English Philology from the University of Granada (Spain) and received her Ph.D. in Translation Studies from the Universitat Jaume I (Castellon, Spain).Her research interests are computer-based linguistics, computer-aided translation, and pedagogical lexicography, among others. She has published several articles related to these lines of research. Currently, she lectures in the Department of Translation Studies at the University of Murcia (Spain).

PATRICIA SALAZAR is a lecturer at Universitat Jaume I (Castellón). She belongs to the research group LAELA (Lingüística Aplicada a l'Ensenyament de la Llengua Anglesa) and her main research interests include foreign language acquisition, negotiation of meaning and form, collaborative discourse and interlanguage pragmatics. Her research has appeared in national and international publications and she is co-editor of the book *Teaching and Learning the English Language from a Discourse Perspective* (2005).

ANNA MAURANEN (University of Tampere, Finland) is Professor of English at Tampere University. She has published widely in corpus linguistics, translation studies and contrastive rhetoric. Her current research focuses on speech corpora, chunks in ELF speech and English as lingua franca. She is running a research project on lingua franca English in academic settings and compiling the *ELFA* (English as a Lingua Franca in the Academia) corpus. She is a member of the editorial board and advisory board in the *International Journal of Corpus Linguistics, Languages in Contrast, Studies in Corpus Linguistics* and *TESOL Quarterly*. Mauranen has contributed extensively to various volumes on corpus linguistics and translation. She is the author of *Cultural Differences in Academic Rhetoric: a Text-Linguistic Study*. She has co-authored *Academic Writing. Intercultural and Textual Issues and Translation Universals: Do They Exist?*. She has recently co-authored *Linear Unit Grammar. Integrating Speech and Writing* with John Sinclair.

VIVIANA CORTES (Iowa State University, USA) is Assistant Professor in the TESL/Applied Linguistics and Technology program at Iowa State University, where she teaches corpus-based English grammar, and discourse analysis. Dr. Cortes holds a B.A. in English from the Universidad Tecnológica Nacional (Buenos Aires, Argentina), an M.A. in TESL from California State University (Los Angeles, California) and a Ph.D. from Northern Arizona University (Flagstaff, Arizona). He research interests are related to descriptive studies of language use and to the investigation of frequently occurring word combinations, such as lexical bundles, in different academic registers. Her latest articles can be read in *English for Specific Purposes, Applied Linguistics,* and in several edited books.

ENIKO CSOMAY (San Diego State University, USA) is an Associate Professor of Linguistics at San Diego State University. As an Applied Linguist, she finished her B.A. at Eotvos University (Hungary), her Master's at the University of Reading (U.K.) and her Ph.D. at Northern Arizona University (Flagstaff, AZ). In her research, she applies corpus-based techniques to analyze discourse patterns and most recently to describe linguistic variation in other dimensions of classroom discourse such as teacher talk versus student talk specific to university classrooms. Her most recent publications in these areas appeared in *Linguistics and Education* and in the *Journal of English for Academic Purposes*.

NANCY DRESCHER (Minnesota State University) earned her doctorate in Applied Linguistics at Northern Arizona University. She is currently teaching courses in the theories and methods of teaching ESL/EFL in the MA TESL program in the English Department at Minnesota State University, Mankato. Some of her current research interests include the use of corpus-based research methodology, identity and language, ESL/EFL program development/evaluation, and ESL/EFL teacher education.

PAULA GARCÍA (Northern Arizona University) PhD, is coordinator for research, pedagogy and practice in the E-Learning Center at Northern Arizona University, where she received her doctorate in applied linguistics in 2004. Her dissertation, titled *Meaning in Academic Contexts: A Corpus-Based Study of Pragmatic Utterances*, was an analysis of a spoken corpus made up of office hours, study groups, and service encounters in university contexts investigating speech act utterances using a customized computer program that searched for linguistic features in addition to processing codes. She has published journal articles and book chapters on pragmatic comprehension, assessment, and the use of technology in tertiary education. She currently works with faculty in designing research studies that demonstrate the effectiveness of technological advances and innovative pedagogies used in their classes, and facilitates the dissemination of successful projects through publications and conference presentations. She also organizes and presents at faculty development events and graduate teacher training sessions.

JAVIER PÉREZ-GUERRA (University of Vigo, Spain) is a tenured lecturer at the Department of English, University of Vigo (Spain), where he coordinates the research unit Language Variation and Textual Categorisation (LVTC). In most of his research Javier has used corpora as evidence for theoretical speculation. Since he is interested in syntactic change the recent history of the English language, he has collected data from historical corpora such as The Helsinki Corpus of English Texts, ARCHER, Chadwyck Healey's 18th- and 19th-century collections, etc. For the contemporary data, Javier has used the British National Corpus, the American National Corpus, (F-)LOB, (F-)Brown, among others. Currently he is focused on multidimensional linguistic variation among genres in late Modern English and Present-day English.

AMÁLIA MENDES (University of Lisbon) is researcher at the Centre of Linguistics of the Lisbon University (CLUL) since 2001. She has been involved since 1989 in the compilation of the Reference Corpus of Contemporary Portuguese (CRPC), a vast corpus covering several Portuguese geographical varieties. She has taken part in the European projects PAROLE and SIMPLE, involving corpus compilation and annotation. She published her PhD thesis in 2005, a corpus-based study on the lexical semantics of Portuguese verbs of emotion.

FERNANDA BACELAR (University of Lisbon) is main researcher and coordinator of the Linguistics Centre in Lisbon (CLUL). Her main research areas are corpus linguistics, lexis, and the syntax of oral language. She has participated in research projects including: TagShare project –tagging and shallow processing tools and resources, *REDIP - Rede de Difusão Internacional do Português: rádio, televisão e imprensa* and *Análise Contrastiva de Variedades do Portugués y Léxico Multifuncional Informatizado del Portugués Contemporáneo*. Bascelar has co-authored: *A Língua Portuguesa em Mudança*, about discourse in social communication media and has contributed to the volume C-ORAL-ROM *Integrated*

Reference Corpora for Spoken Romance Languages. Luísa Alice Pereira and Maria Fernanda Bacelar do Nascimento have published the *Dicionário de Combinatórias do Portugués.*

YUKIO TONO (Meikai University, Tokyo) is Professor at the School of Applied Linguistics at Meikai University, Tokyo. He has previously lectured at Tokyo Gakugei University, Keio University and Seikei University in Japan. Tono has published widely in the area of corpus-based approaches to second language acquisition studies. He has worked on the construction of *JEFLL* Corpus (Japanese EFL Learner). Other projects include the NHK "Ultimate 100 Keywords", a corpus-based TV English conversation program; and the *Standard Speaking Test (SST) Corpus*, a joint collaboration between Communication Research Laboratory and ALC Press, and university advisory members (1-million word corpus of spoken English by Japanese-speaking learners of English). He has recently co-authored (2006) the book *Corpus-Based Language Studies. An Advanced resource book* with Anthony McEnery and Richard Xiao.

JOHN OSBORNE (University of Savoie) is Professor of English Linguistics at the Université de Savoie. He has co-authored (Barbara Lewandowska-Tomasczyk, Frits Schulte) the books *Foreign Language Teaching and Information and Communication Technology* and *Computers in Language Studies*. He is the editor of *La compréhension de l'oral*. Current projects where he is the main researcher include *Constitution et exploitation de corpus d'apprenants* containing both written and an oral data.

WINNIE CHENG (The Hong Kong Polytechnic University) is Director of the Research Centre for Professional Communication in English (RCPCE) and Professor of English at The Hong Kong Polytechnic University. Her main research interests include corpus linguistics, discourse and conversation analysis, pragmatics, discourse intonation, intercultural communication in professional contexts, collaborative assessment and online education. She was involved in the compilation of the *Hong Kong Corpus of Spoken English* (HKCSE). She is the author of *Intercultural Conversation* published by John Benjamins and has published articles in:

International Journal of Corpus Linguistics, English World-Wide, Applied Linguistics, and *ICAME Journal.* Prof. Chen has also contributed to the volumes *Applied Corpus Linguistics. A Multidimensional Perspective* and *Rethinking Language Pedagogy from a Corpus Perspective.*

SYLVIE DE COCK (University of Louvain) is assistant lecturer at the Catholic University of Louvain. She is also a researcher at the UCL Centre for English Corpus Linguistics, directed by Sylviane Granger. This center is the first one which started work on compiling a large computerised corpus of learner language: the *International Corpus of Learner English* (ICLE). De Cock is also involved in the compilation of the *LINDSEI* (*Louvain International Database of Spoken English Interlanguage*) database. De Cock's research interests include lexicology, phraseology, corpus linguistics and learner corpora. She has published widely on learner corpora, in different books and international journals, such as *Learner English on Computer, Lexicographica* or the *International Journal of Corpus Linguistics.*

FIONA FARR (University of Limerick) is a lecturer in English Language Teaching (ELT), and course director of the MA in ELT at the University of Limerick, where she is involved in the education of teachers at both undergraduate and postgraduate levels. She is part of a research group called IVACS (Inter-varietal applied corpus studies) and is co-manager of the *Limerick Corpus of Irish English* (L-CIE), a one-million word corpus of contemporary spoken Irish English. Her professional interests include language teacher education, spoken language corpora and their applications, discourse analysis, and language variety. She has published in journals such as *TESOL Quarterly* and the *Journal of English for Academic Purposes*, and also has chapters in books on corpora and language variety, as well as Irish-English pragmatics, and teacher education.

Linguistic Insights

Studies in Language and Communication

This series aims to promote specialist language studies in the fields of linguistic theory and applied linguistics, by publishing volumes that focus on specific aspects of language use in one or several languages and provide valuable insights into language and communication research. A cross-disciplinary approach is favoured and most European languages are accepted.

The series includes two types of books:

– **Monographs** – featuring in-depth studies on special aspects of language theory, language analysis or language teaching.
– **Collected papers** – assembling papers from workshops, conferences or symposia.

Vol. 1   Maurizio Gotti & Marina Dossena (eds)
          Modality in Specialized Texts. Selected Papers of the
          1st CERLIS Conference.
          421 pages. 2001. ISBN 3-906767-10-8. US-ISBN 0-8204-5340-4

Vol. 2   Giuseppina Cortese & Philip Riley (eds)
          Domain-specific English. Textual Practices across
          Communities and Classrooms.
          420 pages. 2002. ISBN 3-906768-98-8. US-ISBN 0-8204-5884-8

Vol. 3   Maurizio Gotti, Dorothee Heller & Marina Dossena (eds)
          Conflict and Negotiation in Specialized Texts. Selected Papers of
          the 2nd CERLIS Conference.
          470 pages. 2002. ISBN 3-906769-12-7. US-ISBN 0-8204-5887-2

Editorial address:

Prof. Maurizio Gotti   Università di Bergamo, Facoltà di Lingue e Letterature Straniere,
                        Via Salvecchio 19, 24129 Bergamo, Italy
                        Fax: 0039 035 2052789, E-Mail: m.gotti@unibg.it

·

Ana María Hornero / María José Luzón / Silvia Murillo (eds)

Corpus Linguistics

· Applications for the Study of English

Bern, Berlin, Bruxelles, Frankfurt am Main, New York, Oxford, Wien, 2006.
526 pp., num. fig.
Linguistic Insights. Studies in Language and Communication. Vol. 25
Edited by Maurizio Gotti
ISBN 978-3-03910-675-2 / US-ISBN 978-0-8204-7554-7 br.
sFr. 118.– / €* 81.30 / €** 83.60 / € 76.– / £ 53.20 / US-$ 90.95

* includes VAT – valid for Germany   ** includes VAT – valid for Austria

The aim of this volume is to present a state-of-the-art view on corpus studies. This collection of papers, presented at the XII Susanne Hübner Seminar in November 2003 at the University of Zaragoza, comprises both quantitative and qualitative analyses and studies on both written and oral corpora. Structured in seven sections, the book covers a wide range of approaches and methodologies and reflects current linguistic research. The papers have been written by scholars from a large number of universities, mainly from Europe, but also from the USA and Asia.

The volume offers contributions on diachronic studies, pragmatic analyses and cognitive linguistics, as well as on translation and English for Specific Purposes. The book includes several papers on corpus design and reports on research on oral corpora. At a more specific level, the papers analyse aspects such as politeness issues, dialectology, comparable corpora, discourse markers, the expression of evidentiality and writer stance, metaphor and metonymy, conditional sentences, evaluative adjectives, delexicalised verbs and nominalization.

«By way of a general evaluation it must be said that this is a perfect example of a state-of-the-art volume in which the communion between applied discourse analysis and CL is fully brought up. As the editors point out, the papers presented 'give an idea of the great variety of topics which characterize the present state of the art in the research on Corpus Linguistics' (p.11). I find no better compliment than this which is to be understood as an enthusiastic recommendation of this volume. I am sure readers will find in it sufficient food for thought to open up new areas of research in the field of CL.» (Jordi Piqué-Angordans, Ibérica)

PETER LANG
Bern · Berlin · Bruxelles · Frankfurt am Main · New York · Oxford · Wien

Alan Partington / John Morley / Louann Haarman (eds)

Corpora and Discourse

Proceedings of *CamConf 2002*
Università degli Studi di Camerino, Centro Linguistico d'Ateneo
Sept 27th-29th 2002

Bern, Berlin, Bruxelles, Frankfurt am Main, New York, Oxford, Wien, 2004.
420 pp., num. tables and graphs
Linguistic Insights. Studies in Language and Communication. Vol. 9
Edited by Maurizio Gotti
ISBN 978-3-03910-026-2 / US-ISBN 978-0-8204-6262-2 pb.
sFr. 93.– / €* 64.20 / €** 66.– / € 60.– / £ 42.– / US-$ 71.95

* includes VAT – valid for Germany   ** includes VAT – valid for Austria

Corpus linguistics has made impressive strides in the fields of lexicography and grammatical description, but has had relatively little to say as yet in describing features of discourse. This volume, then, examines how it is possible to use concordance technology and the detailed linguistic evidence available in corpora to enhance the study of, among other things, how speakers/writers organise their discourse, how they express evaluation of their topics and the rhetorical strategies they employ to persuade an audience. Particular attention is paid to interrogating specialized corpora and to devising techniques to discover what is going on between speakers and between authors and readers in particular varieties of the language. These studies reveal the value of integrating corpus techniques with other, non-automatic, methods of research into the linguistic record and of combining quantitative and qualitative approaches. In general, they show how it is possible to use corpora to analyse discourse not only as product but also as process.

«...'Corpora and Discourse' represents a collection of interesting and thought-provoking papers which sketch new exciting approaches to discourse, raise a number of intriguing research questions, and call for more and larger specialised corpora and for further corpus studies of what is going on between speakers/writers and listeners/readers.» (Ute Römer, Anglistik)

PETER LANG

Bern · Berlin · Bruxelles · Frankfurt am Main · New York · Oxford · Wien

Roberta Facchinetti / Matti Rissanen (eds)

Corpus-based Studies of Diachronic English

Bern, Berlin, Bruxelles, Frankfurt am Main, New York, Oxford, Wien, 2006. 300 pp.
Linguistic Insights. Studies in Language and Communication. Vol. 31
Edited by Maurizio Gotti
ISBN 978-3-03910-851-0 / US-ISBN 978-0-8204-8040-4 pb.
sFr. 78.– / €* 53.50 / €** 55.– / € 50.– / £ 35.– / US-$ 59.95

* includes VAT – valid for Germany ** includes VAT – valid for Austria

Corpus-based studies of diachronic English have been thriving over the last three decades to such an extent that the validity of corpora in the enrichment of historical linguistic research is now undeniable. The present book is a collection of papers illustrating the state of the art in corpus-based research on diachronic English, by means of case-study expositions, software presentations, and theoretical discussions on the topic. The majority of these papers were delivered at the *25th Conference of the International Computer Archive of Modern and Medieval English* (ICAME), held at the University of Verona on 18-23 May 2004. A number of typological and geographical varieties of English are tackled in the book: from general to specialized English, from British to Australian English, from written to speech-related registers. In order to discuss their tenets, the contributors draw on corpora and dictionaries from different centuries, including the most recent ones; hence, they testify to the fact that past and present are so strongly interlocked and so inextricably entwined that it proves hard – if not preposterous – to fully understand Present-day English structure and features without turning back to the previous centuries for an in-depth knowledge of the 'whys' and 'hows' of the current state of the art.

Contents: Roberta Facchinetti/Matti Rissanen: Introduction – Anne Curzan/Chris C. Palmer: The Importance of Historical Corpora, Reliability, and Reading – Johan van der Auwera/Martine Taeymans: More on the Ancestors of *Need* – Manfred Markus: Spotting Spoken Historical English: The Role of Alliteration in Middle English Fixed Expressions – Irma Taavitsainen/Päivi Pahta/Martti Mäkinen: Towards a Corpus-Based History of Specialized Languages: *Middle English Medical Texts* – Barry Morley/Patricia Sift: Towards the Automatic Identification of Directive Speech Acts – Helena Raumolin-Brunberg: Leaders of Linguistic Change in Early Modern England – Hans Martin Lehmann/Caren auf dem Keller/Beni Ruef: ZEN Corpus 1.0 – Udo Fries: Death Notices: The Birth of a Genre – Franck Zumstein: The Contribution of Computer-Searchable Diachronic Corpora to the Study of Word Stress Variation – Merja Kytö/Erik Smitterberg: 19th-Century English: An Age of Stability or a Period of Change? – Clemens Fritz: The Conventions' Spelling Conventions: Regional Variation in 19th-Century Australian Spelling – Tine Breban: The Grammaticalization of the English Adjectives of Comparison: A Diachronic Case Study – Göran Kjellmer: Panchrony in Linguistic Change: The Case of *Courtesy*.

PETER LANG
Bern · Berlin · Bruxelles · Frankfurt am Main · New York · Oxford · Wien